# Educating the Children of Migrant Workers in Beijing

*Educating the Children of Migrant Workers in Beijing* is a timely book that addresses the gap in the provision of basic education to migrant children in China. It examines the case of Beijing, with a focus on policy implementation at the municipal and district levels and its impacts on migrant schools and their students.

Rural migrant workers in the cities typically lack local *hukou* (household registration) and face serious obstacles in accessing basic social services, including schooling for their children. The educational situation of these children, however, can vary both across and within localities, and, despite policies and regulations from the central government, there have emerged broad and sometimes even extreme differences in the implementation of these policies at the local levels.

This book uses evidence from qualitative interviews and the analysis of policy documents and materials to provide readers with a rare glimpse into the local politics surrounding migrant children's education in China's political center, including the nature of and motives behind policy implementation at the municipal and district levels and the implications for the survival and development of migrant schools in the city.

*Educating the Children of Migrant Workers in Beijing* is a unique and in-depth contribution to an important area and will appeal to scholars and students across a range of disciplines, including China studies, migration studies, education, social policy, and development studies, as well as to practitioners and policymakers working on migrant issues and social welfare provision in China.

**Myra Pong** earned her PhD from the Institute of Development Studies (IDS) at the University of Sussex and was a Fulbright Scholar at the University of Hong Kong in 2014–15. She has Bachelors and Masters degrees in international relations and affairs from Brown University, the London School of Economics and Political Science, and Peking University.

## Critical Studies on Education and Society in China
Series Editor: Gerard A. Postiglione

China's economic rise has been breathtaking and unprecedented. Yet educational opportunities remain highly unequal. China has the essential ingredients to build a great system of education, but educational governance needs an overhaul if China is to realize its goal of dramatically boosting its technological output to world-class levels. As more work by established Chinese and overseas scholars becomes accessible in English to the larger global community, myths will be removed and replaced by more accurate and sophisticated analyses of China's fascinatingly complex educational transformation. This series will provide highly analytical examinations of key issues in China's education system.

Books in the series include:

*School Choice in China: A different tale?*
Wu Xiaoxin

*Educating the Children of Migrant Workers in Beijing:*
*Migration, education, and policy in urban China*
Myra Pong

**Wah Ching Centre of Research on Education in China**
華 正 中 國 教 育 研 究 中 心
The University of Hong Kong 香 港 大 學

# Educating the Children of Migrant Workers in Beijing

## Migration, education, and policy in urban China

Myra Pong

Routledge
Taylor & Francis Group

LONDON AND NEW YORK

First published 2015
by Routledge
2 Park Square, Milton Park, Abingdon, Oxon OX14 4RN

and by Routledge
711 Third Avenue, New York, NY 10017

*Routledge is an imprint of the Taylor & Francis Group, an informa business*

*British Library Cataloguing in Publication Data*
A catalogue record for this book is available from the British Library

*Library of Congress Cataloging in Publication Data*
A catalog record for this book has been requested

ISBN: 978-1-138-78115-3 (hbk)
ISBN: 978-1-315-77021-5 (ebk)

Typeset in Galliard
by Deer Park Productions

To my parents,
for giving me the opportunity to go on this journey

# Contents

# Tables and figures

## Tables

# Figures

# Foreword

China's unprecedented growth over three decades has fuelled many positive developments, from rising incomes to a massive expansion of education at higher levels in the system. But an increasingly uneven pattern of development is generating new social tensions and challenges. This volume tackles an important area where it is easy to discern the reproduction of social inequality and injustice, and the creation of social exclusion for a future generation.

China's migrant population has long been recognised as the labour force powering China's phenomenal growth, but is equally recognised as being marginalised in the distribution of benefits. As migration episodes become longer and more stable, often providing the primary source of income for rural households, migrant men and women have increasingly moved as families to, or have established families in, urban areas. Their children, however, far from accessing the opportunities that cities should offer, also live lives on the margin. The major exclusion for the majority is from mainstream schooling.

This problem has been recognised since the late 1990s, with early studies identifying a growing number of 'migrant schools' in major cities including Beijing, and NGOs and student volunteers becoming involved in their support. Policy, however, has been slow to change and, when it has not always done so constructively. Despite a compulsory education law, decentralised governance places the responsibility for the provision and financing of education on the location of an individual's household registration (*hukou*) – and that remains the rural area. Regulations also require rural children – even if resident as migrants in cities – to take key exams in their place of registration.

This study vividly documents the struggles and commitment of children, their parents and teachers, to ensure some basic education for the millions of children without access to urban schools – without sending them back to their villages. Official discourses have legitimised this education exclusion on a variety of grounds, frequently linked to the cost of financing. Policy shifts have at times had perverse effects, allowing local officials to use concerns about quality and safety to close existing schools without any responsibility to provide better alternatives, thus forcing schools underground. Like their migrant parents, the children, teachers and their schools exist in a shadowy space between legality and illegality – making them also hard to research.

This book is the result of a determined effort by Myra Pong to find the schools, and interview many of those involved from children and parents to head teachers, NGOs and government officials. It reveals the complexity of the situation and hard choices faced by families and teachers, and the risks of being pushed – through an inability to comply with higher-level policy demands – from the shadows of legality into illegality.

On the surface, integrating children into urban schools would not appear to be a major challenge for a capable state that is managing a complex reform process – and addressing it would bring significant individual and social gains. Why is so little progress being made? This study investigates in depth the policies and policy implementation processes that affect educational access and outcomes for migrant children. By examining a number of districts within one city – Beijing – it illuminates considerable variation even among districts as local context, politics and resources shape very different strategies and responses to higher-level policy directives. In the heart of the capital, close to the centre of state and Party power, such variation seems remarkable. The book thus makes an important contribution not only to understanding the educational situation of migrant children, but also in adding to a limited literature on local level policy-making processes and resulting variations in implementation and outcomes within China's decentralised governance system. It generates insights that inform our understanding of the complexity and contradictions of China's reform and policy processes.

As China now embarks on a new phase of development, with a stronger emphasis on inclusion, sustainable urbanisation and reducing the rural–urban divide, this book poses important challenges. Can the central government find the mechanisms to ensure its policies are implemented equitably across locations and generations? Will this generation of children of migrant workers in China's cities also have a chance to be part of the 'China dream'?

Sarah Cook
Director, United Nations Research Institute for Social
Development (UNRISD)
Geneva, May 2014

# Acknowledgments

There are many people I would like to thank for contributing to the completion of this research. I am greatly indebted to Dr Sarah Cook, whose brilliant insight and guidance have been instrumental in shaping this work. It was her commitment to and extensive knowledge about social and economic development in China that drew me to the Institute of Development Studies (IDS) in the first place, and this study would not have been possible without her tutelage, support, and encouragement. I also thank her for introducing me to key contacts in Beijing. In addition, I am extremely grateful to Dr Rachel Sabates-Wheeler, who provided me with invaluable feedback over the course of my research at IDS.

Several other individuals made indelible marks on this study. I would particularly like to thank Dr Zhao Shukai of the Development Research Center of China's State Council and Dr Lü Shaoqing of the Chinese Ministry of Agriculture's Research Center for Rural Economy for sharing their wisdom and experience, introducing me to important contacts in the field, and providing a wealth of practical support. Dr Han Jialing of the Beijing Academy of Social Sciences gave me extensive guidance and was a critical source of feedback. It was they who introduced me to the world of migrant children's education at the start of my fieldwork, and their vital work and early roles in this area paved the way for this study.

I am grateful to Dr Zhang Xiulan of Beijing Normal University's School of Social Development and Public Policy for providing incredibly valuable guidance and help during my fieldwork. I would also like to thank Dr Zhang Linxiu of the Center for Chinese Agricultural Policy at the Chinese Academy of Sciences for her enthusiastic support and for sharing knowledge and relevant data that were immensely useful during the fieldwork and writing stages. Dr Song Yingquan of Peking University's China Institute for Educational Finance Research was an important source of knowledge, especially on the situation of migrant children in public schools. My thanks also go to graduate students Li Qiang and Liu Yu for their enthusiasm and hard work in providing assistance during the earlier stages of my fieldwork.

In addition, several individuals at IDS provided useful feedback at various points during the research process. They include, but are certainly not limited to, Dr Gerry Bloom, Dr Naomi Hossain, Dr Henry Lucas, and Dr Linda

Waldman. I must also thank Dr Rachel Murphy of Oxford University for her extremely helpful comments and suggestions.

I am particularly indebted to Dr Odd Arne Westad of the London School of Economics and Political Science (LSE), who has been a remarkable mentor over the years. It was thanks to his guidance and encouragement that I pursued a double Master's degree program at Peking University and LSE, and the experiences I had and the people I met in Beijing during the program ultimately inspired me to do this research.

This book would not have been possible without the support of my family and close friends. I would like to express my deepest gratitude to my parents, David and Barbara Pong, for their countless sacrifices. My father has been a tremendous source of guidance and wisdom, and his work and contributions to the study of Chinese history have, in many ways, prompted my own interest in China. My mother has been my biggest cheerleader over the years, and she has been a constant source of strength and reassurance throughout all of my endeavors, no matter how far away in the world they have taken me. I also thank my sisters, Amanda and Cynthia, who have, through the pursuit of their personal goals and interests, helped motivate me to pursue my own, and my dear niece, Bo-yi, for being a source of great joy during the final stages of this project.

I am grateful to Suchi Pande and Sabrina Snell for their intellectual and moral support during my time at IDS. Friends in Beijing provided much needed and appreciated support, advice, assistance, and inspiration throughout the research and writing process and particularly during my fieldwork. This journey would not have been the same without them, and I owe them a very special thank you.

I would like to close by extending my thanks and appreciation to all of the individuals who participated in this study, including the migrant school principals and teachers who allowed me into their schools. I am especially grateful to the migrant families who shared their experiences with me. This book aspires to shed greater light on the problems faced by this segment of Chinese society and generate more interest, in the hopes that it may help bring these children and youth one step closer to living and progressing "under the same blue sky."

# 1 Introduction

During its more than 30 years of economic reform and opening up, China has undergone extraordinary social and economic change. A major part of this transformation has been increased internal mobility, especially rural–urban migration. Since the early 1980s, migration without a change of *hukou* (household registration) status[1] has increased steadily, leading many to point to a "tidal wave" of rural migrant workers (*mingong chao*) and "the largest flow of migrant labor in history" (Roberts 1997: 250; see also Li 1996; Chan 1999; Bai and He 2003). According to the Fifth National Population Census of 2000, China's "floating population" – people residing in areas outside their place of household registration – totaled 144 million, including 120 million rural migrant workers (Zheng *et al.* 2008: 1).

This has not only led to a redefinition of the country's internal boundaries, but it has also resulted in a rapidly changing Chinese society. The National Population and Family Planning Commission of China estimated that the country's floating population grew by ten million in 2010 and reached 221 million in 2011, of which almost three-quarters were migrant workers (Wong 2011). According to the National Bureau of Statistics, there were 262.61 million migrant workers in 2012 (An 2013). The bureau also reported that China's urban population (690.79 million) surpassed its rural population (656.56 million) for the first time in 2011. That is, 51.27 percent of China's citizens now reside in cities, compared to about 10 percent back in 1949 (Wines 2012). It is projected that, if the present trend continues, an additional 300 million workers will migrate from rural to urban areas over the next 30 years (Wong 2011).

This large-scale migration has given rise to unique policy challenges for the Chinese government, one being educational provision for the children of these rural migrant workers in the cities (hereafter referred to as migrant children). Along with factors like higher salaries and standards of living, education has been an important motive for the high levels of rural–urban migration (Kwong 2004; Lu and Song 2006: 339, table 1). Many migrant parents view education in the cities as an opportunity for their children to break out of poverty and improve their social status (Kwong 2004: 1077). This has contributed to an increasing number of migrant workers who take their children with them or have children in the cities (Guo 2002: 358; Kwong 2004: 1076–7). It was estimated that there were already close to 20 million children and youth under the age of 18 in the floating population by 2000 (Xinhua News Agency 2004). The All-China Women's Federation reported that the number of children migrating to other localities with their parents reached 35.81 million in 2010, a 41.37 percent increase from 2005, and that over 80 percent of these children were from rural parts of the country (Xinhua News Agency 2013). Migrant families also tend to remain in the cities for longer amounts of time, often for over a decade (cited by Postiglione 2006: 15).

The surge in the number of school-aged migrant children in cities since the early to mid-1990s has increased the urgency of issues concerning the provision of basic education for this group (Lü and Zhang 2004: 65). Despite China's Compulsory Education Law (1986) (*Zhonghua renmin gongheguo yiwu jiaoyufa*), which stipulated that the government would provide nine years of education to all children at the primary and middle school levels free of tuition,[2] migrant children, not having the appropriate household registration, were often left out of the local public school system. They began to attend poor quality, makeshift schools that were set up and run by migrants themselves. In Beijing, these schools – commonly referred to as migrant schools, or *dagong zidi xuexiao* – emerged in the early 1990s as a "self-help" (*zili jiuji*) mechanism in a context in which migrant workers were unable to pay the expensive fees required for their children to enroll in local public schools (Han 2001: 1–4).[3] The result was the emergence of a "rural–urban" gap in education within urban areas themselves, contributing to the image of migrant workers as "willing workers, invisible residents" (Roberts 2002) and migrant families as a "community outside the system" (*tizhiwai qunluo*) (Li 1996: 1144).

In China, the development of the education sector is frequently discussed as a priority for national development. Under former President Hu Jintao, educational development was a critical part of building a "harmonious society" (*hexie shehui*), a central theme of the Communist Party of China (CPC) emphasizing social and economic development based on democracy, the rule of law, equity, justice, sincerity, amity, and vitality. According to China Education and Research Network (2004), with a total of 318 million students enrolled in educational institutions at various levels (the highest in the world), China's government "prioritizes education as a fundamental and guiding cause with an overall importance to social and economic development." At the UNESCO-sponsored Fifth High-Level Group Meeting on Education for All in November 2005, then Premier Wen Jiabao emphasized that China's education agenda would prioritize the spreading of compulsory and vocational education, the elimination of illiteracy, and the development of education in rural areas. He asserted:

> As a large developing country with 1.3 billion people, China is running the largest education system of the world. Our experience has driven home to us that only by speeding up education development and improving the quality of the entire citizenry can we turn our huge population from a sheer

pressure into an enormous resource, put economic development in the orbit of progress in science and technology, and improve the living quality and standards of the entire population.

(Wen 2005)

He further stated:

Fairness is the soul of education for all. There is no social justice to speak of without equitable education opportunities. By tradition the Chinese lay great store by education, and the age-old saying, "In education there should be no class distinction," remains an enduring exhortation to this day. The Chinese government is working to ensure children's equitable right to education, promote balanced development in compulsory education, and bridge the gap between urban and rural areas and between regions in education development.

(Wen 2005)[4]

The government's desire to promote educational equality has also been reflected in central policies concerning migrant children's education since the early 2000s. Most significantly, in 2001, the central government adopted a policy of "two priorities" (*liangweizhu*) towards the provision of compulsory education for migrant children. Under this policy, the two areas of focus would be management by local governments in receiving areas (*liuru diqu zhengfu*) – which, in the case of municipalities like Beijing, refers primarily to the municipal and district governments – and education of migrant children in public schools (*gongban xuexiao*) (see also Qu and Wang 2008: 178–9; Han 2009). This decentralization of responsibilities, however, has created space for differential policy implementation at the local level, and, in the case of Beijing, this has meant that many migrant children still attend privately-run migrant schools. Though these schools have grown in number and size since the 1990s, they remain poor in condition, offer poor quality education, and often lack state recognition. Nevertheless, they continue to be a more feasible option than public school education for many migrant children because of factors like flexible enrollment procedures and low fees (see Kwong 2006: 172; Chen and Liang 2007: 125–6). Thus, while overall access to education in China has been increasing (Postiglione 2006: 3), the quality of and access to compulsory education have become a serious problem for the children of the massive population of migrant workers.

The Chinese government has been making efforts to improve the quality of *rural* education in areas like teaching and facilities to reduce the rural–urban gap in education.[5] Though such efforts might eventually increase the incentive for children to attend school in rural areas, the current reality is that a growing number of migrant workers choose to migrate with their children or have children in the cities, making migrant children's education a critical policy issue. Yet the problems surrounding educational provision for these children have not been afforded equal importance:

[T]here is a growing segment of the population that does not fit neatly into the rural–urban dichotomy traditionally characterizing the economy and the school system. The children of the rural-to-urban migrants that are flooding China's cities have fallen into a conspicuous gap in the provision of public education.

(Rural Education Action Project 2009)

According to Kwong (2006: 175), the situation stems in large part from the "fallout from the lag between educational legislation and the unanticipated nature and pace of social changes introduced by the market economy and the more liberal official stand on population and other social policies." In other words, the problems surrounding migrant children's education are not confined to the educational arena alone.

Although migrant children's education has been garnering an increasing amount of attention from the Chinese government and society, there remain serious gaps in knowledge. For example, even though the policy of "two priorities" calls for the decentralization of responsibilities to receiving governments, there continues to be a strong tendency among scholars to primarily attribute the problems migrant children face in attaining basic education to the *hukou* system. This has resulted in insufficient attention being paid to other potentially significant factors that may be producing and sustaining the problems of migrant schools mentioned above, the role of policy implementation at the local levels being an important one. There is also a tendency to discuss the general problems of migrant children and migrant schools at the *municipal* level, with little attention given to *district*-level dynamics.

Now it is certainly the case that, whatever the conditions are for migrant children's education, there exist widespread problems affecting, for example, rural children, girls, and minority children when it comes to educational provision in China. But, like everything else, there may also exist broad differences in the actual conditions experienced by these children, from province to province, city to city, district to district, and, indeed, even school to school. This said, the ultimate focus of this book is on examining policy processes and specifically policy implementation, rather than on directly analyzing the educational experiences of these children. The decision to do so is based on the recognition that, although it is the central government that sets policies on migrant children's education, lower levels of government, thanks to the consequences of decentralization, often enjoy flexibility in interpreting and implementing them. Therefore, to truly understand the issues and conditions surrounding migrant children's education, especially the situations of migrant schools and their students, it is imperative to conduct in-depth analyses of policy implementation at the local levels. The purpose of this study is to provide such an analysis for the case of Beijing.

## Policy implementation and migrant children's education in Beijing

Beijing attracts migrants from across the country. According to the Sixth National Population Census, the city's permanent resident population reached

19.6 million in November 2010, including about seven million migrants (Xinhua News Agency 2011). Based on data from the 2005 One-Percent Population Survey of China and a 2006 one-percent floating population survey conducted in Beijing by Renmin University of China, it was calculated that there were about 504,000 children in Beijing's floating population aged 14 and under by the mid-2000s (Zhai *et al.* 2007; Duan and Yang 2008: 23). By 2002, over 300 migrant schools had already been established in the city (cited by Kwong 2006: 171). As of mid-2010, 66 of them had been licensed by the government.

Since the policy of "two priorities" calls for the key role of public schools in educating migrant children, it might be assumed that migrant schools are increasingly unimportant. This study emphasizes that migrant schools continue to serve a critical function for migrant communities in Beijing. Yet, nearly two decades after their first appearance in the capital city, they still lack the resources to provide a learning environment on a par with urban public schools and, according to Lai *et al.* (2012: 15–16), even rural schools. Despite central policies calling for increased management of and support for these schools at the local levels, migrant schools in Beijing have not received much assistance from the municipal government. Most are unlicensed and remain vulnerable to government closures. What is more, the city's pursuit of urbanization has meant that these schools – and the migrant enclaves in which they are usually located – have been threatened with ongoing rounds of demolition. The resulting situation is one in which the demand for migrant schools continues to exist, but they remain poor in condition and unstable.

With the rising inflow of migrant families into Beijing, the educational opportunities available to migrant children are becoming an increasingly urgent issue. However, to date, no studies have analyzed in detail the potential causes and consequences of differential policy implementation in the area, especially at the district level. In light of the policy of "two priorities," this study highlights the development of two trends in Beijing: (1) the emergence of variation among district policy approaches towards migrant children's education and particularly migrant schools; and (2) increased civil society involvement. It explores the interaction between these two trends and the consequences for migrant schools and their students.

To address the bigger challenge identified, this book examines two sets of questions. First, what policy attitudes and approaches have the Beijing municipal and selected district governments adopted towards migrant children's education and why? Are there differences among district governments in how they view and approach the policy area and, if so, what factors are driving these differences? How are the municipal and district approaches then affecting the survival and development of migrant schools as a source of education for migrant children, and what are the consequences for the quality of these schools in comparison to state-run public schools? Second, what are the broader implications for the future of migrant children's education in Beijing and subsequently the social exclusion of this segment of society, and what does all of this contribute to understandings of policy implementation and decentralization in urban China?[6]

In tackling these questions, this study aims to: (1) understand the policy history and local policy environment surrounding educational provision for migrant children in Beijing; (2) explore how the selected districts are approaching the policy area and why; and (3) examine how the municipal *and* district policy approaches are shaping the situations of migrant schools (both directly and indirectly, through their relationship to civil society). The objective is to shed light on the complex dynamics surrounding the survival and development of migrant schools, including the extent to which they are supported by government and society, and what this ultimately means for the future provision of education to migrant children in the capital city.

Drawing on evidence from qualitative interviews and analysis of policy documents acquired during fieldwork, this book argues that the situations of migrant schools in Beijing are not only shaped by a general lack of support from the municipal government, but they are also substantially impacted by *district*-level policy implementation. Using Haidian, Shijingshan, and Fengtai districts as cases, it finds that, when it comes to implementing the central and municipal policies, there are broad and even extreme differences among district governments based on local circumstances, even in Beijing, which is under the very nose of the central government. It also shows that exploring the interaction between the government and civil society – including the extent to which district-level policy implementation affects civil society involvement and vice versa – is crucial to understanding the situations of migrant schools in the capital city. Though the general lack of consistent, up-to-date data on migrant children in China makes it difficult to assess the impact of such policy processes on educational outcomes like academic performance and completion rates, this study illustrates that policy implementation at the municipal *and* district levels – and the policy environment in which it operates – has a critical impact on migrant schools in Beijing, including the amount of external attention and support they and their students receive.

## The fieldwork

Understanding decision-making processes in China is a difficult task, to say the least. As Howell (2003: 198) emphasizes:

> In the case of China, charting the policy process is particularly challenging. Though there is greater openness and transparency than in the pre-reform era, institutional structures and decision-making mechanisms remain opaque, information is limited and access by researchers to key players is constrained.

What is more, as will be discussed in Chapter 4, migrant children's education in China – and in Beijing in particular – remains a somewhat delicate policy area for the government given its perceived linkages to population growth and potential social instability. The subsequent challenges I encountered had direct implications for the ways in which I could conduct this research and the relative ease with which I could gain access to the different groups of actors involved. Therefore, as is often the case in qualitative research, the processes of data collection and analysis shaped not only each other but also the design of the entire study.

This book uses case studies to explore migrant children's education and the situations of migrant schools in three districts and thereby provides a more detailed understanding of the potential importance of district-level policy implementation and dynamics within the policy area. I conducted the fieldwork in Beijing between October 2009 and September 2010, with the majority of my time being spent in three of the four inner suburban districts: Haidian, Shijingshan, and Fengtai. The general selection of inner suburban districts as cases was based primarily on the presence of rural–urban transition areas and high concentrations of migrant workers. I chose to focus my research on these three districts in particular based on the recognition that the basic physical, demographic, and economic differences among them would provide a good basis for comparison.

During the first two months of fieldwork, I worked on building relationships with academics and researchers and other contacts and collecting official and secondary data concerning migrant children's education in China. I spent the remaining period conducting qualitative interviews with key government and civil society actors, as well as migrant school principals and teachers and migrant families, and collecting policy documents and materials from various interviewees and sources. In late 2009, I interviewed education commission officials in the three selected districts. I visited migrant schools between December 2009 and June 2010 and interviewed civil society actors primarily during periods when the schools were closed, mainly between mid-January and early March of 2010 for Chinese New Year and during the summer. I conducted interviews with migrant families between March and July 2010. I also made additional trips to Beijing in late 2011 and mid-2013, during which I conducted follow-up conversations with key researchers and migrant school principals about relevant developments.

In order to build an understanding of the municipal and district policy approaches and the reasons behind them, a significant part of the research involved identifying, collecting, and examining central, municipal, and district-level policy documents. I was able to access central and municipal-level policy documents primarily through government websites and local researchers and district-level documents mainly through interviewees. A review of the latter was particularly useful in shedding light on the impact of local context on the policy approaches adopted in the selected districts.

In order to better understand how the municipal and district policy approaches have affected the situations of migrant schools and their students (both directly and through their relationship to civil society), I conducted qualitative interviews with a range of local actors.[7] The main method of data collection was semi-structured interviews and short questionnaires, based on questions catered to each set of actors. Information extracted from informal conversations and encounters served as an additional source of knowledge. I conducted all interviews in Mandarin Chinese. Since the research involved conversing with people from different provinces, each of which has its own dialect and accent, I digitally recorded the interviews when consent was given. Based on guidance from local researchers, I did not digitally record my interviews with migrant parents, allowing me to converse more freely with the individuals.

During the fieldwork, I was able to gain access to 22 migrant schools in Beijing, including 17 in Haidian, Shijingshan, and Fengtai (see Table 1.1). Of these 17, eight offered primary school education and at least two out of three years of middle school education, while the remaining nine only offered primary school education. At each of the schools, I interviewed the principal to gain an understanding of the school's history and situation, including key obstacles faced and the nature of its relationship with the local government and civil society. To better understand the situations of migrant school teachers, I also interviewed 26 teachers across the schools, who were selected based on availability and their willingness to participate. In addition, I collected information from schools in nearby districts (two in Chaoyang, two in Changping, and one in Daxing), which were chosen based on available contact information and access. Talking to principals and teachers from these schools allowed for a contextualization of the findings in the three core districts and a better understanding of the larger situation of migrant schools in Beijing.[8]

I visited the licensed migrant schools first and was able to access these schools through local researchers and principals I met during earlier stages of the research. I chose and contacted unlicensed schools largely based on their proximity to the licensed schools, so that the schools visited would be in relatively similar demographic areas. Again, I used various channels to acquire access. In many cases, the principals interviewed provided me with contact information for nearby migrant schools. In addition, though there is no official comprehensive list of migrant schools in Beijing, I was able to obtain two contact lists from a migrant school principal and a local researcher, which served as an additional channel through which I could contact unlicensed migrant schools.

Between March and July 2010, I conducted interviews with 40 migrant families (14 in Haidian, 16 in Shijingshan, and ten in Fengtai), with the aim of

*Table 1.1* Number and type of migrant schools visited in the three selected districts (2009–10)

| District | Total number of licensed migrant schools | Estimated number of unlicensed migrant schools* | Number of licensed migrant schools visited | Number of unlicensed migrant schools visited | Total number of migrant schools visited |
|---|---|---|---|---|---|
| Haidian | 2 | ≈19 | 2 | 4 | 6 |
| Shijingshan | 3 | ≈6 | 3 | 4 | 7 |
| Fengtai | 3 | ≈6 | 2 | 2 | 4 |

Source: Author's fieldwork (2009–10).

*It is difficult to know the exact number of unlicensed migrant schools at any given time, especially since migrant schools are vulnerable to demolition and government closures and often move within and across districts (sometimes changing their names in the process). These figures are based on estimates from interviews and documents collected during fieldwork.

understanding their experiences and the obstacles they faced in terms of education, including the extent to which they had received support from the government and society. Based on guidance from local researchers, I acquired access primarily through teachers, and families were selected from one licensed and two unlicensed schools in each district. At each school, I requested that the contact list provided reflect a range in terms of grade level, educational performance, and family background, and the number of families interviewed was ultimately determined by availability and the willingness to participate.

In order to acquire an understanding of the district-level policy attitudes and approaches, I conducted interviews with education commission officials from the three selected districts, which were arranged through a local university. Two researchers based in the central government also served as important sources of information throughout the fieldwork. To gain deeper insight into the role of civil society, I interviewed academics and researchers, university student volunteers, and individuals from 14 of the key local NGOs and international organizations involved in migrant children's education in Beijing. I gained access to these actors through multiple channels, including previous contacts and local conferences and symposiums. NGOs in particular were selected based on their level of involvement in the policy area and recommendations from principals and teachers, researchers, and other organizations.

The data collected were analyzed using qualitative content analysis to identify and examine key themes, patterns, issues, and examples, both at the Beijing municipal level and at the district level based on the three selected cases. Using open coding, interview notes and transcripts and field observations were reviewed in order to pinpoint major themes and categories within the data, taking into account those occurring within and across the different groups of actors interviewed and those within and across the three districts. These themes and categories were then compiled, organized, and refined.

It goes without saying that I encountered not a few challenges while conducting this research. Even the simple matter of identifying some of the schools was a major obstacle. Many principals interviewed, for example, expressed that they did not know the locations or contact details of nearby migrant schools. In addition, given the fundamental difficulties of counting and keeping track of these schools, the two contact lists of migrant schools obtained during fieldwork included information that was often incomplete and/or outdated. One of the two lists, for instance, had been compiled around 2004 and therefore included schools that no longer existed and excluded others that were established later. Even when accurate contact information for a school was obtained, the principals were sometimes unwilling or hesitant to talk. Indeed, several declined outright to participate, stating that they were too busy, that their school was about to be demolished or shut down, or, in some cases, that academic research would not benefit their schools. Setting aside the validity of their explanations – and I do empathize with them, given the difficulties they have to confront on a daily basis – their refusal to participate did not make my research any easier.

Access to migrant schools in Fengtai district was especially difficult. As will be discussed in Chapter 5, the district government's extreme approach in shutting down migrant schools, particularly in the early 2000s, meant that there were essentially no migrant schools in the district for a period of time. Around the mid-2000s, migrant schools began to appear again, albeit on a much smaller scale. It became clear to me early on in my fieldwork that these schools are now relatively isolated, not only from migrant schools in other districts, but also from each other in the district itself. As a result, many principals, including a few in Fengtai itself, were unable to provide me with the contact details for schools in the district.

Moreover, the number of migrant families interviewed was limited by the inability of many parents to participate, often because of their long work hours. Another obstacle was related to security concerns. Between March and May 2010, there were five major attacks on schoolchildren across China. A total of 17 people died, and close to 100 were injured (Wong 2010). In this context, the Chinese government instructed all schools (public and private) to adopt stricter security measures. In consequence, many migrant schools became hesitant to share parents' contact information, even if it was purely for research purposes.

Difficulties in accessing local officials are common in this policy area, at least in the case of Beijing, and this was confirmed by academics and researchers in the sample. As a result, municipal-level officials and officials from other relevant organs of the three district governments were not interviewed. Access to public schools was also attempted (through, for example, local researchers) but was not possible, given that such access in Beijing normally requires close relations with the government. Analyzing the situations of migrant children in these schools is important, especially since public schools may vary in terms of, for instance, how accessible they are to migrant children and whether or not migrant students are integrated into their classrooms. It would also provide a critical control group. While I did not explore the situations of migrant children in these schools in depth, I was able to acquire an understanding of key issues concerning their education through conversations with migrant parents with children in public schools, migrant school principals, and civil society actors, as well as by drawing on the findings of Song *et al.* (2009) and Lai *et al.* (2012).

In addition to these challenges, the basic lack of statistical data on migrant children made it difficult to assess the impact of policy implementation on educational outcomes like completion rates. Official surveys and censuses are generally not made public in their entirety, and data that are public, including those in the annual education and area statistical yearbooks, do not usually include figures specifically on migrant children or migrant schools. Indeed, official documents often only provide figures for the "outside population" (*wailai renkou*) or "floating population" (*liudong renkou*), neither of which refers specifically to rural–urban migrant workers. Moreover, usage of the terms "children of the floating population" (*liudong ertong*) and "migrant workers' children" (*nongmingong zinü* or *wailai wugong renyuan suiqian zinü*) is frequently inconsistent and unclear in Chinese documents. The latter is technically a subset of the former, which includes children who do not have the local city's *hukou* but are not the children of rural–urban migrant workers. Some sources, however, use the terms interchangeably or only refer to the "children of the floating population," making analyses of relevant policy materials more difficult.

This lack of consistency and clarity reflects the difficulties of collecting data on rural–urban migrants and has had major consequences for knowledge of migrant children's education. Nevertheless, this book creates a picture of the problems of migrant schools and their students in Beijing and in the selected districts by drawing on data from multiple sources, including interviews, policy documents, government surveys and censuses, research studies, and media reports. When citing such sources throughout the book, the terms used are the same as those originally used by the authors.

Despite the restrictions faced during fieldwork, this study makes a significant contribution to the understanding of migrant children's education by shedding light on the nature and impact of policy implementation in the area and subsequently also the micro-politics of educational provision for these children. While the results cannot be generalized to other cities, particularly in light of the diversity of experiences and differences in the pace and scale of reforms across localities in China, focusing on Beijing provides a good sample of the problems migrant children can encounter in a major city and is a good starting point for future studies in other cities with large migrant populations. The findings have important implications for other localities in terms of the ways in which policy implementation and its impacts on migrant children's education can be understood.

## Conceptual framework and contributions of the study

This study's framework for analysis is set out in Chapter 2, which provides a review of existing knowledge on policy processes and decentralization, both in general and in China, and identifies key themes that can be applied to analyzing the implementation of policies on migrant children's education in Beijing. There is an enormous amount of literature on policy processes. The traditional or linear model of policy processes treats policy making as a rational process in which implementation is a separate, administrative process that occurs after policy decisions, one that is meant to resolve the problem as understood in the policy (Sutton 1999: 9). There is, however, growing agreement that policy processes are not linear and rational but are instead highly complex and context-specific (e.g. Sutton 1999; de Vibe *et al.* 2002; IDS 2006: 8).

Based on this logic, this study examines migrant children's education in Beijing from the perspective of policy and policy processes, with a particular focus on the roles of and interaction among *policy implementation* (including policy attitudes and approaches at the municipal and district levels), *policy history* (including key policies and legislation at different levels), and *local context* (including social, economic, political, and governance factors). In light of the policy of "two priorities," analysis of the effects of decentralization is central to this discussion. Since decentralization frequently increases the number and range of stakeholders involved in the policy process, an examination of civil society involvement in the policy area is also critical to my framework.

The significance of using policy processes and decentralization to frame my analysis of migrant children's education can largely be understood from two angles. First, it enhances the understanding of differential policy implementation within a Chinese city, as well as how local policy processes in an increasingly important but complex policy area operate and the various motives and pressures involved. In doing so, it illustrates the significance of looking beyond the role of institutional factors like the *hukou* system in driving policies concerning rural–urban migrants in China. The study therefore makes a major contribution to the conceptualization of policy processes in an urban Chinese context, particularly valuable in light of the general lack of literature on the effects of decentralization in the realms of migration and education in China. Second, while it is difficult to envision what Chinese society will look like in another 30 years from now, this exploration sheds light on wider issues that may surface in the future, including the longer-term impacts of economic reforms and policy on trends in social stratification and the intergenerational transmission of poverty in China. In other words, this study strengthens the grasp of potential future trends concerning both policy processes and societal development. As Zhong (2003: 4) notes: "[E]conomic reform and decentralization in the past decade have brought about significant changes to local government and politics; these may provide crucial clues as to where China's future development is heading."

Ultimately, as previously mentioned, conducting research concerning policy processes in China is a fundamentally difficult task. Nevertheless, this book draws on visits to migrant schools, interviews with key state and societal actors, and analysis of policy documents and materials to bring together for the first time the range of factors affecting migrant children's education in Beijing and the situations of migrant schools in particular. It provides a useful case study that sheds light on the complexities of decentralization and policy implementation and how they may be contributing to an increasingly stratified urban society, as well as the interactions among local government departments, migrant school principals and teachers, migrant families, and actors like researchers, NGOs, and the media. This analysis of the local policy environment and the actors involved – including their roles, motives, and willingness and capacity to assist migrant schools – adds a fresh and innovative perspective to the dialogue on migrant children's education and, more broadly, the complex linkages between government, migration, educational inequality, policy, and social stratification in China. It provides a much needed framework for the state and civil society actors involved to understand the dynamics surrounding differential policy implementation and serves as a foundation upon which to identify a set of realistic, effective steps to improve educational provision for migrant children in Beijing.

## Outline of the study

This book is organized into three sections. The first section, consisting of Chapters 2–3, provides necessary background information and develops the conceptual framework discussed above. Chapter 2 examines the main bodies of literature relevant to this study. It starts by providing contextual information regarding internal migration policies and patterns in China since 1949. It gives an overview of central policies towards rural migrants in cities over time and high-lights the central government's shift towards the more positive treatment of and better services for migrant workers and their families in the early 2000s. The chapter then examines the emergence of migrant children's education as an important policy issue during the 1990s, particularly in large cities such as Beijing, and identifies important gaps in the understanding of the subject, including how and with what consequences policies in the area are implemented. The rest of the chapter proposes a framework for analysis that draws on the broader literatures on policy processes and decentralization, as well as literature concerning migration–education linkages, educational inequality, urbanization, and policy processes in China. Within this framework, the roles of policy history, local context, and civil society are explored as potential factors shaping policy implementation.

Chapter 3 introduces readers to the selected field sites. It focuses in particular on the emergence of migrant schools as a source of education for migrant children in Beijing and explores the growth and development of these schools since the early to mid-1990s. It provides evidence of their critical role in the provision of compulsory education for migrant children in the city, motivating a closer exami-nation of their situations at the local levels. It then gives an overview of the situ-ations in each of the three selected districts (Shijingshan, Fengtai, and Haidian).

The second section, Chapters 4–7, analyzes the policy environment in Beijing (including the roles of the various actors involved) and the impact on the situations of migrant schools and their students at the municipal and district levels. Chapter 4 evaluates the policy history of migrant children's education in China. It identifies major themes in the evolution of the central and Beijing municipal policies, includ-ing key differences between them, and points to the importance of examining the effects of decentralization within cities. Chapter 5 evaluates the district policy approaches towards migrant children's education and migrant schools in particular and the role of local context in shaping these approaches. It examines the approaches adopted by the Shijingshan, Fengtai, and Haidian district governments and identifies fundamental areas in which the three trajectories diverge.

Chapter 6 analyzes the impact of the municipal and district policy approaches on migrant schools in Beijing and draws attention to the gap between central-level policy ideals and the local reality. Evidence from fieldwork shows that migrant schools in Beijing still face some of the same basic problems as they did during the 1990s – a general lack of resources and poor physical conditions, a low quality of teaching, instability, and difficulties acquiring licenses – and that both the munici-pal and district policy approaches have shaped the situations of the schools in these four areas. Despite the continued existence of these problems, as well as the policy focus on the role of public schools and increased efforts to shut down or demolish migrant schools, the rest of the chapter shows that migrant schools remain a neces-sary source of education for many migrant children in Beijing.

Chapter 7 assesses the role of the civil society actors that have become involved in migrant children's education in Beijing since the mid- to late 1990s. They are mainly academics and researchers, the media, university student organizations, non-governmental organizations (NGOs), migrant school principals' and teachers' associations, and migrant parent activists. It explores the involvement of each set of actors, including their interaction with the government and migrant schools and also among themselves. The chapter argues that, due in large part to the local policy environment, including district-level dynamics, the capacity of these actors to significantly impact the situations of migrant schools and their students remains low.

The final section, Chapter 8, discusses the implications of the study for understanding of policy implementation in urban China, as well as the future of migrant children's education and broader trends in social stratification and exclusion. It highlights key reasons why it is in the best interests of the central, municipal, and district governments not to allow the current situation in Beijing to persist. This is followed by a list of policy and program recommendations and suggestions for future research. The chapter emphasizes the urgent need to adopt targeted measures to assist and improve migrant schools in the city, at least in the short term, and offers suggestions as to how this can be achieved.

## Notes

1 The *hukou* household registration system divides citizens by their place and type of registration (rural or urban, agricultural or non-agricultural).
2 In China, children of compulsory school age are usually defined as being between the ages of six and 15.
3 The translations of quotes from Chinese materials (such as policy documents) and interviews cited throughout this book are my own.
4 "In education there should be no class distinction" is a direct quote from Confucius, *The Analects*, 15: 38.
5 See Hannum *et al.* (2010: 127–9) for a discussion of key policies concerning rural education.
6 As de Haan (1998: 12–13) maintains: "[Social exclusion] refers to exclusion (deprivation) in the economic, social and political sphere. It ... includes power relations, agency, culture and social identity. Social exclusion can refer to a state or situation, but it often refers to *processes*, to the mechanisms by which people are excluded." In the words of Wang (2008: 695), it "includes not only access to services but also discrimination in the delivery of those services through differences in quality, reach and effectiveness."
7 See Appendix A for a list of these actors.
8 One of the schools visited was established through the sponsorship of a local foundation. Though subsidized by the foundation and relatively better resourced, it faced certain obstacles similar to other migrant schools and was therefore included in the sample.

## Bibliography

An, Baijie. "Migrant-Worker Population Hits 262 Million." *China Daily*, May 27, 2013. http://usa.chinadaily.com.cn/china/2013-05/27/content_16537065.htm (accessed September 27, 2013).

Bai, Nansheng and Yupeng He. "Returning to the Countryside Versus Continuing to Work in the Cities: A Study on Rural Urban Migrants and Their Return to the Countryside of China." *Social Sciences in China* 24, no. 4 (Winter 2003): 149–59.

Chan, Kam Wing. "Internal Migration in China: A Dualistic Approach." In *Internal and International Migration: Chinese Perspectives*, ed. Frank N. Pieke and Hein Mallee. Surrey: Curzon Press, 1999, pp. 49–71.

Chen, Yiu Por and Zai Liang. "Educational Attainment of Migrant Children: The Forgotten Story of China's Urbanization." In *Education and Reform in China*, ed. Emily Hannum and Albert Park. Oxford: Routledge, 2007, pp. 117–32.

China Education and Research Network. "MOE: Survey of the Educational Reform and Development in China." December 23, 2004. www.edu.cn/Researchedu_1498/20060323/t20060323_113688.shtml (accessed October 10, 2008).

de Haan, Arjan. "'Social Exclusion': An Alternative Concept for the Study of Deprivation?" *IDS Bulletin* 29, no. 1 (January 1998): 10–19.

de Vibe, Maja, Ingeborg Hovland, and John Young. "Bridging Research and Policy: An Annotated Bibliography." ODI Working Paper No. 174, Overseas Development Institute, London, 2002. www.odi.org.uk/resources/odi-publications/working-papers/174-bridging-research-policy-annotated-bibliography.pdf (accessed November 7, 2008).

Duan, Chengrong and Ge Yang. "Woguo liudong ertong zuixin zhuangkuang: jiyu 2005 nian quanguo 1% renkou chouyang diaocha shuju de fenxi" ["Study on the Latest Situation of Floating Children in China"]. *Renkou xuekan* [*Population Journal*] 6 (2008): 23–31.

Guo, Fei. "School Attendance of Migrant Children in Beijing, China: A Multivariate Analysis." *Asian and Pacific Migration Journal* 11, no. 3 (2002): 357–74.

Han, Jialing. "Beijingshi liudong ertong yiwu jiaoyu zhuangkuang diaocha baogao" [Report on the Investigation of the Compulsory Education Situation of Children of the Floating Population in Beijing]. *Qingnian yanjiu* [*Youth Studies*] 8 and 9 (2001): 1–7, 10–18.

Han, Jialing. "Education for Migrant Children in China." Paper commissioned for the *Education for All Global Monitoring Report 2010: Reaching the Marginalized*, 2009. http://unesdoc.unesco.org/images/0018/001865/186590e.pdf (accessed August 19, 2010).

Hannum, Emily, Meiyan Wang, and Jennifer Adams. "Rural–Urban Disparities in Access to Primary and Secondary Education under Market Reforms." In *One Country, Two Societies: Rural–Urban Inequality in Contemporary China*, ed. Martin King Whyte. Cambridge, MA: Harvard University Press, 2010, pp. 125–46.

Howell, Jude. "Women's Organizations and Civil Society in China: Making a Difference." *International Feminist Journal of Politics* 5, no. 2 (July 2003): 191–215.

IDS. "Understanding Policy Processes: A Review of IDS Research on the Environment." Institute of Development Studies, Knowledge, Technology and Society Team, Brighton, 2006. www.ids.ac.uk/files/Policy_Processes06.pdf (accessed August 3, 2012).

Kwong, Julia. "Educating Migrant Children: Negotiations between the State and Civil Society." *The China Quarterly* 180 (December 2004): 1073–88.

Kwong, Julia. "The Integration of Migrant Children in Beijing Schools." In *Education and Social Change in China: Inequality in a Market Economy*, ed. Gerard A. Postiglione. Armonk, NY: M. E. Sharpe, 2006, pp. 163–78.

Lai, Fang, Chengfang Liu, Renfu Luo, Linxiu Zhang, Xiaochen Ma, Yujie Bai, Brian Sharbono, and Scott Rozelle. "Private Migrant Schools or Rural/Urban Public Schools: Where Should China Educate Its Migrant Children?" REAP Working Paper No. 224, Stanford University, Rural Education Action Project, Stanford, CA, 2012. http://

iis-db.stanford.edu/pubs/23180/migrant_paper_final_sdr_fang_acm_sdr_march26_
sdr.pdf (accessed August 3, 2012).

Li, Cheng. "Surplus Rural Laborers and Internal Migration in China: Current Status and Future Prospects." *Asian Survey* 36, no. 11 (November 1996): 1122–45.

Lü, Shaoqing and Shouli Zhang. "Urban/Rural Disparity and Migrant Children's Education: An Investigation into Schools for Children of Transient Workers in Beijing." *Chinese Education and Society* 37, no. 5 (September/October 2004): 56–83.

Lu, Zhigang and Shunfeng Song. "Rural–Urban Migration and Wage Determination: The Case of Tianjin, China." *China Economic Review* 17, no. 3 (2006): 337–45.

Postiglione, Gerard A. "Schooling and Inequality in China." In *Education and Social Change in China: Inequality in a Market Economy*, ed. Gerard A. Postiglione. Armonk, NY: M. E. Sharpe, 2006, pp. 3–24.

Qu, Zhiyong and Li Wang. "Liudong ertong yiwu jiaoyu wenti he zhengce yingdui" [The Problem of Compulsory Education for Children of the Floating Population and Policy Responses]. In *Zhongguo jiaoyu fazhan yu zhengce 30 nian (1978–2008)* [*China's Education Development and Policy, 1978–2008*], ed. Xiulan Zhang. Beijing: Shehui kexue wenxian chubanshe [Social Sciences Academic Press], 2008, pp. 165–206.

Roberts, Kenneth D. "China's 'Tidal Wave' of Migrant Labor: What Can We Learn from Mexican Undocumented Migration to the United States?" *International Migration Review* 31, no. 2 (Summer 1997): 249–93.

Roberts, Kenneth D. "Rural Migrants in Urban China: Willing Workers, Invisible Residents." *Asia Pacific Business Review* 8, no. 4 (Summer 2002): 141–58.

Rural Education Action Project. "Education for Migrant Children." 2009. http://reap.stanford.edu/docs/education_for_migrant_children/ (accessed April 19, 2011).

Song, Yingquan, Prashant Loyalka, and Jianguo Wei. "Does Going to Public Schools Matter for Migrant Children's Academic Achievement in China?" Manuscript, Peking University, China Institute for Educational Finance Research, Beijing, China, 2009.

Sutton, Rebecca. "The Policy Process: An Overview." ODI Working Paper No. 118, Overseas Development Institute, London, 1999. www.odi.org.uk/resources/odi-publications/working-papers/118-policy-process.pdf (accessed November 2, 2008).

Wang, Lu. "The Marginality of Migrant Children in the Urban Chinese Educational System." *British Journal of Sociology of Education* 29, no. 6 (November 2008): 691–703.

Wen, Jiabao. "Opening Speech." Speech delivered at the Fifth High-Level Group Meeting on Education for All, Beijing, China, November 28–30, 2005. www.unesco.org/education/efa/global_co/policy_group/HLG5_presentations/Opening/china.doc (accessed December 9, 2010).

Wines, Michael. "Majority of Chinese Now Live in Cities." *The New York Times*, January 17, 2012. www.nytimes.com/2012/01/18/world/asia/majority-of-chinese-now-live-in-cities.html (accessed January 19, 2012).

Wong, Edward. "Fifth Deadly Attack on a School Haunts China." *The New York Times*, May 12, 2010. www.nytimes.com/2010/05/13/world/asia/13china.html?ref=asia&pagewanted=all (accessed May 13, 2010).

Wong, Edward. "China: 10 Million More Migrants." *The New York Times*, March 4, 2011. www.nytimes.com/2011/03/04/world/asia/04webbriefs-China.html?_r=1&partner=rssnyt&emc=rss (accessed March 4, 2011).

Xinhua News Agency. "Foundation to Fund Education of Migrant Workers' Children." January 14, 2004. www.china.org.cn/english/culture/84631.htm (accessed April 6, 2012).

Xinhua News Agency. "Beijing's Population Tops 19.6 Mln, Migration Key Contributor to Growth." May 5, 2011. http://news.xinhuanet.com/english2010/china/2011-05/05/c_13860069.htm (accessed February 7, 2011).

Xinhua News Agency. "Left-Behind, Migrant Children in China Nears 100 Mln." May 10, 2013. http://news.xinhuanet.com/english/china/2013-05/10/c_132373256.htm (accessed December 12, 2013).

Zhai, Zhenwu, Chengrong Duan, and Qiuling Bi. "Beijingshi liudong renkou de zuixin zhuangkuang yu fenxi" ["The Floating Population in Beijing: An Update"]. *Renkou yanjiu* [*Population Research*] 31, no. 2 (March 2007): 30–40.

Zheng, Xinrong *et al.* "Cujin nongmingong zinü yiwu jiaoyu xiangmu zongjie baogao" [Summary Report of the Program on Promoting Compulsory Education for Migrant Children]. Completion report prepared for the IDF program entitled Ensuring Access to Basic Education for Rural Migrant Children, under the aegis of the Department of Basic Education of the Ministry of Education, 2008. http://219.234.174.136/snxx/baogao/snxx_20081010092411_6154.html (accessed September 4, 2010).

Zhong, Yang. *Local Government and Politics in China: Challenges from Below*. Armonk, NY: M. E. Sharpe, 2003.

# 2 Migrant children's education in China's cities and the emergence of a new policy area

Despite increased scholarly attention since the late 1990s, there remain serious gaps in the understanding of migrant children's education in China, particularly in terms of the role and impacts of policy and policy implementation. In light of the increasing urgency of the subject, this chapter reviews the main bodies of literature and knowledge relevant to the education of these children. It proposes an analytical framework that allows for a more nuanced understanding of the dynamics surrounding migrant children's education in Beijing and ultimately creates a stronger foundation upon which to improve the situations of the city's migrant schools and their students.

The chapter starts by highlighting key migration patterns and policies in China since 1949, providing useful historical background and motivating a closer examination of education for migrant children. It then explores the literatures on migration–education linkages, rural–urban migration and urbanization, and educational inequality in China and how they relate to migrant children's education and trends in social stratification. The discussion shows that research on the subject often focuses on describing the situations of migrant schools and their students but fails to analyze the potential range of factors leading to those outcomes in the first place. Much of the literature on China's internal migration also emphasizes the predominant impact of the *hukou* system in shaping policies regarding rural–urban migrants and the problems they and their families face in the cities, resulting in a tendency to overlook the effects of differential policy implementation *within* localities. Given these gaps, the chapter then turns to the literature on policy processes – in which policy history, local context (including issues related to decentralization), and the involvement of civil society are increasingly relevant considerations – and creates a framework for analyzing policy implementation and its consequences for the situations of migrant schools and their students at the local levels.

## Internal migration patterns and policies since 1949

### 1949–78

Though internal migration in China is often discussed in the post-1978 context of China's economic reforms, it is useful to highlight some of the pre-1978 developments, given that "[t]he roots of China's present migration problems lie in the policies of the first decades of the People's Republic" (Davin 1999: 18). Before 1978, a substantial amount of migration was initiated and controlled by the state. The government was able to regulate internal migration processes through mechanisms such as labor planning, residency control, monopoly of employment, and the work unit (*danwei*) system (Liu and Chan 2001: 76).[1]

Still, migration outside these initiatives did occur. The period between 1951 and 1960 was one of increasing rural–urban migration; about 19.8 million people migrated from rural to urban areas between 1953 and 1956 alone (Roberts 1997: 255; Liang 2001: 500). This, according to Lary (1999: 34), "was an ideological problem for the Communist leadership, whose development strategy was posited on rural revolution, on bringing a better life to peasants; this did not mean letting them run away to the cities." The result was the emergence of policies to address this migration, most notably the Ministry of Public Security's "Interim Regulations on Urban Household Administration" (*Chengshi hukou guanli zanxing tiaoli*) (July 1951). The regulations set up the *hukou* system in urban areas, primarily meant to monitor, rather than control, population mobility (Cheng and Selden 1994: 649; Chan and Zhang 1999: 819–20). The "Decision on Labor Employment Problems" (*Guanyu laodong jiuye wenti de jueding*), issued by the State Council in August 1952, is another example. It was one of the earliest policies to more thoroughly tackle the issue of rural–urban migration, though it did not create ways to regulate or stop the population flows (Cheng and Selden 1994: 650).

As rural–urban migration increased, however, the government strengthened efforts to end the "blind flows" of rural labor. The "Joint Directive to Control the Blind Influx of Peasants into Cities" (*Guanyu jixu guanche quanzhi nongmin mangmu liuru chengshi de zhishi*), issued by the Ministry of Internal Affairs and Ministry of Labor in March 1954, is an early example. It stipulated that the state would be responsible for regulating labor mobility and employment. In December 1954, the Standing Committee of the National People's Congress issued the "Regulations for Public Security Substations" (*Gongan paichusuo zuzhi tiaoli*) and the "Organic Regulations of Urban Street Offices" (*Jiedao banshichu zuzhi tiaoli*). Both increased government control over migration within and between rural and urban areas (Cheng and Selden 1994: 654–5).

In June 1955, the State Council's "Directive Concerning the Establishment of a Permanent System of Household Registration" (*Guanyu jianli jingchang hukou dengji zhidu de zhishi*) extended the *hukou* system to rural areas. This led to the "Regulations on Household Registration in the People's Republic of China" (*Zhonghua renmin gongheguo hukou dengji tiaoli*), issued by the Standing Committee of the National People's Congress in January 1958 (Cheng and Selden 1994: 655–6, 662). The regulations applied the *hukou* system to all citizens, "establish[ing] a fully-fledged *hukou* institution and grant[ing] state agencies much greater powers in controlling citizens' geographical mobility through a system of migration permits and recruitment and enrolment certificates" (Chan and Zhang 1999: 820). Citizens would be divided by their place of registration (*hukou suozaidi*), rural or urban, and type of registration (*hukou leibie*), agricultural or non-agricultural.[2] The impact was extensive. Under this new system, migrants lacking an employment certificate or school admission certificate had to first acquire a moving-in certificate (*zhunqian zheng*) from the local police in the city to which they planned to migrate, and this certificate would then be used to acquire a moving-out certificate (*qianyi zheng*) that would be required for migrants to depart from their home areas. In other words, it was no longer possible for people in rural areas to look for jobs in urban areas freely. Enterprises in the cities could still recruit rural workers when needed, but it was increasingly the case that these workers were granted short-term contracts, were not provided the same benefits as offered to long-term workers, and had to go back to their home areas after their contracts expired (Davin 1999: 8). All of these developments meant that, by the mid- to late 1950s, the household registration system had already created "a deep but not impermeable divide between urban and rural areas, between workers and collective farmers, between the state sector and the collective sector" (Cheng and Selden 1994: 660–1).

### Post-1978

While the levels of *hukou* migration – migration involving a formal change of residency (Chan and Buckingham 2008: 590) – have been relatively stable since 1978, migration without a change in household registration has been rising since the early 1980s.[3] The number of out of township rural–urban migrants, for example, increased from two million in 1982 to 62 million in 1993 and reached 102.6 million in 2004 (cited by Wang and Cai 2007: 16, table 4). According to Wu (2001: 60–1), this post-1978 rural–urban migration can be broken down into four stages: the early 1980s, during which population movement primarily took place within the coastal areas; the mid-1980s, during which there were increases in intra-provincial migration (due in large part to the rapid growth of township and village enterprises) and inter-provincial migration; the late 1980s and mid-1990s, during which labor migration reached new heights; and the late 1990s, during which labor migration somewhat stabilized.[4]

To understand this chronology, it is useful to examine the interaction between these migration patterns and key policy changes. As internal migration started to increase in the early 1980s, the government responded by adopting a policy of promoting small towns and rural industry to minimize rural–urban migration and keep migrants out of cities with populations of at least 500,000 people (Davin 1999: 40).[5] Concerns about migration also led to the State Council's "Measures for the Custody and Repatriation of Vagrants and Beggars in Cities" (*Chengshi liulang qitao renyuan shourong qiansong banfa*) in May 1982, which stated that cities would need to create "custody and repatriation stations" (*shourong qiansong zhan*) for rural beggars in cities, urban vagrants and beggars, and other people without homes and send them back to their place of *hukou* registration (see Li 2004: 17).

By the mid-1980s, however, it became clear that this strategy could not solve the problems posed by large-scale rural–urban migration, resulting in new rules for temporary residence. The "Interim Regulations on the Management of Temporary Residents in Cities and Towns" (*Guanyu chengzhen zanzhu renkou guanli de zanxing guiding*), issued by the Ministry of Public Security in July 1985, stipulated that migrants who were 16 or older and were residing in towns and cities for a period of over three months would need to apply for temporary residence permits (Wang and Cai 2007: 17–18). After paying for the permits, migrants occasionally had to pay an additional fee to the local public security bureau for using urban services. The objectives of establishing this system of temporary residence included strengthening the control of local authorities over migrants, as well as helping with the preservation of social order and urban planning. It also made it easier for local governments to differentiate between migrants who were relatively more stable and successful and those who were either unemployed or underemployed. This regulation, along with the introduction of an identity card system in 1986, was designed to discourage, or even control, rural–urban migration. Registration assigned temporary migrants a status that would prevent them from enjoying the same privileges and services as urban residents (Davin 1999: 21–2, 43–4, 46). It can be argued, though, that the document actually led to a relaxation of barriers to migration and urban residency during the mid-1980s, making it possible for people in rural areas to reside in the cities as temporary residents, as long as they met their own needs in terms of employment, housing, and services (Yang and Guo 1999: 932).

Indeed, the 1985 regulation enabled many migrants from rural areas to stay in urban areas for substantial amounts of time and, as a result, helped stimulate rural–urban migration in the late 1980s. The government response was, again, to introduce measures to try to limit such migration. This included new measures concerning *hukou* transfers and sales. Many cities, for example, started selling permanent registration certificates, with prices ranging, for instance, from 3,500 to 60,000 RMB. Such measures allowed cities to selectively attract wealthier permanent residents (cited by Davin 1999: 36, 44–6).

Still, internal migration continued to increase in the early 1990s.[6] In 1992, Deng Xiaoping's Southern Tour stimulated further economic growth, and the resulting development of private economic sectors increased the demand for rural laborers, leading to higher levels of interregional migration (Wang and Cai 2007: 15–16). The sheer magnitude of migration in the late 1980s and early 1990s set the stage for a tightening of policies in the mid-1990s. The government made increasing efforts to limit the flow of rural laborers, as well as the jobs and services they would be eligible for at the destination. For example, the Ministry of Labor issued the "Interim Regulations on the Management of Cross-Provincial Employment of Rural Workers" (*Nongcun laodongli kuasheng liudong jiuye guanli zanxing guiding*) in November 1994. The document stated that rural migrants must acquire an employment registration card from the local labor and employment agency before departing and an employment registration certificate after reaching their destination. Together, the card and certificate would serve as an employment certificate, which would function as an identification card and make them eligible for services offered by career centers. The regulation also introduced restrictions on the capacity of urban employers to hire employees from other provinces; a worker from another province could only be hired when there were no qualified local workers and when the local labor and employment agency had approved (see Li 2004: 22; Wang and Cai 2007: 19).[7]

Moreover, the "blue stamp *hukou*" (*lanyin hukou*), formally introduced in 1992, became widespread in big cities during the mid- to late 1990s (Chan and Zhang 1999: 836–40; Fan 2002: 108). It entitled one to the same privileges as local residents in terms of education and welfare (cited by Shen and Huang 2003: 53–4). Its attainment, however, would depend on a considerable fee and conditions involving age, skills, education, and major investments or home purchases, making most rural migrants ineligible (Chan and Zhang 1999: 838; Fan 2002: 108). Also during this period, many cities, including Shanghai and Beijing, resorted to more forceful measures, including sending migrants back to their places of registration and demolishing migrant villages (Li 1996: 1123). Such measures corresponded to a period in which rural–urban migration continued to increase, albeit at a slower speed (Mallee 2003: 143).

Starting in the early 2000s, rural–urban migration sped up once again (Wang and Cai 2007: 16–17). This can be attributed to efforts by the central government to actually *facilitate* migration and improve the treatment of migrant workers in a context in which migrants' rights had begun to attract more attention (due, for instance, to occurrences like the Sun Zhigang incident).[8] Indeed, the government "made a serious effort to fundamentally review the official approach to labour migration" during this period, including adopting policy measures aimed at freeing the labor market and ensuring that migrant workers would be given equitable opportunities (Huang and Zhan 2005: 72).

In March 2001, for example, the government made the decision to reform the *hukou* system, beginning with small towns.[9] The reforms include the elimination of the fee previously charged to temporary residence permit applicants and restrictions on the length of stay. Also in 2001, the National Development and Planning Commission (known as the National Development and Reform Commission since 2003) outlined a five-year plan to create a unified labor market, as well as remove restrictions on rural labor mobility and build an employment registration system and a new social security scheme. In January 2002, the CPC Central Committee and the State Council issued the "Opinions on Carrying Out Agricultural and Rural Work in 2002" (*Guanyu zuohao 2002 nian nongye he nong-cun gongzuo de yijian*). The document emphasizes the contributions of migrant workers to urban development since the 1980s and discusses rural–urban migration as a natural outcome of economic development. It calls for efforts to provide migrants with better services and management and to treat them fairly and eliminate unreasonable restrictions (Huang and Pieke 2005: 113–14).

Of particular significance is the "Circular of the General Office of the State Council on Strengthening Employment Management and Service Work for Rural Migrant Workers" (*Guowuyuan bangongting guanyu zuohao nongmin jincheng wugong jiuye guanli he fuwu gongzuo de tongzhi*), issued in January 2003, which Zhao (2003: 168) refers to as "a turning point in public policy."

The document emphasizes the importance of rural–urban migration to urbanization and industrialization and highlights key problems faced by migrants, including the lack of protection of their rights and limitations concerning job eligibility.[10] It discusses several steps to address the unreasonable restrictions placed on migrant workers, such as improving living conditions and access to services like vocational training, and its comprehensiveness "makes it by far the most important policy statement of the central authorities in this area" (Huang and Pieke 2005: 115).

In June 2003, the State Council also replaced the "Measures for the Custody and Repatriation of Vagrants and Beggars in Cities" (1982) – which, in the words of Li (2004: 17), "had become the nightmare of rural workers for more than 20 years" – with the "Administrative Measures for Assisting Vagrants and Beggars with No Means of Support in Cities" (*Chengshi shenghuo wuzhe de liulang qitao renyuan jiuzhu guanli banfa*). Instead of "custody and repatriation stations," vagrants and beggars are encouraged to go to "assistance stations" (*jiuzhu zhan*), which, for example, provide food and accommodation, send patients to hospitals, and provide assistance in contacting family members or employers (see Li 2004: 17–18).

Furthermore, in September 2003, the Ministry of Agriculture, Ministry of Labor and Social Security, Ministry of Education, Ministry of Technology, Ministry of Construction, and Ministry of Finance launched the "Nationwide Training Plan for Rural Migrants (2003–2010)" (*2003–2010 nian quanguo nongmingong peixun guihua*), which calls for stronger efforts to provide basic training to migrant workers (Wang and Cai 2007: 20). In addition, the "Opinions of the State Council on Solving the Problems of Migrant Workers" (*Guowuyuan guanyu jiejue nongmingong wenti de ruogan yijian*), issued in January 2006, discusses protecting the rights of migrant workers and improving their treatment and the services available to them. As Chan and Buckingham (2008: 601) contend, "the generally pro-*mingong* rhetoric of the document is a welcome move in setting a more positive tone for creating a better work and living environment for migrant labour." And, in June 2007, the Standing Committee of the National People's Congress approved the Labor Contract Law (*Zhonghua renmin gongheguo laodong hetongfa*), calling for a range of protections to enhance migrant workers' capacity to acquire long-term jobs (China Labour Bulletin 2007).

In sum, there has been a major shift towards improving the treatment of and services available to rural–urban migrants since the early 2000s. Ultimately, however, "how many of these 'good intentions' will get implemented remains to be seen" (Chan and Buckingham 2008: 601). Indeed, there remain serious questions surrounding the local effects of such recent policies, including the consequences for migrant children's education in the cities.

## Migration–education linkages

Although there is little theoretical analysis of the linkages between migration and education, it is possible to draw on the growing body of migration literature and empirical evidence from case studies to illustrate the importance of exploring them. There is, for example, increasing discussion of the educational attainment of migrants (e.g. Waddington 2003: 30–1; Quinn and Rubb 2005; Skeldon 2005: 14–19), as well as increasing discussion of education as a motive for internal and international migration (e.g. Todaro 1980: 377; Waddington 2003: 31; Hashim 2005: 18–21).

Migration can also have a critical impact on children's educational opportunities. In the United States, for instance, the children of migrant farmworkers are usually extremely poor and live in immigrant households. Many work to support their families, and those who attend school typically face a range of educational problems given their socioeconomic status and high mobility (Branz-Spall *et al.* 2003: 55–6). Kandel and Kao (2001: 1206, 1227) find that, while the financial gains of Mexican labor migration to the United States may help in allowing migrants' children to continue their education, migration has also helped perpetuate the cycle of low-skilled, low-paid immigrants in the United States labor market, not to mention the emergence of barriers to higher educational development within the sending areas in Mexico itself. In Europe, migrant students can be at a disadvantage in terms of enrollment and dropout rates, length of schooling, achievement indicators, and types of diplomas obtained, though educational attainment among them is generally greater in countries with stronger preschool and childcare systems and less economic inequality (Heckmann 2008: 74). In Bangladesh, children who migrate from rural to urban areas – on their own, with other children, or with family members – can face different situations as well. In cases where families migrate, children's schooling depends on factors including the reasons behind the family's decision to migrate and how well they adjust to living in a city. In cases of short-term migration and/or multiple movements, migrant children may be unable to go to school on a regular basis. Autonomous migration can have complex effects on education that are closely tied to issues of child labor (Giani 2006: 1, 16). Thus migrant children in different localities may face the combined impacts of migration, poverty, and cultural barriers in attaining education. However, there is no universal relationship between migration and education, and the nature and impact of these linkages are often shaped by the local context (Hashim 2005: 13; Quinn and Rubb 2005: 154; Whitehead and Hashim 2005: 3, 27).

In China, the relationship between internal migration and education is not straightforward. On the one hand, migration can encourage expenditure on rural education (e.g. through remittances). Migrants contribute financially to the household, which may increase parents' investment in their children's schooling (Murphy 2002: 97). Many migrants also view education in the cities as a tool to help their children break out of poverty and enhance their social status (Kwong 2004: 1077).[11] On the other hand, many parents in rural areas may see education as being ultimately pointless since they can easily acquire unskilled jobs in cities, and they may see school-related fees as burdens inflicted by the government (Qin 1997: 60; Murphy 2002: 92–3). Similarly, many rural children of middle school age may feel that an extra year or two of education will not substantially improve their job opportunities, so they stop attending school and migrate to cities (Murphy 2002: 93). Many migrant children may also be pressured to make financial contributions to their families, which may sometimes lead them to work – e.g. selling flowers, shining shoes, or recycling garbage – rather than attend school (Wu 2001: 85; Murphy 2002: 107).

Moreover, migration can negatively affect education for China's "left-behind children" (*liushou ertong*), the children of migrant laborers who are left behind in rural areas, usually under the care of grandparents. While official estimates suggest there are 20 million left-behind children, a study by the All-China Women's Federation used 2005 census data to argue that there were 58 million left-behind children under 18 years old, making up 28 percent of all rural children and 21 percent of all children in the country (cited by China Labour Bulletin 2008). The federation reported that, by 2010, the number had increased to 61.02 million, making up 37.7 percent of all rural children and 21.88 percent of all children in the country (Xinhua News Agency 2013). Lü (2007: 28, table 3.1) contends that left-behind children attending primary and middle school constitute 86 percent of all left-behind children. Being left behind can have major consequences for their education; academic performance tends to decline after their parents migrate, and many suffer from behavioral and psychological problems (Lü 2007: 151–6, 164–70; China Labour Bulletin 2008).

Thus the relationship between migration and education can be highly complex. Since China has the world's most rapidly growing market economy, largest student population, and largest internal migrant population, much benefit would come from further research on the linkages between migration, educational inequality, and social stratification in China (Postiglione 2006: 18–19).

## Migrant children's education in China

As mentioned in Chapter 1, an increasing number of migrant workers take their children with them or have children in the cities (Guo 2002: 358; Kwong 2004: 1076–7).[12] Based on data from the 2005 One-Percent Population Survey of China, the number of children in the floating population aged 14 and under reached 18.34 million, accounting for 12.45 percent of the floating population; this was a 30 percent increase from the figure provided in the Fifth National Population Census in 2000. The 2005 survey data also indicated that children of the floating population made up a significant proportion of the children in cities (e.g. one-third of the children in Shanghai and 23.83 percent of the children in Beijing) (Bi 2009). These families usually remain in the cities for longer amounts of time. The average length of stay for migrants in Beijing, for instance, is roughly two years, but many migrant families stay for over a decade (cited by Postiglione 2006: 15). This surge in the number of school-aged migrant children in cities since the early 1990s has significantly increased the urgency of issues concerning their education (Lü and Zhang 2004: 65).

Despite the policy reforms discussed earlier, rural migrant workers and their families are not considered to be urban residents under the *hukou* system, and they have frequently faced discrimination through local policies and practices, affecting not only their employment, but also their housing, health care, and education (Zhou 2000: 31–2). They have, in the words of Li (2004: 28), become "the largest group of the underclass living in urban areas," with important consequences for the schooling of migrant children. China's Compulsory Education Law (1986) stipulated that the government would provide nine years of primary and middle school education to students free of tuition; this would apply to "[a]ll children who have reached the age of six ... regardless of sex, nationality or race,"[13] adding that the start of schooling could be delayed to the age of seven in areas where this is not possible. Under this system, however, local governments were only in charge of providing education to children with *local* household registration (Han 2001: 17; Kwong 2006: 168–9).

As a result, in the early to mid-1990s, migrant parents began to find other ways to educate their children. Initially, this involved tutoring or teaching classes in makeshift settings like vegetable sheds and shanties, and eventually migrants' homes and deserted buildings (Han 2001: 1–5). Over time, the number of migrant schools increased, particularly in major cities like Beijing, Shanghai, Guangzhou, Nanjing, and Wuhan (Project Team on Rural Labor Migration 2001: 119). In one Shanghai district, for instance, the number of migrant schools grew from eight to 105 between 1995 and 2000 (cited by Kwong 2006: 171). As will be discussed in Chapter 6, these schools have become a critical source of education for migrant children because of factors like their low fees and the sense of community they offer (Chen and Liang 2007: 125–6). That is, they have emerged as important local informal sector providers of education for this segment of society in China's cities.[14]

Yet knowledge of the nature and scale of the educational exclusion of migrant children and the situations of migrant schools remains limited. First, there is a lack of consistent and up-to-date data. For example, China's Department of Basic Education reported in 1996 that the enrollment rate among migrant children in the country was 96.2 percent (cited by Nielsen *et al.* 2006: 462). Based on 1997 Beijing Migrant Census data, it was estimated that 88 percent of Beijing's migrant children were enrolled in school (Guo 2002: 357). Another estimate, however, suggested that only 40 percent of Beijing's migrant children aged five to 12 were attending school in 1995, compared to 100 percent of local children in the same age group (cited by Solinger 1999: 266). In addition, whereas the China News Agency stated that as few as 12.5 percent of Beijing's migrant children were attending school in 2001, the Xinhua News Agency claimed that nearly 80 percent of the city's migrant children were in public schools in 2002 (cited by Kwong 2006: 169). Such variation reflects to a large extent the challenges of establishing a sampling frame for migrant children and has greatly limited the understanding of the educational exclusion of this group and, ultimately, educational inequality in China (Hannum *et al.* 2010: 145).

Additional problems also exist. Official data may often only include migrants with temporary residence permits, leaving a large number uncounted, while statistics such as those in the 1997 Beijing Migrant Census do not necessarily differentiate between government-sponsored schools and migrant schools (Guo 2002: 359, 372). Moreover, many migrant children in school are overage, making it more difficult to assess their situations (Lü and Zhang 2004: 63–4). For example, a 2004 study by the National Working Committee for Children and Women and UNICEF estimated that 47 percent of six-year-old migrant children were still not attending school and that a number of children aged 11 to 14 were only in the first or second grade (cited by Nielsen *et al.* 2006: 462).

Second, there is a lack of extensive research. Literature on migrant children's education tends to be descriptive, usually discussing the common problems of migrant schools and general barriers to public school education. To the best of my knowledge, only two major studies have compared aspects of migrant and public schools in Beijing (Song *et al.* 2009; Lai *et al.* 2012). Both indicate gaps between migrant and public schools in terms of the quality of education and the educational performance of migrant children, though, because of limited access, Lai *et al.* (2012) included only four public schools in their sample. Indeed, there remain serious difficulties in gaining access to public schools for research purposes in Beijing, further limiting the understanding of migrant children's education.

What is more, the discussion of policies on migrant children's education tends to place great emphasis on the impact of the *hukou* system and only points to the general role of local governments in providing education for these children (see Guo 2002; Han 2003; Lü and Zhang 2004; Kwong 2006; Liang and Chen 2007; Wang 2009). It falls short of analyzing the role of policy implementation, and there is also a tendency to discuss municipal-level situations, with very little attention given to district-level dynamics (e.g. China Labour Bulletin 2008). Li (2004: 28), for instance, writes that in some cities, like Beijing, the government exerts strict control over migrant schools, while in others, like Shanghai, the government is working to improve them. Such generalizations inherently overlook potential variation *within* cities, making additional research critical.

## Rural–urban migration, the *hukou* system, and urbanization

As discussed earlier, the Chinese government initiated efforts to improve the treatment of rural–urban migrants in the early 2000s, raising important questions surrounding the continued relevance of the *hukou* system (Liang and Ma 2004: 484; Lu 2008: 56). Since the 1980s, a series of reforms have led to a relaxation of previous restraints on internal migration. For one, with the dismantling of the commune system and the establishment of the household responsibility system, agricultural production became more efficient, and this increased the capacity of peasants to seek employment in the service and industrial sectors (Lin 1988; Liang 2001: 500–1). In addition, in order to further develop the service sector in the cities, the government started to permit rural peasants to migrate to urban areas and set up small businesses (Wu and Xie 2003). The increasing market sector in the cities also resulted in a greater demand for cheap rural labor (Wu and Treiman 2004: 365).

Despite such reforms, there remains a strong tendency to emphasize the *hukou* system's continued impact on trends in social stratification (see Davin 1999: 48; Cai 2003: 120; Liang and Ma 2004: 484; Wu and Treiman 2004: 365; Chan and Buckingham 2008; Lu 2008: 56). As Wang (2010: 335) asserts:

> Functioning as a legal Great Wall, a great floodgate, China's *hukou* (household registration) system has divided people and regulated internal migration for more than a half century in the People's Republic of China (PRC). Much of China's profound gap between the rural and urban sectors, and among the different regions, is either directly created by or essentially maintained by the *hukou* system. Despite repeated efforts at reforming it since the 1980s, the *hukou* system remains a fundamental institution that helps to define politics, social life, and economic development in the PRC today.

Accordingly, it is also regularly discussed as being at the root of migrant children's educational problems (see Guo 2002; Lü and Zhang 2004; Kwong 2006; Liang and Chen 2007; Wang 2008). Chen and Liang (2007: 128), for instance, maintain: "Policies that would allow migrant children to be enrolled in local public schools without paying prohibitively high fees are ultimately linked to the reform of China's *hukou* system."

It is difficult to discuss rural–urban migration and social stratification in China without also mentioning urbanization. Urbanization – which Gu and Wu (2010: 1–2) define as "a complex and multifaceted process involving population migration from rural to urban areas, rural and urban land conversions, spatial reconfiguration of settlements, and changing governance and management" – has become a critical part of China's post-1978 societal transformation (Heikkila 2007: 65). Because of factors including the system of administrative hierarchy in urban areas and institutional barriers to labor migration like the *hukou* system, it is often referred to as "urbanization with Chinese characteristics" (Chan 2010: 65–70).

Though relatively slow between 1949 and 1978, urbanization has since entered into a period of rapid growth, involving a growing urban population and an increasing number of cities and towns (Zhou 2004: 445; Li and Piachaud 2006: 1).[15] Despite being difficult to measure given the complexities surrounding urban borders and definitions of "urban" (Chan 2010: 64), estimates have been high. Yusuf and Nabeshima (2008: 1–2, table 1.2), for example, draw on data from various sources to argue that, between 1980 and 2005, the percentage of China's population residing in urban areas increased from 19.6 percent to 42.9 percent, and the urban population grew from 191.4 million to 562.1 million.[16] A key factor contributing to this trend has been rural–urban migration (Heikkila 2007: 68).[17] Such migration has increased the pressures on local governments in large cities, with important outcomes for migrant workers (Li and Piachaud 2006: 7; Saich 2008: 181).[18]

Indeed, while it can be viewed as "the best long-term solution to the problems of inequality in service provision, which primarily reflect urban-rural differences"

(Saich 2008: 182), urbanization has had major consequences for the exclusion of rural–urban migrants in areas like service provision and housing. The implications are serious. Urban development, and the focus on physical infrastructure in particular, takes government resources away from developing human capital, when investing in human capital not only improves technological and manufacturing capabilities, but it also plays a critical role in fighting unemployment and urban crime (Yusuf and Nabeshima 2008: 24).

Thus rural–urban migration, the *hukou* system, urbanization, and social stratification in China can be seen as being closely interlinked. As Heikkila (2007: 77–8) puts it: "These [migrant] workers are essential to successful urbanization, yet that very success can undermine their ability to partake in it, as housing costs and basic services are priced beyond their reach." Yet a part of this picture that remains largely unexplored is the politics surrounding policy implementation and the potential outcomes for migrant families and the services available to them locally. While it is difficult to deny the fundamental importance of the *hukou* system, the tendency to emphasize its central impact on policies concerning migrants might lead to the conclusion that such institutional mechanisms operate in relative isolation. Deeper analyses of the local policy processes at work would shed much needed light on the extent to which central-level objectives to improve the treatment of rural–urban migrants are being realized and why.

## Educational inequality and social stratification in China

The significance of examining the consequences of policy implementation for migrant children's education in particular can be understood by looking at the basic relationship between educational inequality and social stratification in China.[19] China's student population – the largest in the world – totaled 234 million by 1996 (including roughly 136 million at the primary school level) and grew to 318 million by late 2002 (cited by UNDP 1998: 39; China Education and Research Network 2004). Access to education in the country is at an all-time high. Though the government has only allotted a small proportion of its GDP to education over recent decades,[20] it has achieved rates of enrollment at the primary and middle school levels surpassing that in the majority of other low-income countries (Postiglione 2006: 3). China's primary school net enrollment rate increased from 97.8 percent to 98.7 percent between 1990 and 2003, and the gross enrollment rate for middle school increased from 66.7 percent to 90 percent between 1990 and 2002 (Ministry of Foreign Affairs of the People's Republic of China and United Nations System in China 2005: 22).

Still, such figures are only part of the picture, and there is general consensus that education is an increasingly crucial factor influencing patterns of social stratification and inequality in China (see Hannum 1999: 210–11; Rong and Shi 2001; Li 2003: 62; Ding and Lu 2006: 25; Ross 2006). Between 1978 and 1996, China's GDP increased nearly fourfold, bringing an overall improvement in living standards (cited by Wu and Xie 2003: 426–7). Post-1978 economic reforms, however, have also contributed to rising inequalities; according to

Gustafsson *et al.* (2008: 20, table 1.3), for example, the Gini coefficient in China rose from 0.395 to 0.450–0.468 between 1988 and 2002. This has had major consequences for education. As Postiglione (2006: 3) asserts, "educational inequalities continue to widen, compliments of a hot-wired market economy and the easing of pressure on the central government over the responsibility to ensure access and equity."

Indeed, economic reforms have created disparities in the allocation of educational investment, leading to gaps in educational attainment and opportunities and consequences for income and work-related disparities (Rong and Shi 2001: 121).[21] These inequalities exist in terms of area (between and within urban and rural areas), region (western, central, and eastern/coastal), gender, and ethnicity. In fact, the rural poor, girls, ethnic minorities, and the children of migrants have the lowest enrollment and highest dropout rates (Postiglione 2006: 3–5). For instance, based on 2000 census data, the enrollment rate for children aged seven to 16 was 89 percent in rural areas and 94 percent in urban areas, and the percentage of the population that was not enrolled in school and had less than middle school attainment was 13.17 percent in rural areas and 3.75 percent in urban areas (Hannum *et al.* 2010: 132, 141, table 6.8). By the early 2000s, roughly one-fifth of China's inhabited rural areas had not yet been able to guarantee nine years of compulsory education. What is more, about 70 percent of school-aged children under 11 years of age who were not attending school were female (Postiglione 2006: 3–4). These groups can also overlap. Hannum *et al.* (2010: 135, table 6.5), for example, reported an enrollment rate of 76.84 percent for rural minority girls between seven and 16 years old, compared to 91.54 percent for urban minority girls in the same age group in 2000.

Such trends can significantly impact patterns of social stratification (Hannum 1999: 210–11). As Postiglione (2006: 6) contends:

> China is approaching a key historical educational juncture in education – the first time that children from nearly every family, region, and nationality in China will attend school. As schooling reaches into virtually all regions and households, it comes to play a larger role in determining China's social stratification.

The educational exclusion of migrant children can therefore have serious implications for trends in social stratification, motivating a deeper exploration of the local dynamics shaping their educational situations. The rest of this chapter turns to the literatures on policy processes and decentralization to create a framework for analyzing policy implementation and its consequences for migrant children's education. This will shed light on the micro-politics of educational provision for these children and subsequently also the potential range of factors that can affect the situations of migrant schools and their students in one city, strengthening the capacity to improve educational opportunities for these children at the local levels.

## Policy implementation in the realm of migrant children's education: a framework for analysis

This section draws on existing knowledge on policy processes and decentralization, both in general and in China, and identifies key themes that can be applied to analyzing the implementation of policies on migrant children's education. There is a vast amount of literature surrounding policy processes. Most simply, the term refers to "the process through which policy is made and implemented" (Blaikie and Soussan 2001: 11). The linear model (or the rational or mainstream model) discusses policy making as "a problem-solving process which is rational, balanced, objective and analytical" (Sutton 1999: 9). According to this model, policy decisions are the result of several stages: agenda setting, investigation of the options for addressing the problem, assessment of the costs and benefits of those options, decision making, implementation, and possible evaluation (IDS 2006: 7).

There is, however, growing agreement that policy processes are not linear and rational. Instead, they are "incremental, complex and messy" processes in which facts and values interact, "overlapping and competing agendas" are present, and the perspectives of the vulnerable and marginalized are frequently ignored (IDS 2006: 8; see also Sabatier 1986; Thomas and Grindle 1990; Crosby 1996; Sutton 1999; de Vibe *et al.* 2002). Following from this logic, policy processes can be understood by examining the roles of *knowledge and discourse* (what is the narrative and how is it being framed), *actors and networks* (which individuals and groups are involved and how are they related), and *politics and interests* (what power dynamics are involved) (IDS 2006: 9).

Policy processes tend to be context-specific and can even differ within political systems (Atkinson and Coleman 1992: 157). Still, a few general themes are worth highlighting. First is the fundamental importance of policy implementation, which Lampton (1987: 4) defines as "the stage between the high politics of policy formulation and feedback once the effects of policies become apparent." The linear model treats it as a separate process that occurs after policy decisions, one that is meant to resolve the problem as understood in the policy and is administrative in nature. There is increasing agreement, however, that implementation itself can be intensely complex and political (Thomas and Grindle 1990; Crosby 1996; Sutton 1999: 22–3; Little 2008: 14–17). It can be non-linear and interactive and require management through, for example, collaboration, involvement from stakeholders, and the mobilization of resources (Grindle and Thomas 1991; Sutton 1999: 22–3). Lipsky (1980), for instance, introduced the idea of "street-level bureaucracies" to describe the role of actors like schools in shaping implementation and policy outcomes.

Second is the role of policy history. Key policy milestones are critical in understanding policy making and implementation. These can include previous policies and legislation; major conferences, projects, and events; media and public campaigns; and global policy developments (Blaikie and Soussan 2001: 10). Third, policy processes can be significantly influenced by the local social, economic, political, and governance contexts (Grindle and Thomas 1989; Blaikie and

Soussan 2001: 10). The interaction between local contextual factors and differing levels of involvement among actors and networks can have major consequences for the policy process, including implementation (Keeley and Scoones 2000: 90). Indeed, the implementation process can be shaped by both the policy's content (including the decision-making sites, designated implementers, and expected outcomes) and the local context (including institutional arrangements and the interests of and balance of power among different stakeholders) (Little 2008: 16).

Within this discussion of local context, decentralization is often discussed as an important factor (e.g. Blaikie and Soussan 2001). There is a large body of literature on decentralization. In many developing countries and transition economies, the term refers to the transfer of actual *decision-making power* to the local level. In countries where centralized control has been long-established (like China and India), it commonly refers to the transfer of *responsibilities* in implementing policies. There is also a distinction between political and administrative decentralization and fiscal decentralization (Bardhan 2002: 186). For example, in discussing the decentralization of responsibility for the provision of basic education, King and Cordeiro Guerra (2005: 179) write:

> This transfer has taken various forms, including devolving fiscal responsibility and management to lower levels of government, making public schools autonomous, requiring the participation of communities in operating schools, expanding community financing, allowing families to choose their schools, and stimulating private provision of education.

Decentralization is frequently seen as a way of increasing accountability and the efficiency of governments (Bardhan 2002: 185). Yet there is growing discussion in the policy processes literature of its complex effects as well; it can, for instance, lead to "new challenges for citizen action, the negotiation of expertises and participation in the policy process" (Keeley and Scoones 1999: 6). Ultimately, its outcomes vary and are often shaped by local political, institutional, and social circumstances (Azfar *et al.* 2001: 8). As Shankland (2000: 7) maintains, "an extensive literature has already documented the fact that [participation and decentralisation] are also far from unproblematic, and that there is a need for a better understanding of what they mean in specific policy contexts."

In China, the decentralization of power and responsibilities to local governments extends back to the 1950s (Lin *et al.* 2006: 308). Starting in the 1980s, decentralization significantly increased the role of local governments in the delivery of services (Davis 1989). Since then, the complex nature and effects of decentralization have been garnering an increasing amount of scholarly attention, especially in regard to fiscal management and in rural areas (e.g. West and Wong 1995; Riskin 2000; Tang and Bloom 2000; Wong 2007). According to Heilmann (2008: 1, 28), decentralization in China, or "decentralized experimentation" – where local officials are encouraged by the central government to experiment with different methods of problem resolution, and these experiences are subsequently fed back into central-level policy making – can be highly political given "competing interests, ideological frictions, personal rivalries, tactical opportunism or ad hoc policy compromises." Decentralization has thus become a crucial factor influencing policy making and implementation. The resulting gap between policy and local realities then has serious implications for the delivery of social services such as health care and education (Wong 2007). In other words, despite the tendency to emphasize the *hukou* system's impact on social stratification highlighted earlier, there is a general recognition of the important role of local governments, local politics, and local considerations in social welfare provision in China.

The role of civil society is an additional factor. Indeed, decentralization increases the number of stakeholders and can create space for civil society to influence the policy process (King and Cordeiro Guerra 2005: 200). Starting in the 1980s, decentralization in China transferred the responsibility for public policy to local governments. Decisions concerning funding, however, were typically not transferred. In other words, local governments became responsible for providing particular welfare services but lacked the formal budgets to do so and also faced the effects of downsizing. These circumstances created room for civil society actors to take on many of the service provision tasks previously managed by local governments (Teets 2008: 7–8). Policy processes in China have, as a result, become more and more messy and disjointed and are increasingly shaped by local factors (Howell 2007: 21).[22]

Yet knowledge of policy processes in China remains limited, particularly in the realms of migration and education. Much of the academic discourse on policy-making and implementation in China is focused on structural aspects like bureaucratic hierarchies and central–local relations, often in rural areas (Lieberthal and Oksenberg 1988; Bo 2000; Zhong 2003; Lieberthal 2004). There have been some efforts to apply aspects of the policy processes literature to China. Lampton (1987: 3–4), for instance, highlights the absence of references to China in the literature on implementation and the importance of understanding the interaction between policy content, the institutional context of policy implementation, and the broader social and political environment. A more recent example is Bloom *et al.* (2008), which examines the making and implementation of health policies in China, Cambodia, and Lao PDR, including the roles of policy networks and different stakeholder interests.

In the academic discourse on migrant children's education, however, there has been a general lack of attempts to analyze the implementation process, including the roles of policy history and local context. Moreover, despite increasing discussion of civil society in China in areas like the environment (e.g. Ho 2001) and, as will be discussed in Chapter 7, labor and gender, very few studies have explored the role of civil society in migrant children's education, perhaps the only exception being Kwong (2004). Thus knowledge of how policies on migrant children's education are implemented, including which actors are involved and why, remains extremely limited. Yet, as King and Cordeiro Guerra (2005: 179) maintain: "In countries as large and diverse as China ..., generating local solutions to educational problems and mobilizing local energies and resources can yield dividends for all." The opportunity then arises to think about how existing understandings of policy processes may resonate in the realm of migrant children's education. This would not only shed light on the micro-politics of migrant children's education in Beijing and the consequences for migrant schools, but it would also help in identifying more targeted ways to improve the educational situations of these children.

This study draws on the above discussion – including the work of Grindle and Thomas (1989), Sutton (1999), Riskin (2000), Blaikie and Soussan (2001), King and Cordeiro Guerra (2005), IDS (2006), Howell (2007), Wong (2007), Little (2008), and Teets (2008) – to analyze the local policy environment concerning migrant children's education in Beijing. In light of the decentraliza-tion of responsibilities called for by the policy of "two priorities," it explores the potential impacts of three key areas on policy implementation: (1) *policy history* (including central and municipal policies); (2) *local context* (including municipal and district-level factors); and (3) *the role of civil society actors* (including their capacity to interact with the government) (see Figure 2.1). As Blaikie and Soussan (2001: 2) emphasize, analyses of policy processes must include the impacts on the people the policies are meant to affect. Examining the conse-quences of the above for migrant schools and their students is therefore critical to the research, informing the understanding of educational provision for this group and larger trends in social stratification.

Because of the way in which central policies on migrant children's education have been designed, lower levels of government often enjoy flexibility in interpret-ing and implementing them. In Beijing, the municipal government sets the tone of the local policy environment by interpreting central policies and designing local ones and by setting guidelines for the district governments to follow. The frame-work proposed above therefore involves examining the policy approaches adopted at both the municipal and district levels and the reasons behind them, shedding light on the nature of this flexibility and the roles these two levels of government

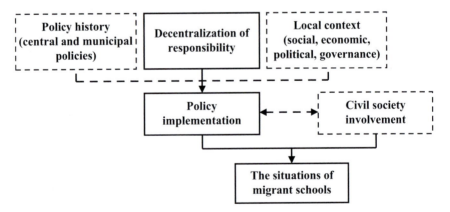

*Figure 2.1* Factors shaping policy implementation and its impact on migrant schools in Beijing.

Source: Author's fieldwork (2009–10).

play in the policy area. Analysis also shows, however, that the shift towards local responsibility for educating migrant children has increased the number and range of local actors involved. In addition to actors within the government, academics and researchers, the media, university student organizations, NGOs, businesses, migrant school principals' and teachers' associations, and migrant parent activists have become involved as well. This has greatly increased the potential for interaction in the policy process, not only between the government and civil society, but also among civil society actors themselves (see Figure 2.2).

This study explores the roles of the government and civil society actors involved, including the extent to which there is room for such interaction and how their relationships with each other and with migrant schools shape the environment in which education is provided to migrant children in Beijing. It tackles questions involving the balance of power between stakeholders, why some voices are included or excluded, and what the consequences are for migrant schools and their students. Given the unique historical development of the migration policies and patterns discussed earlier in this chapter, as well as the distinctive nature of Chinese policy making, such an analysis will make a valuable contribution to the discourse on policy implementation in China and its relationship to trends in social inequality.

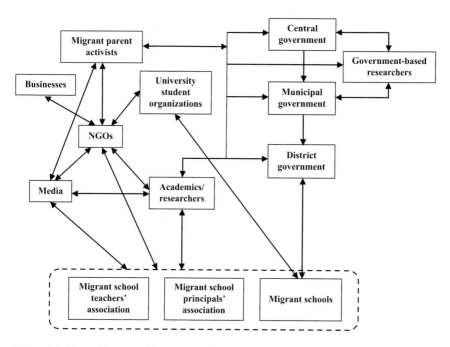

*Figure 2.2* Potential areas of interaction between government, civil society, and migrant schools in Beijing.

Source: Author's fieldwork (2009–10).

Ultimately, this framework allows for a deeper examination of the potential complexities surrounding policy implementation – including the effects of local context at the municipal and district levels – and the consequences for migrant schools and their students. This will shed important light on the local policy environment, including the relationship between decentralized decision making and local politics, and the implications for broader trends in social stratification. Furthermore, this exploration will help demonstrate that assumptions about the *hukou* system's predominant impact on policies concerning rural–urban migrants are grounded in a more linear interpretation of policy processes, in which such institutional regulations operate in a relatively straightforward and insulated manner. The above discussion makes it clear that policy processes are far from straightforward. By applying this framework to migrant children's education in Beijing, this study underscores the need to look beyond the *hukou* system's impact and creates a more nuanced understanding of the situations of migrant schools and their students at the local levels.

China has a long history of decentralization and therefore provides useful lessons, including those concerning the different factors that have shaped its experiences, the various sources of support or opposition that have emerged, and the obstacles and risks that have been encountered over time (King and Cordeiro Guerra 2005: 196). Drawing on existing knowledge on policy processes and decentralization, as well as migration, urbanization, and educational inequality in China, this study fills major gaps in the understanding of how policies in this area are implemented (including which actors are involved), why certain approaches are adopted (including the roles of policy history and local context), and what the consequences are for migrant schools and their students (including district-level outcomes). This will greatly enhance the understanding of why migrant schools and their students face the situations that they do at the municipal *and* district levels, with the ultimate objective of creating a stronger foundation upon which to improve educational opportunities for these children.

## Notes

1 Such migration was often driven by the government's desire to achieve policy objectives like economic growth via state planning (Lary 1999: 30–1). The relocation of millions of people to inland "Third Front" areas in the 1950s and 1960s and the "rustification" (*xiafang*) of intellectuals and youths from urban areas to rural areas and other remote parts of the country in the 1960s and 1970s are two major examples (see Fan 1999: 956).
2 See Chan and Zhang (1999: 821–3) for a more detailed explanation of this dual classification system.
3 According to Chan (1999: 50), six key factors contributed to this wave of migration: "(1) rural decollectivization, which has set free surplus labourers previously tied to the place of residence in the countryside; (2) rapid expansion of the urban economy, especially in the labour intensive sectors, creating ten of millions of low-skilled jobs; (3) continuing large gaps in living standards between cities and the countryside in many regions, especially since the mid-1980s; (4) concurrent relaxation of migratory controls and development of urban food and labour markets; (5) increasing regional specialization of skills, partly based on different traditions; and (6) the development and expansion of migrant networks …."

4 Much of this has been chain migration, where previous migrants interact with later migrants and provide them with knowledge and support in terms of relocation, housing, and employment, thereby creating linkages between particular places of origin and particular destinations (Mallee 2003: 143). Native-place networks have helped guide migrants into various sectors, jobs, and destinations (Ma and Xiang 1998; Roberts 2002: 150). Most of this migration has also been circular (i.e. every year some migrants leave for the cities and others return) (Davin 1996: 662).

5 To an extent, the results were significant; the number of rural enterprises, for example, increased from 1.5 million to 18.5 million between 1978 and 1990 and reached 23 million in 1996 (cited by Davin 1999: 41).

6 The 1990s was also a period during which street children began to attract more attention. According to the Ministry of Civil Affairs, there were at least 150,000 street children in Chinese cities by the mid-2000s, and most came from poor rural areas (Xinhua News Agency 2005). In 2008, the same ministry estimated that the number of street children lacking parental care was between one and 1.5 million, the majority of whom had migrated to cities from rural areas (UNICEF China 2011). These children often make a living by begging, scavenging, and/or stealing, or by doing jobs such as selling flowers, polishing shoes, and doing temporary work on construction sites. Most have unstable living situations and may frequently find shelter in abandoned buildings, in parks, on construction sites, or on the street. Some move to the cities with their parents or other adults and are cared for by them (Wu 2001: 87).

7 The document provided the impetus for local governments to introduce their own regulations. In 1995, Shanghai's labor bureau issued the "Administrative Measures for the Categorized Usage and Employment of Labor from Outside Shanghai by Local Employers" (*Shanghaishi danwei shiyong he pinyong waidi laodongli fenlei guanli banfa*), which introduced three categories of jobs: jobs that allowed outside laborers, jobs that allowed only the limited employment of outside laborers, and jobs that were not open to outside laborers. Similarly, in 1996, Beijing's labor bureau issued "The 1996 List of Industries and Jobs for which the Usage of People from Outside Beijing is Allowed or Restricted" (*1996 nian benshi yunxu he xianzhi shiyong waidi renyuan de hangye gongzhong fanwei*) and the "Notice of the Beijing Bureau of Labor on Issues Concerning Employers Recruiting Workers from Outside Beijing" (*Beijingshi laodongju guanyu yongren danwei zhaoyong waidi wugong renyuan youguan wenti de tongzhi*), which were both based on the notion of "urban first, rural second" and "Beijing first, outside second" (Li 2004: 22–3).

8 In 2003, Sun Zhigang, a 27-year-old migrant worker and university graduate, was detained at a custody and repatriation center in Guangzhou after failing to produce a temporary residence permit during a random identity check by local police. Sun was severely beaten while in custody and died three days after being detained (Liu 2003).

9 The new policies following the *hukou* reform can be summarized as follows: (1) in small towns and townships, rural laborers who legally work and have housing can obtain residency; (2) in medium-sized cities and the capitals of certain provinces, the maximum number of rural workers who can apply for permanent residency has been eliminated; and (3) in large cities like Beijing and Shanghai, the number of rural workers who can acquire permanent residency continues to be limited by a policy of "widening the gate, raising the price" (Huang and Pieke 2005: 114).

10 Such sentiments were expanded on in 2004 and 2005 circulars (Davies and Ramia 2008: 142–3).

11 One factor leading to the emergence of education as a motive for migration during the 1980s was the declining educational situation in rural areas, where economic and educational policies were limiting the number of schools and increasing the costs of educational provision. The result was rural–urban stratification in the education system, prohibiting rural children from moving up the social ladder (Hannum 1999: 210).

12 The exact period during which migrant children began to move with their parents into cities on a large scale cannot be discussed with certainty. There was a major underreporting of children in the 1982, 1990, and 2000 censuses, and underreporting in 2000 was three times greater than that in the earlier censuses. This was largely because of incentives faced by government officials and parents to underreport; for example, since the early 1990s, local officials have been held accountable in cases where family planning regulations were violated (Goodkind 2004: 281–2, 288).

13 See www.edu.cn/20050114/3126820.shtml (accessed January 24, 2012).

14 The informal sector is a difficult concept to measure and define, particularly given the substantial variation in the problems and needs of those working in it (Gërxhani 2004; Ruffer and Knight 2007: 15). Nevertheless, "[t]hese different groups have been termed 'informal' because they share one important characteristic: they are not recognised or protected under the legal and regulatory frameworks" (Ruffer and Knight 2007: 15).

15 See Zhou (2004) and Li and Piachaud (2006) for an overview of urbanization in China since 1949.

16 The most urbanized populations in China are in the eastern and coastal provinces and municipalities (Chen 2006: 104).

17 Though pre-reform urbanization was government-controlled, post-1978 urbanization has been driven by industrial development in rural areas, the market economy, and large-scale rural–urban migration (Li and Piachaud 2006: 6).

18 The focus on urbanization in small cities and towns has, since the Eleventh Five-Year Plan (2006–10), also been extended to large cities (Li and Piachaud 2006: 11).

19 In the realm of human resource development, there are several key "energizers," mainly education, health and nutrition, employment, the environment, and economic and political freedom. Though all interconnected, education is often treated as the foundation for improving the rest (cited by Rong and Shi 2001: 108). If provided equally and efficiently, it can help break the intergenerational transmission of poverty (Todaro and Smith 2009: 371).

20 In 1990, the Chinese government spent 2.5 percent of its GNP on education, ranking 114th in the world (Rong and Shi 2001: 120). Despite pledges to allocate 4 percent of its GDP to education since 1993, educational expenditure was still only 3.33 percent of GDP in 2008 (Chen 2010). The problem is amplified by the failure to fully utilize existing resources for education (Tsang 1994: 309).

21 Between 1990 and 1998, the government's share in the total expenditure on education dropped from 64.6 percent to 53.1 percent. During the same period, the share of tuition and incidental fees increased from 2.3 percent to 12.5 percent. This has resulted in an increased financial burden on poor families with school-aged children, making it more difficult for them to complete the nine years of compulsory education and increasing the potential for greater educational inequality (Zhang and Kanbur 2005: 194).

22 Relevant literature on civil society in social welfare provision in China will be discussed in Chapter 7.

# Bibliography

Atkinson, Michael M. and William D. Coleman. "Policy Networks, Policy Communities and the Problems of Governance." *Governance: An International Journal of Policy and Administration* 5, no. 2 (April 1992): 154–80.

Azfar, Omar, Satu Kähkönen, and Patrick Meagher. "Conditions for Effective Decentralized Governance: A Synthesis of Research Findings." IRIS Working Paper No. 256, University of Maryland, IRIS Center, College Park, MD, 2001. www.iris.umd.edu/download.aspx?ID=b587c7e7-919f-46f1-b166-1297ba15818a (accessed May 6, 2011).

Bardhan, Pranab. "Decentralization of Governance and Development." *Journal of Economic Perspectives* 16, no. 4 (Fall 2002): 185–205.

Bi, Jianhong. "'Zhongguo yiwu jiaoyu caizheng gaige: chengxiao yu zhanwang' xueshu yanjiuhui zongshu" [A Summary of the Academic Forum Entitled Financial Reform of Compulsory Education in China: Achievements and Prospects]. CIEFR Briefing No. 13, Peking University, China Institute for Educational Finance Research, Beijing, 2009. http://ciefr.pku.edu.cn/html/c12_KeYanJianBao/2009-12/285.html (accessed April 3, 2012).

Blaikie, Piers and John Soussan. "Understanding Policy Processes." Livelihood-Policy Relationships in South Asia Working Paper No. 8, University of Leeds, Leeds, 2001. www.york.ac.uk/inst/sei/prp/pdfdocs/2_livelihoods.pdf (accessed May 10, 2009).

Bloom, Gerald, Lijie Fang, Kristina Jönsson, Chean Rithy Men, Bounfeng Phoummalaysith, Anonh Xeuatvongsa, Yunping Wang, and Hongwen Zhao. "Health Policy Processes in Asian Transitional Economies." *Studies in HSO&P* 23 (2008): 85–105. www.itg.be/itg/Uploads/Volksgezondheid/povill/Health%20policy%20processes%20in%20Asian%20transitional%20economies.pdf (accessed October 9, 2010).

Bo, Zhiyue. "Introduction: Local Government in Post-Deng China." *Journal of Contemporary China* 9, no. 24 (2000): 157–8.

Branz-Spall, Angela Maria, Roger Rosenthal, and Al Wright. "Children of the Road: Migrant Students, Our Nation's Most Mobile Population." *The Journal of Negro Education* 72, no. 1 (Winter 2003): 55–62.

Cai, Fang. "How the Market Economy Promotes the Reform of the Household Registration System." *Social Sciences in China* 24, no. 4 (Winter 2003): 118–25.

Chan, Kam Wing. "Internal Migration in China: A Dualistic Approach." In *Internal and International Migration: Chinese Perspectives*, ed. Frank N. Pieke and Hein Mallee. Surrey: Curzon Press, 1999, pp. 49–71.

Chan, Kam Wing. "Fundamentals of China's Urbanization and Policy." *The China Review* 10, no. 1 (Spring 2010): 63–94.

Chan, Kam Wing and Will Buckingham. "Is China Abolishing the *Hukou* System?" *The China Quarterly* 195 (September 2008): 582–606.

Chan, Kam Wing and Li Zhang. "The *Hukou* System and Rural–Urban Migration in China: Processes and Changes." *The China Quarterly* 160 (December 1999): 818–55.

Chen, Aimin. "Urbanization in China and the Case of Fujian Province." *Modern China* 32, no. 1 (January 2006): 99–130.

Chen, Jia. "Government to Increase Spending on Education." *China Daily*, March 1, 2010. www.chinadaily.com.cn/china/2010-03/01/content_9515384.htm (accessed April 24, 2012).

Chen, Yiu Por and Zai Liang. "Educational Attainment of Migrant Children: The Forgotten Story of China's Urbanization." In *Education and Reform in China*, ed. Emily Hannum and Albert Park. Oxford: Routledge, 2007, pp. 117–32.

Cheng, Tiejun and Mark Selden. "The Origins and Social Consequences of China's *Hukou* System." *The China Quarterly* 139 (September 1994): 644–68.

China Education and Research Network. "MOE: Survey of the Educational Reform and Development in China." December 23, 2004. www.edu.cn/Researchedu_1498/20060323/t20060323_113688.shtml (accessed October 10, 2008).

China Labour Bulletin. "National People's Congress Approves New Labour Contract Law." 2007. www.clb.org.hk/en/node/46445 (accessed August 3, 2012).

China Labour Bulletin. "The Children of Migrant Workers in China." 2008. www.clb.org.hk/en/node/100316 (accessed December 3, 2008).

Crosby, Benjamin L. "Policy Implementation: The Organizational Challenge." *World Development* 24, no. 9 (September 1996): 1403–15.

Davies, Gloria and Gaby Ramia. "Governance Reform towards 'Serving Migrant Workers': The Local Implementation of Central Government Regulations." *The China Quarterly* 193 (March 2008): 140–9.

Davin, Delia. "Migration and Rural Women in China: A Look at the Gendered Impact of Large-Scale Migration." *Journal of International Development* 8, no. 5 (September 1996): 655–65.

Davin, Delia. *Internal Migration in Contemporary China*. London: Macmillan, 1999.

Davis, Deborah. "Chinese Social Welfare: Policies and Outcomes." *The China Quarterly* 119 (September 1989): 577–97.

de Vibe, Maja, Ingeborg Hovland, and John Young. "Bridging Research and Policy: An Annotated Bibliography." ODI Working Paper No. 174, Overseas Development Institute, London, 2002. www.odi.org.uk/resources/odi-publications/working-papers/174-bridging-research-policy-annotated-bibliography.pdf (accessed November 7, 2008).

Ding, Weili and Ming Lu. "Are Equity and Efficiency Irreconcilable Goals in Education? A General Equilibrium Analysis of Basic Education Finance." *Social Sciences in China* 27, no. 3 (Autumn 2006): 21–31.

Fan, C. Cindy. "Migration in a Socialist Transitional Economy: Heterogeneity, Socioeconomic and Spatial Characteristics of Migrants in China and Guangdong Province." *International Migration Review* 33, no. 4 (Winter 1999): 954–87.

Fan, C. Cindy. "The Elite, the Natives, and the Outsiders: Migration and Labor Market Segmentation in Urban China." *Annals of the Association of American Geographers* 92, no. 1 (March 2002): 103–24.

Gërxhani, Klarita. "The Informal Sector in Developed and Less Developed Countries: A Literature Survey." *Public Choice* 120, no. 3/4 (September 2004): 267–300.

Giani, Laura. "Migration and Education: Child Migrants in Bangladesh." Sussex Migration Working Paper No. 33, University of Sussex, Sussex Centre for Migration Research, Brighton, 2006. www.sussex.ac.uk/migration/documents/mwp33.pdf (accessed December 5, 2008).

Goodkind, Daniel M. "China's Missing Children: The 2000 Census Underreporting Surprise." *Population Studies* 58, no. 3 (November 2004): 281–95.

Grindle, Merilee S. and John W. Thomas. "Policy Makers, Policy Choices, and Policy Outcomes: The Political Economy of Reform in Developing Countries." *Policy Sciences* 22, no. 3/4 (1989): 213–48.

Grindle, Merilee S. and John W. Thomas. *Public Choices and Policy Change: The Political Economy of Reform in Developing Countries*. Baltimore, MD: Johns Hopkins University Press, 1991.

Gu, Chaolin and Fulong Wu. "Urbanization in China: Processes and Policies." *The China Review* 10, no. 1 (Spring 2010): 1–10.

Guo, Fei. "School Attendance of Migrant Children in Beijing, China: A Multivariate Analysis." *Asian and Pacific Migration Journal* 11, no. 3 (2002): 357–74.

Gustafsson, Björn, Shi Li, and Terry Sicular. "Inequality and Public Policy in China: Issues and Trends." In *Inequality and Public Policy in China*, ed. Björn A. Gustafsson, Shi Li, and Terry Sicular. Cambridge: Cambridge University Press, 2008, pp. 1–34.

Han, Jialing. "Beijingshi liudong ertong yiwu jiaoyu zhuangkuang diaocha baogao" [Report on the Investigation of the Compulsory Education Situation of Children of the Floating Population in Beijing]. *Qingnian yanjiu* [*Youth Studies*] 8 and 9 (2001): 1–7, 10–18.

Han, Jialing. "Beijingshi 'dagong zidi xuexiao' de xingcheng, fazhan yu weilai" [The Formation, Development, and Future of Migrant Schools in Beijing]. In *Zhongguo minban jiaoyu zuzhi yu zhidu yanjiu* [Research on the Organization and System of Private Education in China], ed. Xiaobing Sun. Beijing: Zhongguo qingnian chubanshe [China Youth Press], 2003, pp. 402–16.

Hannum, Emily. "Political Change and the Urban–Rural Gap in Basic Education in China, 1949–1990." *Comparative Education Review* 43, no. 2 (May 1999): 193–211.

Hannum, Emily, Meiyan Wang, and Jennifer Adams. "Rural–Urban Disparities in Access to Primary and Secondary Education under Market Reforms." In *One Country, Two Societies: Rural–Urban Inequality in Contemporary China*, ed. Martin King Whyte. Cambridge, MA: Harvard University Press, 2010, pp. 125–46.

Hashim, Iman M. "Exploring the Linkages between Children's Independent Migration and Education: Evidence from Ghana." DRC Working Paper No. T12, University of Sussex, Development Research Centre on Migration, Globalisation and Poverty, Brighton, 2005. www.migrationdrc.org/publications/working_papers/WP-T12.pdf (accessed December 8, 2008).

Heckmann, Friedrich. *Education and Migration: Strategies for Integrating Migrant Children in European Schools and Societies, A Synthesis of Research Findings for Policy-Makers*. Report submitted to the European Commission by the NESSE network of experts, 2008. www.interculturaldialogue2008.eu/fileadmin/downloads/resources/education-and-migration_bamberg.pdf (accessed May 9, 2009).

Heikkila, Eric J. "Three Questions Regarding Urbanization in China." *Journal of Planning Education and Research* 27, no. 1 (Fall 2007): 65–81.

Heilmann, Sebastian. "From Local Experiments to National Policy: The Origins of China's Distinctive Policy Process." *The China Journal* 59 (January 2008): 1–30.

Ho, Peter. "Greening without Conflict? Environmentalism, NGOs and Civil Society in China." *Development and Change* 32, no. 5 (November 2001): 893–921.

Howell, Jude. "Civil Society in China: Chipping Away at the Edges." *Development* 50, no. 3 (September 2007): 17–23.

Huang, Ping and Frank N. Pieke. "China Labor Migration: Some Policy Issues." *Social Sciences in China* 26, no. 3 (Autumn 2005): 112–24.

Huang, Ping and Shaohua Zhan. "Internal Migration in China: Linking It to Development." In *Migration, Development and Poverty Reduction in Asia*, ed. International Organization for Migration. Geneva: International Organization for Migration, 2005, pp. 65–84. www.iom.int/jahia/webdav/site/myjahiasite/shared/shared/mainsite/published_docs/books/migration_development.pdf (accessed April 2, 2012).

IDS. "Understanding Policy Processes: A Review of IDS Research on the Environment". Institute of Development Studies, Knowledge, Technology and Society Team, Brighton, 2006. www.ids.ac.uk/files/Policy_Processes06.pdf (accessed August 3, 2012).

Kandel, William and Grace Kao. "The Impact of Temporary Labor Migration on Mexican Children's Educational Aspirations and Performance." *International Migration Review* 35, no. 4 (Winter 2001): 1205–31.

Keeley, James and Ian Scoones. "Understanding Environmental Policy Processes: A Review." IDS Working Paper No. 89, Institute of Development Studies, Brighton, 1999. www.ids.ac.uk/files/dmfile/wp89.pdf (accessed November 10, 2008).

Keeley, James and Ian Scoones. "Knowledge, Power and Politics: The Environmental Policy-Making Process in Ethiopia." *The Journal of Modern African Studies* 38, no. 1 (March 2000): 89–120.

King, Elizabeth M. and Susana Cordeiro Guerra. "Education Reforms in East Asia: Policy, Process, and Impact." In *East Asia Decentralizes: Making Local Government Work*, ed. World Bank. Washington, DC: World Bank, 2005, pp. 179–207. http://siteresources. worldbank.org/INTEAPDECEN/Resources/dc-full-report.pdf (accessed November 4, 2008).

Kwong, Julia. "Educating Migrant Children: Negotiations between the State and Civil Society." *The China Quarterly* 180 (December 2004): 1073–88.

Kwong, Julia. "The Integration of Migrant Children in Beijing Schools." In *Education and Social Change in China: Inequality in a Market Economy*, ed. Gerard A. Postiglione. Armonk, NY: M. E. Sharpe, 2006, pp. 163–78.

Lai, Fang, Chengfang Liu, Renfu Luo, Linxiu Zhang, Xiaochen Ma, Yujie Bai, Brian Sharbono, and Scott Rozelle. "Private Migrant Schools or Rural/Urban Public Schools: Where Should China Educate Its Migrant Children?" REAP Working Paper No. 224, Stanford University, Rural Education Action Project, Stanford, CA, 2012. http:// iis-db.stanford.edu/pubs/23180/migrant_paper_final_sdr_fang_acm_sdr_march26_ sdr.pdf (accessed August 3, 2012).

Lampton, David M. "The Implementation Problem in Post-Mao China." In *Policy Implementation in Post-Mao China*, ed. David M. Lampton. Berkeley, CA: University of California Press, 1987, pp. 3–24.

Lary, Diana. "The 'Static' Decades: Inter-Provincial Migration in Pre-Reform China." In *Internal and International Migration: Chinese Perspectives*, ed. Frank N. Pieke and Hein Mallee. Surrey: Curzon Press, 1999, pp. 29–48.

Li, Bingqin. "Urban Social Exclusion in Transitional China." CASE Paper No. 82, London School of Economics and Political Science, Centre for Analysis of Social Exclusion, London, 2004. http://sticerd.lse.ac.uk/dps/case/cp/CASEpaper82.pdf (accessed February 3, 2007).

Li, Bingqin and David Piachaud. "Urbanization and Social Policy in China." *Asia-Pacific Development Journal* 13, no. 1 (June 2006): 1–26.

Li, Cheng. "Surplus Rural Laborers and Internal Migration in China: Current Status and Future Prospects." *Asian Survey* 36, no. 11 (November 1996): 1122–45.

Li, Chunling. "Social and Political Changes and Inequality in Educational Opportunities: On the Impact of Family Background and Institutional Factors on Educational Attainment (1940–2001)." *Social Sciences in China* 24, no. 4 (Winter 2003): 62–79.

Liang, Zai. "The Age of Migration in China." *Population and Development Review* 27, no. 3 (September 2001): 499–524.

Liang, Zai and Yiu Por Chen. "The Educational Consequences of Migration for Children in China." *Social Science Research* 36, no. 1 (March 2007): 28–47.

Liang, Zai and Zhongdong Ma. "China's Floating Population: New Evidence from the 2000 Census." *Population and Development Review* 30, no. 3 (September 2004): 467–88.

Lieberthal, Kenneth. *Governing China: From Revolution through Reform*, 2nd edn. New York, NY: W. W. Norton, 2004.

Lieberthal, Kenneth and Michel Oksenberg. *Policy Making in China: Leaders, Structures, and Processes*. Princeton, NJ: Princeton University Press, 1988.

Lin, Justin Yifu. "The Household Responsibility System in China's Agricultural Reform: A Theoretical and Empirical Study." *Economic Development and Cultural Change* 36, no. 3, "Supplement: Why Does Overcrowded, Resource-Poor East Asia Succeed: Lessons for the LDCs?" (April 1988): S199–S224.

Lin, Justin Yifu, Ran Tao, and Mingxing Liu. "Decentralization and Local Governance in China's Economic Transition." In *Decentralization and Local Governance in Developing*

*Countries: A Comparative Perspective*, ed. Pranab Bardhan and Dilip Mookherjee. Cambridge, MA: MIT Press, 2006, pp. 305–27.

Lipsky, Michael. *Street-Level Bureaucracy: Dilemmas of the Individual in Public Services.* New York, NY: Russell Sage Foundation, 1980.

Little, Angela W. *EFA Politics, Policies and Progress.* CREATE Pathways to Access Research Monograph No. 13. London: University of London, Institute of Education, 2008. http://sro.sussex.ac.uk/1861/1/PTA13.pdf (accessed June 18, 2011).

Liu, Ta and Kam Wing Chan. "National Statistics on Internal Migration in China: Comparability Problems." *China Information* 15, no. 2 (October 2001): 75–113.

Liu, Zhiming. "Zhongguo xinwen zhoukan nianzhong tegao: Sun Zhigang, yi shengming juanke muzhi" [China Newsweek Year-End Special Feature: Sun Zhigang, Inscribing His Tombstone with His Life]. *Zhongguo xinwen zhoukan* [*China Newsweek*], December 22, 2003. www.people.com.cn/GB/shizheng/1026/2258792.html (accessed July 12, 2012).

Lü, Shaoqing. *Liushou haishi liudong? "Mingong chao" zhong de ertong yanjiu* [*Left Behind or Migration? An Empirical Study on Children of Rural Migrants*]. Beijing: Zhongguo nongye chubanshe [China Agriculture Press], 2007.

Lü, Shaoqing and Shouli Zhang. "Urban/Rural Disparity and Migrant Children's Education: An Investigation into Schools for Children of Transient Workers in Beijing." *Chinese Education and Society* 37, no. 5 (September/October 2004): 56–83.

Lu, Yilong. "Does *Hukou* Still Matter? The Household Registration System and Its Impact on Social Stratification and Mobility in China." *Social Sciences in China* 29, no. 2 (May 2008): 56–75.

Ma, Laurence J. C. and Biao Xiang. "Native Place, Migration and the Emergence of Peasant Enclaves in Beijing." *The China Quarterly* 155 (September 1998): 546–81.

Mallee, Hein. "Migration, *Hukou* and Resistance in Reform China." In *Chinese Society: Change, Conflict and Resistance*, 2nd edn, ed. Elizabeth J. Perry and Mark Selden. London: RoutledgeCurzon, 2003, pp. 136–57.

Ministry of Foreign Affairs of the People's Republic of China and United Nations System in China. *China's Progress towards the Millennium Development Goals 2005.* Beijing: Department of International Organizations, Ministry of Foreign Affairs of the People's Republic of China, and the United Nations Country Team in China, 2005. www.un. org.cn/cms/p/resources/30/354/content.html (accessed August 3, 2012).

Murphy, Rachel. *How Migrant Labor is Changing Rural China.* Cambridge: Cambridge University Press, 2002.

Nielsen, Ingrid, Berenice Nyland, Chris Nyland, Russell Smyth, and Mingqiong Zhang. "Determinants of School Attendance among Migrant Children: Survey Evidence from China's Jiangsu Province." *Pacific Economic Review* 11, no. 4 (December 2006): 461–76.

Postiglione, Gerard A. "Schooling and Inequality in China." In *Education and Social Change in China: Inequality in a Market Economy*, ed. Gerard A. Postiglione. Armonk, NY: M. E. Sharpe, 2006, pp. 3–24.

Project Team on Rural Labor Migration. "Rural Labor Migration in China: Retrospect and Prospect." In *Labor Mobility in China: A Review of Ford Foundation Grantmaking 1997–2001*, ed. Ford Foundation. Beijing: Ford Foundation, 2001, pp. 105–33.

Qin, Hui. "'Nongmin fudan' wenti de fazhan qushi: Qinghua daxue xuesheng nongcun diaocha baogao zhi fenxi" [The Trend of the "Farmers' Burden" Issue: Analysis of the Rural Survey Report by Tsinghua University Students]. *Gaige* [*Reform*] 2 (1997): 57–62, 87.

Quinn, Michael A. and Stephen Rubb. "The Importance of Education-Occupation Matching in Migration Decisions." *Demography* 42, no. 1 (February 2005): 153–67.

Riskin, Carl. "Decentralization in China's Transition." Bratislava Policy Paper No. 4, UNDP, Bratislava, 2000. http://211.71.86.12/uploadfile/teacher/rwlijun/teaching-plan/200709/1095302541236.pdf (accessed October 21, 2013).

Roberts, Kenneth D. "China's 'Tidal Wave' of Migrant Labor: What Can We Learn from Mexican Undocumented Migration to the United States?" *International Migration Review* 31, no. 2 (Summer 1997): 249–93.

Roberts, Kenneth D. "Rural Migrants in Urban China: Willing Workers, Invisible Residents." *Asia Pacific Business Review* 8, no. 4 (Summer 2002): 141–58.

Rong, Xue Lan and Tianjian Shi. "Inequality in Chinese Education." *Journal of Contemporary China* 10, no. 26 (2001): 107–24.

Ross, Heidi. "Challenging the Gendered Dimensions of Schooling: The State, NGOs, and Transnational Alliances." In *Education and Social Change in China: Inequality in a Market Economy*, ed. Gerard A. Postiglione. Armonk, NY: M. E. Sharpe, 2006, pp. 25–50.

Ruffer, Tim and John Knight. "Informal Sector Labour Markets in Developing Countries." Oxford Policy Management, Oxford, 2007. www.opml.co.uk/sites/opml/files/Informal%20sector%20labour%20markets%20in%20developing%20countries_0.pdf (accessed October 21, 2013).

Sabatier, Paul A. "Top-Down and Bottom-Up Approaches to Implementation Research: A Critical Analysis and Suggested Synthesis." *Journal of Public Policy* 6, no. 1 (January–March 1986): 21–48.

Saich, Tony. "The Changing Role of Urban Government." In *China Urbanizes: Consequences, Strategies, and Policies*, ed. Shahid Yusuf and Tony Saich. Washington, DC: World Bank, 2008, pp. 181–206. http://siteresources.worldbank.org/INTEAECOPRO/Resources/3087694-1206446474145/China_Urbanizes_Complete.pdf (accessed June 28, 2011).

Shankland, Alex. "Analysing Policy for Sustainable Livelihoods." IDS Research Report No. 49, Institute of Development Studies, Brighton, 2000. http://biblioteca.hegoa.ehu.es/system/ebooks/11157/original/Analysing_Policy_for_Sustainable_Livelihoods.pdf (accessed May 20, 2011).

Shen, Jianfa and Yefang Huang. "The Working and Living Space of the 'Floating Population' in China." *Asia Pacific Viewpoint* 44, no. 1 (April 2003): 51–62.

Skeldon, Ron. "Globalization, Skilled Migration and Poverty Alleviation: Brain Drains in Context." DRC Working Paper No. T15, University of Sussex, Development Research Centre on Migration, Globalisation and Poverty, Brighton, 2005. www.migrationdrc.org/publications/working_papers/WP-T15.pdf (accessed December 8, 2008).

Solinger, Dorothy J. *Contesting Citizenship in Urban China: Peasant Migrants, the State, and the Logic of the Market*. Berkeley, CA: University of California Press, 1999.

Song, Yingquan, Prashant Loyalka, and Jianguo Wei. "Does Going to Public Schools Matter for Migrant Children's Academic Achievement in China?" Manuscript, Peking University, China Institute for Educational Finance Research, Beijing, China, 2009.

Sutton, Rebecca. "The Policy Process: An Overview." ODI Working Paper No. 118, Overseas Development Institute, London, 1999. www.odi.org.uk/resources/odi-publications/working-papers/118-policy-process.pdf (accessed November 2, 2008).

Tang, Shenglan and Gerald Bloom. "Decentralizing Rural Health Services: A Case Study in China." *International Journal of Health Planning and Management* 15, no. 3 (July/September 2000): 189–200.

Teets, Jessica C. "Improving Governance in China: The Role of Civil Society in Local Public Policy." Paper presented at the annual meeting of the Midwest Political Science Association National Conference, Chicago, IL, April 3, 2008. www.allacademic.com/meta/p_mla_apa_research_citation/2/6/7/4/9/p267492_index.html (accessed November 4, 2008).

Thomas, John W. and Merilee S. Grindle. "After the Decision: Implementing Policy Reforms in Developing Countries." *World Development* 18, no. 8 (August 1990): 1163–81.

Todaro, Michael P. "Internal Migration in Developing Countries: A Survey." In *Population and Economic Change in Developing Countries*, ed. Richard A. Easterlin. Chicago, IL, University of Chicago Press, 1980, pp. 361–402.

Todaro, Michael P. and Stephen C. Smith. *Economic Development*, 10th edn. Harlow: Pearson Education, 2009.

Tsang, Mun C. "Costs of Education in China: Issues of Resource Mobilization, Equality, Equity and Efficiency." *Education Economics* 2, no. 3 (1994): 287–312.

UNDP. *China Human Development Report: Human Development & Poverty Alleviation 1997*. Beijing: UNDP, 1998. www.undp.org.cn/downloads/nhdr/nhdr1997.pdf (accessed November 7, 2007).

UNICEF China. "In-depth: A Renewed Effort on Street Children." September 2, 2011. www.unicef.cn/en/index.php?m=content&c=index&a=show&catid=53&id=108 (accessed May 9, 2014).

Waddington, Clare. "Livelihood Outcomes of Migration for Poor People." DRC Working Paper No. T1, University of Sussex, Development Research Centre on Migration, Globalisation and Poverty, Brighton, 2003. www.migrationdrc.org/publications/working_papers/WP-T1.pdf (accessed December 8, 2008).

Wang, Dewen and Fang Cai. "Migration and Poverty Alleviation in China." IOM Migration Research Series No. 27, International Organization for Migration, Geneva, 2007. http://publications.iom.int/bookstore/free/MRS_27.pdf (accessed January 25, 2012).

Wang, Fei-Ling. "Renovating the Great Floodgate: The Reform of China's *Hukou* System." In *One Country, Two Societies: Rural–Urban Inequality in Contemporary China*, ed. Martin King Whyte. Cambridge, MA: Harvard University Press, 2010, pp. 335–64.

Wang, Lu. "The Marginality of Migrant Children in the Urban Chinese Educational System." *British Journal of Sociology of Education* 29, no. 6 (November 2008): 691–703.

Wang, Zhichao. "Systematic Barriers to Schooling of Migrant Workers' Children and Policy Recommendations." *Frontiers of Education in China* 4, no. 2 (June 2009): 298–311.

West, Loraine A. and Christine P. W. Wong. "Fiscal Decentralization and Growing Regional Disparities in Rural China: Some Evidence in the Provision of Social Services." *Oxford Review of Economic Policy* 11, no. 4 (Winter 1995): 70–84.

Whitehead, Ann and Iman Hashim. "Children and Migration." Background paper for DFID Migration Team, Department for International Development, London, 2005. www.childmigration.net/dfid_whitehead_hashim_05 (accessed December 8, 2008).

Wong, Christine. "Fiscal Management for a Harmonious Society: Assessing the Central Government's Capacity to Implement National Policies." BICC Working Paper No. 4, British Inter-University China Centre, Oxford, 2007. http://bicc.blogs.ilrt.org/files/2012/06/04-Wong.pdf (accessed October 21, 2013).

Wu, Weiping. "Labor Mobility in China: A Review of the Program Redressing Discrimination against Labor Migrants 1997–2001." In *Labor Mobility in China:*

*A Review of Ford Foundation Grantmaking 1997–2001*, ed. Ford Foundation. Beijing: Ford Foundation, 2001, pp. 57–104.

Wu, Xiaogang and Donald J. Treiman. "The Household Registration System and Social Stratification in China: 1955–1996." *Demography* 41, no. 2 (May 2004): 363–84.

Wu, Xiaogang and Yu Xie. "Does the Market Pay Off? Earnings Returns to Education in Urban China." *American Sociological Review* 68, no. 3 (June 2003): 425–42.

Xinhua News Agency. "China to Help More Street Children." March 7, 2005. www.china.org.cn/english/2005/Mar/121989.htm (accessed May 9, 2011).

Xinhua News Agency. "Left-Behind, Migrant Children in China Nears 100 Mln." May 10, 2013. http://news.xinhuanet.com/english/china/2013-05/10/c_132373256.htm (accessed December 12, 2013).

Yang, Xiushi and Fei Guo. "Gender Differences in Determinants of Temporary Labor Migration in China: A Multilevel Analysis." *International Migration Review* 33, no. 4 (Winter 1999): 929–53.

Yusuf, Shahid and Kaoru Nabeshima. "Optimizing Urban Development." In *China Urbanizes: Consequences, Strategies, and Policies*, ed. Shahid Yusuf and Tony Saich. Washington, DC: World Bank, 2008, pp. 1–40. http://siteresources.worldbank.org/INTEAECOPRO/Resources/3087694-1206446474145/China_Urbanizes_Complete.pdf (accessed June 28, 2011).

Zhang, Xiaobo and Ravi Kanbur. "Spatial Inequality in Education and Health Care in China." *China Economic Review* 16, no. 2 (2005): 189–204.

Zhao, Shukai. "Peasant Migration: Order Building and Policy Rethinking." *Social Sciences in China* 24, no. 4 (Winter 2003): 168–76.

Zhong, Yang. *Local Government and Politics in China: Challenges from Below*. Armonk, NY: M. E. Sharpe, 2003.

Zhou, Weilin. "China's Urbanisation: A Study of Its Evolution." *China Report* 40, no. 4 (November 2004): 445–59.

Zhou, Xuejun. "Report on Participatory Urban Poverty Analysis in Beijing: Voice of the Urban Poor". Chinese Agricultural University, Center for Integrated Agricultural Development, Beijing, 2000. www.adb.org/documents/reports/voice_urban_poor/urban_poverty_analysis.pdf (accessed November 7, 2007).

# 3 The growth and development of migrant schools in Beijing

This chapter focuses on the emergence of privately-run migrant schools as a source of education for migrant children in Beijing and provides useful background information that motivates this book's focus on the capital city. Following on from the review of migration patterns and policies and migrant children's education in China in Chapter 2, this chapter starts by highlighting the substantial growth in the number and size of migrant schools in Beijing since the early 1990s. In doing so, it provides evidence of their critical role in the provision of compulsory education for migrant children in the city, making a closer examination of their situations at the local levels important. The rest of the chapter presents a brief overview of the situations in each of the three selected districts (Shijingshan, Fengtai, and Haidian), including basic physical, demographic, and economic differences between them.

## The growth and development of migrant schools in Beijing

According to the Sixth National Population Census, Beijing's permanent resident population reached 19.6 million in November 2010, including about seven million migrants (Xinhua News Agency 2011). The 1997 Beijing Migrant Census indicated that roughly one-third of the migrants in the city were already family units (Mallee 2003: 153). Based on data from the 2005 One-Percent Population Survey of China and a 2006 one-percent floating population survey conducted in Beijing by Renmin University of China, it was estimated that there were about 504,000 children aged 14 and under in the city's floating population by the mid-2000s, an increase of about 310,000 since 2000 (Zhai *et al.* 2007; Duan and Yang 2008: 23). By late 2002, there were around 350 migrant schools in the city (Han 2003: 402).

The discovery of the existence of migrant schools in Beijing is generally attributed to a local researcher at the Development Research Center of China's State Council named Zhao Shukai, whom one long-time migrant school principal in the sample referred to as "the Columbus of Beijing's migrant schools" (HL1P1). While conducting research on migrant workers in 1996, Zhao first came across a migrant school by chance after enquiring about some young children he had seen in a migrant village. He went on to bring the issue to the attention of the media and subsequently the government and society. Despite the media coverage, however, research on migrant children's education in Beijing was rather limited during the late 1990s and early 2000s. The main studies conducted during this period were Lü (2007), the research for which was primarily conducted in 1999 and 2000, and Han (2001), the research for which was conducted in late 2000. Much of the early knowledge of this subject is based on this research. Though the focus of these studies is primarily on describing the situations of migrant schools (e.g. in terms of the backgrounds of the principals and teachers and the numbers of students) and the general problems of the schools and their students, their findings nevertheless provide important and necessary historical context for this study's analysis.

According to Han (2003: 404–6), the emergence and development of migrant schools in Beijing can be divided into three stages: the appearance of migrant schools (1993–7), a period of competitive development (1998–2000), and a period of expansion and self-improvement in an attempt to acquire legal status (2001–3). The first appearance of migrant schools in the city occurred in the early 1990s.[1] These schools – set up for children whose parents made up the lower income segment of the floating population[2] – were run without government permission and operated as "underground schools" (*dixia xuexiao*). They emerged as a "self-help" (*zili jiuji*) or "self-resolution" (*zixing jiejue*) mechanism in a context in which migrants were unable to pay fees like the temporary schooling fee (*jiedufei*) and sponsorship fee (*zanzhufei*) to enroll their children in local public schools (Han 2001: 1–4, 6). That is, it was the migrant workers themselves who took on the responsibility of educating migrant children – children of their friends and relatives, children of other migrants from their home provinces, and their own children – to prevent them from becoming illiterate.[3] Classes were held in makeshift settings or small buildings in the migrant enclaves (Han 2001: 1; 2003: 403–4).

The number of migrant children in Beijing continued to rise during this period. According to the 1997 Beijing Migrant Census, the city's floating population (*Beijing diqu wailai liudong renkou*) reached 2.859 million (including a resident outside population, or *zai Jing juzhu de wailai renkou*, of 2.299 million, accounting for 21.18 percent of the total registered population, or *huji renkou*). This included 162,030 children under the age of 15 and 66,392 children between six and 15 years of age. Also, 32.84 percent of the city's outside population were family units by 1997, and many were beginning to stay for longer periods of time; the census found that 19.42 percent of the outside population had already been in Beijing for over three years, and 10.4 percent had been in the city for at least five years (Han 2001: 1). At the same time, however, the estimated percentage of migrant children in the city who were attending school remained low. Lü and Zhang (2004: 63), for example, write that only 12.5 percent of migrant children aged six to 14 were enrolled in school in the city around the late 1990s.[4] In addition, the dropout rate among children of the city's floating population was estimated to be 13.9 percent based on the 1997 census (Han 2001: 4). These dropouts would sometimes enter the workforce at an early age (Lü and Zhang 2004: 64).

As a result, there was a remarkable increase in the number of migrant schools between 1998 and 2000, during what Han (2003: 404) refers to as a period of competitive growth (*chengzhang jingzheng qi*).[5] Lü (2007: 227) estimated that, by 1999–2000, Beijing had 150–160 migrant schools with 15,000–20,000 students, while Han (2001: 2) estimated that there were at least 200 migrant schools with over 40,000 students by late 2000. By late 2002, the estimate had risen to about 350, with nearly 100,000 students. It was not uncommon for villages to have more than one migrant school, and some schools opened multiple branches.[6] This was then followed by a stage of expansion and self-improvement between 2001 and 2003, in which many schools strove to acquire licenses from the government (Han 2001: 3; 2003: 402, 404–6).

Given the high mobility and often illegal status of migrant schools, figures for the numbers of these schools at any given time have varied. Overall, however, estimates for the number of migrant schools in Beijing – as well as the number of children attending these schools – have substantially increased since the mid-1990s. Over a decade and a half after their first documented appearance in Beijing, it was estimated that there were still over 300 migrant schools, with more than 90,000 students (Rural Education Action Project 2009). At the time of fieldwork, 66 of these schools had been licensed by the government.[7]

Not only has there been a considerable rise in the number of migrant schools in Beijing over time, but the average size of these schools has also increased. According to Lü (2007: 225), these schools varied in size early on; among the 114 migrant schools surveyed in 1999–2000, the number of students at each school ranged from seven to over 1,300 (though the average number of students was 93). There does continue to be a range. Within this study's sample of 22 migrant schools, the number of students at any particular location ranged from about 280 to over 1,600, and the number of teachers ranged from slightly over ten to over 70 (see Table 3.1). However, the average size has increased. For example, nine of the 22 schools I visited had at least 900 students.[8] Indeed, as will be further discussed in Chapter 6, migrant schools remain a critical source of education for migrant children in Beijing, motivating a closer examination of their situations at the local levels.

## The selected districts: Shijingshan, Fengtai, and Haidian

At the time of fieldwork, Beijing was divided into 18 administrative divisions: the *city proper* (Dongcheng, Xicheng, Chongwen, and Xuanwu districts); the *inner suburbs* (Chaoyang, Fengtai, Shijingshan, and Haidian districts); and the *outer suburbs* (Mentougou, Fangshan, Tongzhou, Shunyi, Changping, Daxing, Huairou, and Pinggu districts and Miyun and Yanqing counties) (see Figure 3.1).[9] Since policy implementation may vary among the districts and have differing consequences for migrant schools and their students, a comparative analysis is a crucial step towards building a more comprehensive understanding of migrant

*Table 3.1* A general overview of the migrant schools in the sample

| District | Legal status | Year founded | Number of students* | Number of teachers* |
|---|---|---|---|---|
| Haidian | Licensed (unlicensed branch)** | 1994 | >900 | >50 |
| | Licensed | 1999 | ≈900 | ≈40 |
| | Unlicensed | 1994 | ≈360 | ≈16 |
| | Unlicensed | 1994 | >300 | >10 |
| | Unlicensed | 1995 | 400–500 | >20 |
| | Unlicensed | 1996 | >410 | 17 |
| Shijingshan | Licensed | 1997 | ≈900 | ≈40 |
| | Licensed | 1998 | 1,600–1,700 | >70 |
| | Licensed | 1998 | ≈1,400 | 58 |
| | Unlicensed | 1999 | >800 | ≈35 |
| | Unlicensed | 2000 | >480 | 19 |
| | Unlicensed | 2000 | ≈280 | 14 |
| | Unlicensed | 2000 | ≈520 | 20 |
| Fengtai | Licensed | 2000 | ≈1,300 | 50 |
| | Licensed | 2005 | >1,100 | 45 |
| | Unlicensed | 1999 | >800 | 46 |
| | Unlicensed | 2005 | >600 | 18 |
| Chaoyang | Licensed | 1998 | >1,000 | >40 |
| | Licensed | 2007 | 400–500 | ≈16 |
| Changping | Licensed | 2000 | >1,000 | 46 |
| | Unlicensed | 2003 | ≈400 | 14 |
| Daxing | Unlicensed | 1996 | 712 | 29 |

Source: Author's fieldwork (2009–10).
*Some figures for the numbers of students and teachers are more precise than others given the often high levels of student and teacher mobility, as well as the fact that some principals keep closer records than others.
**Though this school is referred to as licensed, only one of its three branches had a license at the time of fieldwork. Information provided for this school in this and subsequent tables is based on data on one of the unlicensed branches because of reasons concerning access. According to the principal interviewed, however, there were no significant differences between the school's three branches.

children's education. The focus of this study is on three of the four inner suburban districts: Shijingshan, Fengtai, and Haidian.

The general selection of inner suburban districts is based primarily on their high concentrations of migrant workers and the presence of rural–urban transition areas (see Table 3.2). The tendency for rural migrants to concentrate in the inner and to a lesser extent outer suburbs stems largely from the high demand for migrant labor in these areas, as well as considerations concerning housing. Indeed, people in the floating population in Beijing are typically unable to access low-cost public housing and therefore tend to rely on private housing, making location and the costs of rent important factors affecting where in the city they live (Gu and Shen 2003: 118). According to the 1997 Beijing Migrant Census, 62.9 percent of the city's floating population was already residing in the inner suburbs, compared to 21.1 percent in the outer suburbs and 16 percent in the city proper (Wu 2002: 92, table 1). As a result,

*Figure 3.1* Map of Beijing's administrative divisions (2009).
Source: Author.

most migrant schools are also located in the inner and outer suburban areas (Lü and Zhang 2004: 72).

The selection of Shijingshan, Fengtai, and Haidian districts in particular provides a good basis for comparison in light of the basic physical, demographic, and economic differences between them.[10] Shijingshan is the smallest of the four inner suburban districts and, at 84.32 square kilometers, is less than one-fifth the size of Chaoyang district (the largest of the four). By 2007, the district had a permanent resident population (*changzhu renkou*) of 546,000 and an outside population (*wailai renkou*) of 167,000. Its GDP was about 22.64 billion RMB, less than half of Fengtai's and about one-eighth of Haidian's (Beijing Municipal Statistics Bureau and National Bureau of Statistics Beijing Survey Team 2008). Despite its smaller size, it is an important rural–urban transition area and indus-trial zone.

Table 3.2 Area and population of Beijing's administrative divisions

| Administrative unit | Area (km²)* | Total population (2000 census)** | Total population (2010 census)** | Permanent resident population (changzhu renkou)* (10,000 persons)* | Outside population (wailai renkou) (10,000 persons)* | Outside population as a percentage of the permanent resident population |
|---|---|---|---|---|---|---|
| Beijing (total) | 16,410.54 | 13,569,194 | 19,612,368 | 1633.0 | 419.7 | 25.7 |
| **City proper** | | | | | | |
| Dongcheng | 25.34 | 535,558 | 919,000 | 55.2 | 10.1 | 18.3 |
| Xicheng | 31.62 | 706,691 | 1,243,000 | 66.5 | 11.0 | 16.5 |
| Chongwen | 16.52 | 346,205 | – | 29.9 | 5.5 | 18.4 |
| Xuanwu | 18.91 | 526,132 | – | 55.3 | 10.9 | 19.7 |
| **Inner suburbs** | | | | | | |
| Chaoyang | 455.08 | 2,289,756 | 3,545,000 | 300.1 | 96.3 | 32.1 |
| Fengtai | 305.80 | 1,369,480 | 2,112,000 | 169.3 | 44.7 | 26.4 |
| Shijingshan | 84.32 | 489,439 | 616,000 | 54.6 | 16.7 | 30.6 |
| Haidian | 430.73 | 2,240,124 | 3,281,000 | 281.4 | 84.8 | 30.1 |
| **Outer suburbs** | | | | | | |
| Mentougou | 1,450.70 | 266,591 | 290,000 | 27.0 | 3.2 | 11.9 |
| Fangshan | 1,989.54 | 814,367 | 945,000 | 88.7 | 13.0 | 14.7 |
| Tongzhou | 906.28 | 673,952 | 1,184,000 | 96.5 | 27.8 | 28.8 |
| Shunyi | 1,019.89 | 636,479 | 877,000 | 73.6 | 17.3 | 23.5 |
| Changping | 1,343.54 | 614,821 | 1,661,000 | 89.6 | 30.5 | 34.0 |
| Daxing | 1,036.32 | 671,444 | 1,365,000 | 97.8 | 33.7 | 34.5 |
| Huairou | 2,122.62 | 296,002 | 373,000 | 31.6 | 4.5 | 14.2 |
| Pinggu | 950.13 | 396,701 | 416,000 | 42.4 | 3.2 | 7.5 |
| Miyun | 2,229.45 | 420,019 | 468,000 | 44.9 | 4.0 | 8.9 |
| Yanqing | 1,993.75 | 275,433 | 317,000 | 28.6 | 2.5 | 8.7 |

*Source: Beijing Municipal Statistics Bureau and National Bureau of Statistics Beijing Survey Team (2008). Figures in the last column were calculated based on the previous two columns.

**Source: National Bureau of Statistics of China (2000, 2011); Sixth National Census Leading Group Office of Beijing Municipality, Beijing Municipal Statistics Bureau, and National Bureau of Statistics Beijing Survey Team (2011).

Fengtai is the second smallest of the inner suburban districts. At 305.80 square kilometers, it is roughly two-thirds the size of Chaoyang. By 2007, its permanent resident population was 1,693,000, and its outside population was 447,000. Its GDP was approximately 46.32 billion RMB, about one-quarter of Haidian's. Fengtai is one of the city's poorer districts; in 2007, its GDP per capita was only about 27,361 RMB, compared to 41,465 RMB in Shijingshan, 64,988 RMB in Haidian, and 56,562 RMB in Chaoyang (calculated using figures for the permanent resident population) (Beijing Municipal Statistics Bureau and National Bureau of Statistics Beijing Survey Team 2008).

Haidian is the second largest of the inner suburban districts and, at 430.73 square kilometers, is only 24.35 square kilometers smaller than Chaoyang. By 2007, it had a permanent resident population of 2,814,000 and an outside population of 848,000. Its GDP was around 182.88 billion RMB, the highest among the four districts (exceeding Chaoyang's by more than 13 billion RMB) (Beijing Municipal Statistics Bureau and National Bureau of Statistics Beijing Survey Team 2008). Haidian is also known for its high concentration of academic and research institutions, including Peking University and Tsinghua University, and it is one of the country's leading districts in terms of education (particularly higher education), science and technology, and high-tech industry.

Following from the framework created in Chapter 2, exploring the policy environments in these three neighboring districts allows for an interesting look into the potentially different ways in which district governments approach migrant children's education (including the nature of their relationships with migrant schools and civil society) and the consequences for the situations of migrant schools and their students. Moreover, the basic differences between the three districts provide a valuable opportunity to examine the effects of local context on their responses to central and municipal policies, as well as their approaches towards civil society.

The situations in Beijing's other regions were not explored in depth. Chaoyang district, the largest of the city proper and inner suburban districts in area, is usually associated with its high concentration of foreign embassies, international organizations, and businesses. It does, however, have a large number of migrant schools and, while not a core case, is referred to throughout the discussion. The outer suburban districts were also not core cases. As was mentioned in Chapter 1, though, visits were made to several migrant schools in Chaoyang, Changping, and Daxing. In addition, given the tendency of migrant workers to concentrate in the inner and outer suburbs, the city proper districts were not considered for this study.

Using the framework outlined in Figure 2.1 in the previous chapter, the rest of this book presents the main research findings. Chapter 4 starts with an examination of the policy history by exploring the central and Beijing municipal policies on migrant children's education. To contextualize my research in Beijing, the chapter also includes a discussion of the situations in other large cities with sizeable rural migrant populations, including Shanghai and Guangzhou, based on available evidence. This is followed by an analysis of the policy attitudes and approaches adopted in Shijingshan, Fengtai, and Haidian districts in Chapter 5; an examination of the consequences of the municipal and district policy approaches for migrant schools and their students in Chapter 6; and an exploration of the role of civil society actors within this picture, including their capacity to impact migrant children's education and the situations of migrant schools, in Chapter 7.

## Notes

1 The earliest migrant schools in Shanghai were established in 1992, while Shenzhen's earliest migrant schools appeared around 1985 (cited by Han 2003: 404).
2 The higher income segment of the floating population could usually afford to enroll their children in public schools or private "aristocratic" schools (*guizu xuexiao*) (Han 2001: 14).
3 The backgrounds of these early principals varied. While some had teaching experience, others came from backgrounds such as selling vegetables or growing crops, and their educational attainment ranged from no schooling to junior college graduate (Lü 2007: 231–2).
4 Of those attending school, many were overage; it was not unusual for there to be a five- or six-year age gap between children in the same grade level (Lü 2007: 195).
5 For example, in the study by Lü (2007: 226), 57 percent of the 114 schools surveyed in 1999–2000 were established from 1998 onwards.
6 An important result of this second stage was the emergence of a tendency, particularly among academics and researchers, to discuss migrant schools as part of a trend of marketization (e.g. Han 2001: 4; Lü 2007: 233). The following quote is a case in point: "As the number of migrants rose, the potential profitability of meeting the growing demand for migrant schools attracted all kinds of entrepreneurs – even some without any background in teaching. Because migrant schools were privately run and mostly unregulated, there were no standards" (Rural Education Action Project 2009). As will be discussed in Chapter 7, this tendency continues to exist.
7 According to a prominent principal in the sample, the first district in Beijing to start licensing migrant schools was Tongzhou in 2001, followed by Changping in 2002, Haidian in 2003, and Shijingshan, Chaoyang, and Daxing in 2004. By 2004, fewer than 30 had been licensed (CCTV 2004).
8 The number of students at one school in the sample grew from 22 to about 900 between 1997 and 2010 (SL1P1). In another case, the number grew from over 60 in 1995 to over 2,600 students across three branches in 2010 (HL1P1).
9 In mid-2010, it was announced that Chongwen and Xuanwu districts would be merged with Dongcheng and Xicheng districts, respectively, making the new number of administrative divisions 16 (Guo and Li 2010).
10 Further information regarding the situations of these districts will be provided in Chapter 5.

## Bibliography

Beijing Municipal Statistics Bureau and National Bureau of Statistics Beijing Survey Team. *Beijing Area Statistical Yearbook 2008.* Beijing: Tongxin chubanshe [Tongxin Publishing House], 2008.

CCTV. "Migrant School Finally Gains License." October 19, 2004. http://china.org.cn/english/null/109784.htm (accessed April 25, 2009).

Duan, Chengrong and Ge Yang. "Woguo liudong ertong zuixin zhuangkuang: jiyu 2005 nian quanguo 1% renkou chouyang diaocha shuju de fenxi" ["Study on the Latest Situation of Floating Children in China"]. *Renkou xuekan* [*Population Journal*] 6 (2008): 23–31.

Gu, Chaolin and Jianfa Shen. "Transformation of Urban Socio-Spatial Structure in Socialist Market Economies: The Case of Beijing." *Habitat International* 27, no. 1 (March 2003): 107–22.

Guo, Qiang and Shuang Li. "Beijing Redraws Administrative, District Boundaries." *Global Times*, July 2, 2010. http://china.globaltimes.cn/society/2010-07/547640. html (accessed January 19, 2012).

Han, Jialing. "Beijingshi liudong ertong yiwu jiaoyu zhuangkuang diaocha baogao" [Report on the Investigation of the Compulsory Education Situation of Children of the Floating Population in Beijing]. *Qingnian yanjiu* [*Youth Studies*] 8 and 9 (2001): 1–7, 10–18.

Han, Jialing. "Beijingshi 'dagong zidi xuexiao' de xingcheng, fazhan yu weilai" [The Formation, Development, and Future of Migrant Schools in Beijing]. In *Zhongguo minban jiaoyu zuzhi yu zhidu yanjiu* [Research on the Organization and System of Private Education in China], ed. Xiaobing Sun. Beijing: Zhongguo qingnian chubanshe [China Youth Press], 2003, pp. 402–16.

Lü, Shaoqing. *Liushou haishi liudong? "Mingong chao" zhong de ertong yanjiu* [*Left Behind or Migration? An Empirical Study on Children of Rural Migrants*]. Beijing: Zhongguo nongye chubanshe [China Agriculture Press], 2007.

Lü, Shaoqing and Shouli Zhang. "Urban/Rural Disparity and Migrant Children's Education: An Investigation into Schools for Children of Transient Workers in Beijing." *Chinese Education and Society* 37, no. 5 (September/October 2004): 56–83.

Mallee, Hein. "Migration, *Hukou* and Resistance in Reform China." In *Chinese Society: Change, Conflict and Resistance*, 2nd edn, ed. Elizabeth J. Perry and Mark Selden. London: RoutledgeCurzon, 2003, pp. 136–57.

National Bureau of Statistics of China. "Biao 1: Zong renkou, huji renkou, shaoshuminzu renkou bizhong, feinongye hukou renkou bizhong, chengxiang renkou, jiatinghu renkou, jiatinghu leibie (quanbu shuju)" [Table 1: Total Population, Registered Population, National Minority Population as a Percentage, Agricultural Population as a Percentage, City and Countryside Population, Household Population, Household Type (Complete Data)]. 2000. www.stats.gov.cn/tjsj/ndsj/renkoupucha/2000fenxian/htm/ table1.htm (accessed March 29, 2012).

National Bureau of Statistics of China. "2010 nian diliuci quanguo renkou pucha zhuyao shuju gongbao (di er hao)" [Bulletin of Key Data from the Sixth National Population Census of 2010 (No. 2)]. 2011. www.stats.gov.cn/tjgb/rkpcgb/qgrkpcgb/ t20110429_402722510.htm (accessed March 29, 2012).

Rural Education Action Project. "Education for Migrant Children." 2009. http://reap. stanford.edu/docs/education_for_migrant_children/ (accessed April 19, 2011).

Sixth National Census Leading Group Office of Beijing Municipality, Beijing Municipal Statistics Bureau, and National Bureau of Statistics Beijing Survey Team. "Beijingshi 2010 nian diliuci quanguo renkou pucha zhuyao shuju gongbao" [Bulletin of Key Data on Beijing from the Sixth National Population Census of 2010]. 2011. www.bjstats. gov.cn/xwgb/tjgb/pcgb/201105/t20110504_201363.htm (accessed March 29, 2012).

Wu, Weiping. "Migrant Housing in Urban China: Choices and Constraints." *Urban Affairs Review* 38, no. 1 (September 2002): 90–119.

Xinhua News Agency. "Beijing's Population Tops 19.6 Mln, Migration Key Contributor to Growth." May 5, 2011. http://news.xinhuanet.com/english2010/china/2011-05/05/c_13860069.htm (accessed February 7, 2011).

Zhai, Zhenwu, Chengrong Duan, and Qiuling Bi. "Beijingshi liudong renkou de zuixin zhuangkuang yu fenxi" ["The Floating Population in Beijing: An Update"]. *Renkou yanjiu* [*Population Research*] 31, no. 2 (March 2007): 30–40.

# 4 "Under the same blue sky"?

## Central and Beijing municipal policies on migrant children's education

As emphasized in Chapter 2, policies are typically influenced by previous developments and context-specific changes, making an understanding of policy history critical when analyzing policy processes (Blaikie and Soussan 2001: 10). Despite increasing scholarly attention towards migrant children's education in China, there has been little detailed examination of policies on the subject, especially below the central level.[1] To the best of my knowledge, this chapter brings together for the first time the body of published and grey literature, complemented by primary fieldwork, to provide a more comprehensive picture of the policy history of migrant children's education at the central and particularly Beijing municipal levels. In doing so, it sheds light on the interaction between migration and education patterns and policies against the backdrop of China's economic reforms and also lays the groundwork for a closer analysis of policy implementation.

Drawing on previous research and information from policy documents collected during fieldwork, the chapter begins by exploring key central policies in the area. It highlights that, with the policy shift towards the more positive treatment of migrant workers in the early 2000s (discussed in Chapter 2), central policies on migrant children's education, the first of which was issued in 1996, shifted towards a focus on the equal treatment of migrant children and their right to basic education. A closer look reveals that recent policies in this area not only emphasize the integral role of public schools, but they also call for increased support for migrant schools.

With the introduction of the policy of "two priorities" in 2001, however, the central government gave the responsibility for migrant children's education to local governments and public schools, creating space for different policy approaches across localities. The rest of the chapter explores the nature of these differences. Using available evidence on Wuhan, Xiamen, Shanghai, and Guangzhou, it starts by pointing to key areas in which municipal policy approaches can diverge, illustrating the importance of examining the effects of decentralization in different localities. This discussion then sets the stage for a more detailed evaluation of the Beijing municipal policies on migrant children's education. Evidence from interviews and policy documents collected during fieldwork shows that, while Beijing municipal policies do reiterate many of the general sentiments found in the central policies, they have largely omitted discussion of support for migrant schools, resulting in a policy environment in which barriers to the fulfillment of central-level aspirations have emerged. The chapter therefore raises critical questions about how central policies in this area are implemented and why, as well as the consequences for migrant schools and their students at the local levels.

## Central policies on migrant children's education

"Under the same blue sky, grow up and progress together" (*tongzai lantian xia, gongtong chengzhang jinbu*). These were words written by then Premier Wen Jiabao on a blackboard at a Beijing public primary school attended mainly by migrant children in 2003, and they reflected a recognition at the central level of migrant children's right to equal opportunities. The policy goal of seeking educational equality is certainly not a recent development. Article 46 of the Chinese Constitution (1982) states: "Citizens of the People's Republic of China have the duty as well as the right to receive education."[2] Article 5 of the Compulsory Education Law (1986) stipulates: "All children who have reached the age of six shall enroll in school and receive compulsory education for the prescribed number of years, regardless of sex, nationality or race."[3] Article 9 of the Education Law of the People's Republic of China (1995) (*Zhonghua renmin gongheguo jiaoyufa*) asserts: "Citizens of the People's Republic of China shall have the right and duty to be educated. Citizens shall enjoy equal opportunity of education regardless of their nationality, race, sex, occupation, property or religious belief etc." Article 36 of the law maintains: "Education receivers shall enjoy equal rights in going to school, entering higher school, employment and etc."[4] In 2005, the Ministry of Education also drew up the "Outline for Educational Development in China by 2020" (*2020 nian Zhongguo jiaoyu fazhan gangyao*), which discusses approaches to reduce educational inequality.[5]

Calls for educational equality have been echoed in statements made by high-level officials. For example, at the Fifth High-Level Group Meeting on Education for All in November 2005, then Premier Wen Jiabao stated:

> [N]ational education in China is not without its difficulties. Disparities between urban and rural areas and between regions remain a stern reality. The nation's foundation for education as a whole is still weak. We must keep on working hard to attain the goals of education for all.
>
> (Wen 2005)

While chairing a study of the Political Bureau of the CPC Central Committee concerning educational development and human resources in February 2011, then President Hu Jintao urged schools to place more emphasis on the all-around growth of children, saying: "Education is the foundation for national prosperity and social progress ... It carries hundreds of millions of families' expectations for a better life" (Xinhua News Agency 2011).

Important questions subsequently arise regarding the extent to which such senti- ments have been articulated in policies concerning educational provision for migrant children. In light of the evolution of migration policies discussed in Chapter 2, this section examines the central policies on migrant children's education. It explores the common shift made by both sets of policies during the early 2000s and highlights the larger trend towards the more positive treatment of rural–urban migrants.

For several years after migrant schools first began to appear in the cities, the central government did not adopt an official position (see Table 4.1). While the government viewed these schools as encroaching on its authority, it could also not deny these children an education for moral reasons. The government therefore found itself in a position in which it could neither denounce the schools for educat- ing migrant children nor shut them down without adequate alternatives (Kwong 2004: 1079). The result was a government strategy of "do not ban, do not recog- nize, let it run its course" (*bu qudi, bu chengren, zisheng zimie*) (Han 2001: 3; Kwong 2004: 1079).

The lack of government action created space for migrant schools to rapidly grow in number. This started to gain more attention by the mid- to late 1990s, which was also the period during which the central government was tightening its policies towards migrant workers (see Chapter 2). Indeed, the first two policies on migrant children's education reflected the government's broader desire to limit rural labor migration and the jobs and services migrant workers would be eligible for. In

*Table 4.1* General policy trends in migrant children's education

| Period | General situation | Policy response (central level) | Policy response (Beijing municipal level) |
|---|---|---|---|
| Early to mid-1990s | Rising number of migrant children in urban areas; emergence of migrant schools | No official response | |
| Mid- to late 1990s | Rapid rise in the number of migrant schools in large cities like Beijing | Started attracting attention from the central government, leading to efforts to restrict the numbers of migrant children in cities | No major response |
| Since 2001 | | Shift of responsibility for migrant children's education to local governments and public schools, with an emphasis on migrant children's right to education and equal treatment | Appearance of the municipality's first policies directly addressing migrant children's education |

Source: Han (2001, 2003, 2009); Kwong (2004); author's fieldwork (2009–10).

1996, the State Education Commission (known as the Ministry of Education since 1998) issued the "Trial Measures for the Schooling of Children and Youth among the Floating Population in Cities and Towns," which was applied to six pilot sites (see Table 4.2).[6] The document stated that sending governments should create a strict management system for monitoring school-aged children in their areas of jurisdiction to ensure that children who have guardians in their place of *hukou* registration receive their education in that locality. Receiving governments should create the environment and opportunities for children of the floating population to receive basic education. However, only children who could not be taken care of in their place of *hukou* registration could apply to be educated as "temporary students" (*jiedusheng*) in public schools in receiving areas.

This was followed by the "Provisional Measures for the Schooling of Children and Youth in the Floating Population," issued by the State Education Commission and the Ministry of Public Security in 1998. These provisional measures essentially only made suggestions to local governments on how to address the issue, mainly involving admitting migrant children into local public schools, creating new government schools, promoting the role of private schools, or assisting enterprises in setting up migrant schools. In other words, local governments would have the freedom and flexibility to adopt responses based on local circumstances and interests (Kwong 2004: 1080). The document also stated that children of the floating population could be *temporarily* educated in public schools, but their admission would depend on an application process and various conditions. Moreover, public schools could charge these students temporary schooling fees each semester.

In line with the central government's efforts to improve the treatment of rural–urban migrants, policies on migrant children's education have shown a desire to improve educational opportunities for these children since the early 2000s. Most significantly, the government introduced a policy of "two priorities" for educating migrant children, under which the two areas of focus would be management by local governments in receiving areas and education in public schools. Indeed, according to the "Decision of the State Council on the Reform and Development of Basic Education," issued in May 2001, receiving governments are responsible for providing compulsory education to children of the floating population primarily via public schools.[7]

Most policies since then have focused on ensuring migrant children's *right* to education (Gu and Wang 2008: 73). The "Circular of the General Office of the State Council on Strengthening Employment Management and Service Work for Rural Migrant Workers" (2003) (discussed in Chapter 2) states that migrant children's right to compulsory education should be protected and that the provision of education to migrant and local children, including entrance requirements, should be equal. In September 2003, the Ministry of Education and five other departments issued the "Suggestions to Provide Better Compulsory Education to the Children of Migrant Workers in Cities." The document stipulates that public primary and middle schools are mainly responsible for educating migrant children and that receiving governments should incorporate migrant

Table 4.2 Key central policies and legislation on migrant children's education

| Year | Document | Key content |
|---|---|---|
| 1996 | "Trial Measures for the Schooling of Children and Youth among the Floating Population in Cities and Towns" <br> *Chengzhen liudong renkou zhong shiling ertong shaonian jiuxue banfa (shixing)* | • Applied to selected pilot sites <br> • Sending governments should strictly monitor the mobility of school-aged children in their areas of jurisdiction [Article 6] <br> • Only compulsory school-aged children without guardians in their place of *hukou* registration can apply to be temporarily educated in public schools in receiving areas [Articles 6 and 9] |
| 1998 | "Provisional Measures for the Schooling of Children and Youth in the Floating Population" <br> *Liudong ertong shaonian jiuxue zanxing banfa* | • Sending governments should strictly control the migration of compulsory school-aged children in their localities [Article 3] <br> • Children of the floating population without guardians in their place of household registration can be temporarily educated in public schools in receiving areas; admission would require an application process, and public schools can charge them temporary schooling fees (*jiedufei*) [Articles 3, 8, and 11] |
| 2001 | "Decision of the State Council on the Reform and Development of Basic Education" <br> *Guowuyuan guanyu jichu jiaoyu gaige yu fazhan de jueding* | • Importance should be attached to resolving education for children of the floating population, and the primary responsibility belongs to receiving governments (*liuru diqu zhengfu*) and public schools [Section 2, Article 12] |
| 2002 | Law on Promoting Private Education <br> *Zhonghua renmin gongheguo minban jiaoyu cujinfa* | • Private (*minban*) schools and public schools have the same legal status, and the state guarantees their autonomy [Section 1, Article 5] |
| 2003 | "Circular of the General Office of the State Council on Strengthening Employment Management and Service Work for Rural Migrant Workers" <br> *Guowuyuan bangongting guanyu zuohao nongmin jincheng wugong jiuye guanli he fuwu gongzuo de tongzhi* | • Receiving governments (*liurudi zhengfu*) should increase support for migrant schools (referred to as *shehui liliang xingban de nongmingong zinü jianyi xuexiao*) and incorporate them into their educational systems and educational development planning [Section 6] <br> • Educational departments should actively provide guidance for "simple schools" (*jianyi xuexiao*) in areas like teaching, provide assistance to improve school conditions, and gradually standardize how the schools are run; they must not simply adopt a strategy of shutting down schools, which would result in migrant children being unable to go to school [Section 6] <br> • Receiving governments should specially set aside funding for migrant children's education [Section 6] |

*(Continued)*

Table 4.2 Continued

| Year | Document | Key content |
|---|---|---|
| 2003 | "Suggestions [of the Ministry of Education and Five Other Departments] to Provide Better Compulsory Education to the Children of Migrant Workers in Cities" *Guanyu jinyibu zuohao jincheng wugong jiuye nongmin zinü yiwu jiaoyu gongzuo de yijian* | • The main responsibility for educating migrant children lies with receiving governments (*liurudi zhengfu*) and public primary and middle schools [Article 2]<br>• Finance departments of receiving governments should provide subsidies for schools with relatively large numbers of migrant children [Article 5]<br>• Receiving governments should formulate standards for the charging of fees to migrant children, eliminate relevant fees, and ensure that migrant and local children are treated equally (*yishi tongren*) in terms of the fees required [Article 6]<br>• Increased support and management should be provided for migrant schools [Article 8] |
| 2003 | "Notification [of the Ministry of Finance and Four Other Departments] on Issues Concerning the Incorporation of Management Funds for Migrant Workers and Other Related Funds into the Scope of the Financial Budget and Expenditure" *Guanyu jiang nongmingong guanli deng yongguan jingfei naru caizheng yusuan zhichu fanwei yongguan wenti de tongzhi* | • Funding for issues concerning the management of migrant workers (such as public security management and community management) should be included in the regular financial budgets and expenditures of receiving governments (*laodongli shurudi zhengfu*) [Section 1]<br>• Regional educational administrative departments should create a mechanism to guarantee funds for migrant children's education [Section 6] |
| 2004 | "Notification [of the Ministry of Finance] on Regulating the Management of Fees and Promoting Higher Incomes for Peasants" *Guanyu guifan shoufei guanli cujin nongmin zengjia shouru de tongzhi* | • To protect the legal rights of migrant workers, unreasonable fees should be eliminated [Section 4]<br>• Migrant and local children should be treated equally (*yishi tongren*) in terms of the fees charged by public schools; aside from the collection of miscellaneous fees (*zafei*), tuition fees (*xuefei*), and accommodation and textbook fees, schools are not permitted to charge temporary schooling fees and school selection fees (*zexiaofei*), nor are they permitted to require migrants to pay subsidies or other costs [Section 4] |

**2005**

"Suggestions of the Ministry of Education on Further Promoting the Balanced Development of Compulsory Education"

*Jiaoyubu guanyu jinyibu tuijin yiwu jiaoyu junheng fazhan de ruogan yijian*

- Local governments should make serious efforts to address migrant children's education, including ensuring that migrant and local children are treated equally (*yishi tongren*) in the charging of fees and strengthening support and management of private (*minban*) schools primarily attended by migrant children; local educational administrative departments at all levels and schools should adopt targeted measures to address the educational problems of left-behind children [Article 13]

**2006**

"Opinions of the State Council on Solving the Problems of Migrant Workers"

*Guowuyuan guanyu jiejue nongmingong wenti de ruogan yijian*

- Local receiving governments (*shuruadi zhengfu*) should ensure that migrant children have equal access to basic education and should include them in their educational development planning and educational budget [Section 7, Article 21]
- Public schools should treat migrant and local children equally in areas like the charging of fees and management and must not charge extra temporary schooling fees or other fees [Section 7, Article 21]
- To improve school quality, receiving governments should provide support and guidance for private (*minban*) schools educating migrant children in areas like school funding and teacher training [Section 7, Article 21]

**2006**

"Suggestions of the Ministry of Education on Implementing 'Opinions of the State Council on Solving the Problems of Migrant Workers'"

*Jiaoyubu guanyu jiaoyu xitong guanche luoshi "Guowuyuan guanyu jiejue nongmingong wenti de ruogan yijian" de shishi yijian*

- To ensure that migrant children have equal access to compulsory education, educational administrative departments in receiving areas should incorporate migrant children's education into local educational planning and, based on local circumstances, allocate public resources to compulsory education and fully tap into the capacity of public schools [Section 4, Article 13]
- Support for and management of privately-run migrant schools should be strengthened and included in the management of private (*minban*) schools; educational administrative departments should give special care and assistance to this type of school and should, in cooperation with other relevant departments, give vigorous support and guidance to the schools in areas such as location, school funding, teacher training, and teaching [Section 4, Article 17]
- For migrant schools that do not meet the standards, deadlines for improvement should be set; schools with serious safety and health hazards and a low quality of teaching should be shut down as quickly as possible, and arrangements regarding the continued schooling of the students should be made [Section 4, Article 17]

*(Continued)*

Table 4.2 Continued

| Year | Document | Key content |
|------|----------|-------------|
| 2006 | Compulsory Education Law of the People's Republic of China (2006 Amendment) *Zhonghua renmin gongheguo yiwu jiaoyufa (2006 xiuding)* | • Local governments (*dangdi renmin zhengfu*) are responsible for providing equal educational opportunities to migrant children when both parents/guardians are residing/working outside their location of registration [Section 2, Article 12] |
| 2008 | "Notification of the State Council on Waiving Tuition and Miscellaneous Fees for Compulsory School-Aged Children in Cities" *Guowuyuan guanyu zuohao mianchu chengshi yiwu jiaoyu jieduan xuesheng xuezafei gongzuo de tongzhi* | • Local governments at all levels (*difang geji renmin zhengfu*) should incorporate migrant children into the public education system [Section 2]<br>• Public schools should not charge migrant children tuition and miscellaneous fees (*xuezafei*) and temporary schooling fees [Section 2] |

Source: Author's fieldwork (2009–10). See also Qu and Wang (2008: 182–3, table 4.2) and Han (2009).

children's education into urban social development planning. It also maintains that access to compulsory education among migrant children should be the same as that enjoyed by local children and that migrant and local children should be treated equally in terms of the fees required. The "Opinions of the State Council on Solving the Problems of Migrant Workers," issued in January 2006, reiterates that migrant children are entitled to equal access to education and that it is the responsibility of local governments to ensure this. What is more, in June 2006, the Compulsory Education Law was amended to include a provision stating that receiving governments are responsible for providing education to migrant children when both parents/guardians are residing and working in that locality but lack local household registration (see Mo 2006).

Not only do recent policies encourage the integration of migrant children into public schools, but they also highlight the need to support migrant schools.[8] Deeper analysis shows that key policies – including the "Circular of the General Office of the State Council on Strengthening Employment Management and Service Work for Rural Migrant Workers" (2003), the "Suggestions to Provide Better Compulsory Education to the Children of Migrant Workers in Cities" (2003), the "Suggestions of the Ministry of Education on Further Promoting the Balanced Development of Compulsory Education" (2005), and the "Suggestions of the Ministry of Education on Implementing 'Opinions of the State Council on Solving the Problems of Migrant Workers'" (2006) – call for an increase in both the "management" (*guanli*) of migrant schools and "support" (*zhichi*) or "assistance" (*fuchi*) for the schools (see Table 4.2). The significance of these calls for increased support for migrant schools should be underscored, as they indicate the recognition at the central level of the continued role these schools play in providing education for migrant children.

The above discussion demonstrates that central policies shifted towards improving educational opportunities for migrant children in the early 2000s. Though recent policies emphasize the primary role of public schools in this area, they also point to the need to assist migrant schools, a major change compared to the government's initial attitude towards these schools during the 1990s. This more positive approach towards educational provision for these children reflects the government's broader efforts to improve the treatment of rural–urban migrants, as well as reduce educational inequality.

## Decentralization and municipal policy approaches towards migrant children's education

Although the central government has adopted an increasingly positive stance towards migrant children's education and migrant schools, the policy of "two priorities" also made it clear that the responsibility for providing education to these children ultimately belongs to local governments. Decentralization has subsequently created serious problems for migrant children (X. Wang 2008). Local governments have acquired an unprecedented level of autonomy, leading to unclear and conflicting views and approaches that can hinder successful policy implementation (Kwong 2004: 1087). As Froissart (2003) argues, the way central policies in this area are designed has provided local governments with space for maneuver, illustrating the "unofficial slogan of decentralisation: 'the centre proposes, local government disposes' (*zhongyang you zhengce, difang you duice*)." Indeed, there are "different rules, regulations and policies in different cities – as schooling in many ways is still a locally provided public service" (Rural Education Action Project 2009).

To demonstrate the importance of examining decentralized decision making in this area and its effects at the municipal level, it is useful to briefly explore the situations in a few other cities, including the estimated proportion of migrant children attending public schools – though, for reasons discussed in Chapters 1 and 2, the accuracy of such estimates is inevitably uncertain – and the amount of support given to migrant schools. The limited amount of research on migrant children's education has, for the most part, been focused on Beijing (and to a lesser extent Shanghai). Nevertheless, it is possible to shed some light on the variation among municipal-level situations by drawing on available information and data on a few other cities, mainly Wuhan, Xiamen, Shanghai, and Guangzhou (see Table 4.3).[9]

Evidence of variation can already be seen in the cases of Wuhan and Xiamen. According to a researcher in the sample, Wuhan was one of the earliest cities in China to allow migrant children to attend local public schools (see also Fan and Peng 2008: 323). Xinhua News Agency (2005) reported that, with a migrant

*Table 4.3* Basic information on Wuhan, Xiamen, Shanghai, Guangzhou, and Beijing (2008)

| | *Wuhan* | *Xiamen* | *Shanghai* | *Guangzhou* | *Beijing* |
|---|---|---|---|---|---|
| Permanent resident population (*changzhu renkou*) | 8,970,000 | 2,490,000 | 18,884,600 | 10,182,000 | 16,950,000 |
| GDP per capita (RMB) | 44,290 | 62,651 | 73,124 | 81,233 | 63,029 |
| Per capita annual disposable income of urban households (RMB) | 16,712 | 23,948 | 26,675 | 25,317 | 24,725 |
| Educational expenditure (million RMB) | 5,609 | 4,264 (2010) | 32,606 | 9,572 | 26,300 (2007) |
| Educational expenditure per capita (RMB)* | 625 | 1,712 | 1,727 | 940 | 1,552 |

Source: Beijing Municipal Statistics Bureau and National Bureau of Statistics Beijing Survey Team (2008, 2009); Chen and Li (2009); Guangzhou Municipal Statistics Bureau and National Bureau of Statistics Guangzhou Survey Team (2009); Shanghai Municipal Statistics Bureau (2009); Shanghai Municipal Statistics Bureau and National Bureau of Statistics Shanghai Survey Team (2009); Wuhan Municipal Statistics Bureau (2009); Xiamen Municipal Statistics Bureau and National Bureau of Statistics Xiamen Survey Team (2009); Ye (2009); Xiamen Municipal Government (2010).

* These were calculated based on figures for the permanent resident population from 2008.

worker population of more than 400,000, the city had 127,620 migrant children in 298 public schools and over 40,000 in 102 migrant schools by the mid-2000s (i.e. over 75 percent were in public schools). The same source also reported that the city waived over 44 million RMB in temporary schooling fees for migrant children attending public primary and middle schools in 2005. In addition, Wuhan is one of the few cities that permits migrant children to stay for high school, though they still have to return to their place of *hukou* registration for the university entrance exam (*gaokao*) (China Labour Bulletin 2008).

The situation in Xiamen – a special economic zone where the size of the floating population has gradually been approaching that of its permanent resident population of over 1.8 million (Zhu 2011) – has been somewhat different. There were roughly 30,000 migrant children aged six to 14 in the city by 2000, but, out of the 9,158 migrant children estimated to be attending primary schools in 2002, only about one-third were in public schools. Based on concerns about the capacity of its public schools, Xiamen's approach towards the area has, instead, been focused more on the role of migrant schools. Indeed, an estimated more than 70 percent of the migrant children not attending public schools in the city are enrolled in licensed migrant schools that are managed by the local government (L. Wang 2008: 692–3, 700).

Yet, as a prominent researcher in the sample cautioned, because of the large size of Beijing's migrant population, the capital city's situation can only be compared with those of two other cities: Shanghai and Guangzhou (see Table 4.4). A brief examination of the situations in these two major cities also reveals fundamental differences between the policy approaches adopted towards migrant children's education.

In Shanghai, the permanent resident population reached 23.8 million in 2012, including a permanent migrant population of 9.6 million (Zhou 2013). Based on various estimates, the city has 500,000–700,000 migrant children between the ages of six and 14, and there were 519 migrant schools by 2001, including 124 licensed schools (see Ming 2009: 43, table 2.4). It was estimated that 57.1 percent of these children were attending public schools in 2007 (Dai 2008). Not unlike Beijing, migrant schools in Shanghai were poor in quality during the

*Table 4.4* Estimated numbers of migrant children in Shanghai, Guangzhou, and Beijing (2000)

|  | *Shanghai* | *Guangzhou* | *Beijing* |
| --- | --- | --- | --- |
| Number of children in the floating population | 470,000 | 300,000 | 250,000 |
| Children of the floating population as a percentage of the floating population | 10.99 | 34.52 | 9.76 |
| Number of school-aged children in the floating population | ≈270,000 | ≈270,000 | ≈140,000 |
| Children of migrant workers as a percentage of children of the floating population | 65.84 | 78.00 | 80.08 |

Source: These figures were obtained from Zheng *et al.* (2008: 11, table 4) and are based on data from the Fifth National Population Census.

1990s and early 2000s (Zhu 2001). In 2001, it was reported that 140,000 of the 240,000 migrant students in the city were attending roughly 500 migrant schools (China Daily 2001).

However, since 2007 or 2008, Shanghai's municipal government has adopted steps to both reduce the barriers migrant children face in attending public schools and improve the quality of migrant schools. In 2009, Shanghai's education commission announced plans to ensure that all compulsory school-aged migrant children would be attending either public schools or government-subsidized migrant schools by 2010 (Wang 2009). To increase the number of migrant children in public schools, it reduced the requirement for migrant children to enroll in these schools from "five certificates" (*wu zheng*) to two. This, according to Ming (2009: 225), was a significant step forward in terms of improving migrant children's access to public schools in Shanghai, particularly in light of the fact that the city is known for its not very welcoming locals and discrimination against outsiders. Shanghai has also made efforts to improve the quality of migrant schools by closing down substandard ones and helping to improve those in relatively better condition. According to Beijing Migrant School Principals' Association (2009), it adopted measures to license over 60 migrant schools per year.

In 2009, Shanghai's municipal government spent 3.69 billion RMB on increasing the number of migrant children enrolled in local schools, and, by early 2010, the city's education commission stated that 97.3 percent of the city's 400,000 migrant children were attending either public schools or government-subsidized private schools, while 2.7 percent were attending 22 unlicensed or unqualified private schools (Xinhua News Agency 2010). It now provides a subsidy of 2,300 RMB (about 340 USD) per year to students attending licensed migrant schools, eliminating their need to pay tuition (Beijing Migrant School Principals' Association 2009).[10] Moreover, principals in the sample expressed that, because of government financial support, the average monthly salary of migrant school teachers in Shanghai is at least 1,500 RMB (roughly 220 USD), which is more than 500 RMB higher than that in Beijing. According to a staff member of an NGO working in both Beijing and Shanghai, migrant school teachers in Shanghai also receive regular training from the local education commission.

Thus, in describing Shanghai's progress, interviewees in the sample used words such as "all-around support" (*gefangmian de zhichi*), "comprehensive subsidization" (*suoyou buzhu*), "proper management" (*zhenggui guanli*), and "open-minded" (*kaiming*). In addition, migrant schools in the city were described as being in better condition than those in Beijing. As one researcher explained:

> In terms of Shanghai, and why it's done relatively well now, it's because the Secretary of the CPC Shanghai Municipal Committee has attached a great deal of importance to the issue. He has treated it as an indication of [the city's] image. ... He had previously come over from Hubei, which has done pretty well in the area. His view is: If Hubei can do it, why can't Shanghai? (A1)

In contrast, Guangzhou has primarily promoted the role of private (*minban*) schools in providing education for migrant children, rather than focusing on increasing the numbers of migrant children in public schools. The city – with a population of about 12 million – was reported to have a migrant population of over five million by 2007 (Zhan 2007). By 2008, there were over 430,000 children in the city's floating population (Zhang 2008). It was estimated that roughly two-thirds were attending privately-run schools (cited by China Labour Bulletin 2008). As one researcher in the sample described, though the physical conditions of migrant schools in Guangzhou are relatively better than those in Beijing, the city's reliance on private schools has placed much of the financial burden on the migrant families themselves. That is, unlike Shanghai, it has mainly been relying on migrant workers' money. At the same time, enrollment in public schools has become increasingly expensive for migrant children. For example, the school selection fee (*zexiaofei*) charged by public middle schools in Guangzhou between 2003 and 2005 was estimated to be 30,000–60,000 RMB. Temporary schooling fees have also been on the rise. At one public primary school in the city, for instance, the temporary schooling fee charged in 2006 was 30,000 RMB, which was reportedly ten times higher than the year before (China Labour Bulletin 2008).

Ultimately, one should be cautious in generalizing about any particular city's experiences in this policy area, and, even in places with stronger reputations like Shanghai, restrictions may exist. Nevertheless, the above review of available information and data on the situations in these various cities does demonstrate that cities can face different circumstances and adopt differing approaches towards the policy area. This existence of variation provides initial evidence to suggest that educational provision for these children can be influenced by a range of factors beyond the *hukou* system, and it illustrates the fundamental importance of understanding the nature and impact of policy implementation within different localities, especially in light of the potential implications it may have for trends in social stratification (see Chapter 2). Yet, while there are clearly areas in which localities can diverge, more detailed knowledge of the situations within different cities remains sparse, highlighting the need for more in-depth analyses at the local levels. The rest of this book therefore explores such local dynamics for the case of Beijing, creating a more nuanced understanding of the local politics surrounding migrant children's education and the consequences for migrant schools and their students.

## Beijing municipal policies on migrant children's education

In light of the central-level shift towards improving educational opportunities for migrant children, as well as the municipal-level variations discussed above, this section draws on information from policy documents collected during fieldwork and interviews to examine the policy response in Beijing. The Beijing municipal government was relatively late in responding to the central government's initial policies (discussed earlier). While cities including Shanghai and Wuhan reportedly responded soon after the 1998 measure, Beijing's only response in 1998 was a discussion paper entitled "Beijing's Plan towards School-Aged Children and Youth," which, according to Kwong (2004: 1081), was "not very sympathetic towards the migrant children."

The Beijing municipal government did not begin to address migrant children's education until the early 2000s. The first major mention of the subject came in 2001 with the "Suggestions of the Beijing Municipal People's Government on Implementing 'Decision of the State Council on the Reform and Development of Basic Education'" (see Table 4.5). Its first policy focused solely on migrant children's education – its first real response to the 1996 and 1998 central-level measures – was the "Provisional Measures for the Implementation of Compulsory Education for Children and Youth of the Floating Population in Beijing," issued by Beijing's education commission in 2002. Composed of 12 brief articles, the document reiterates the notion that children of the floating population who have guardians in their place of household registration should return there for schooling. It also states that public schools in Beijing can charge these children temporary schooling fees and other miscellaneous fees. Though it does say that all school-aged children of the floating population who have migrated to Beijing with their parents should receive compulsory education, the language used in discussing how this would be achieved is vague. Article 2, for example, says that all relevant government departments and offices (including those related to education, public security, business, labor, prices, health, and housing management) should carry out their respective responsibilities, and Article 3 states that educational administrative departments should adopt measures to create the conditions for these children to attend school. Yet there is a failure to specify what those responsibilities are and what specific measures should be adopted. The document also sets the tone for the municipality's approach towards migrant schools; Article 10 states that migrant schools may exist as long as they have been reviewed and approved by local educational administrative departments, while Article 11 says that district and county educational administrative departments and educational supervision departments should strengthen their "management and supervision" (*guanli he jiandu*) of these schools and shut down substandard ones.

This was followed in 2004 by the "Suggestions on Implementing the General Office of the State Council's Working Documents on Providing Better Compulsory Education to the Children of Migrant Workers in Cities." A response to the 2003 central policy, the document was issued jointly by ten departments: Beijing's education commission, development and reform commission, commission office for public sector reform, public security bureau, finance bureau, civil affairs bureau, health bureau, labor and social security bureau, land and resources bureau, and education supervision office. Using a more positive tone, it emphasizes the policy of "two priorities" and the need to protect the *right* of migrant children to receive compulsory education in Beijing. Moreover, school fees should be the same for local and migrant children, and, starting in September 2004, public primary and middle schools

Table 4.5 Key Beijing municipal policies on migrant children's education

| Year | Document | Key content |
|------|----------|-------------|
| 2001 | "Suggestions of the Beijing Municipal People's Government on Implementing 'Decision of the State Council on the Reform and Development of Basic Education'" *Beijingshi renmin zhengfu guanche "Guowuyuan guanyu jichu jiaoyu gaige yu fazhan jueding" de yijian* | • Receiving governments are primarily responsible for the compulsory education of children of the floating population [Section 2, Article 8] <br>• To ensure that children of the floating population who are legally residing in Beijing receive compulsory education, various channels should be used (including placing them in public schools as temporary students and using extra school buildings and teachers to open special schools) [Section 2, Article 8] |
| 2002 | "Provisional Measures [of the Beijing Municipal Education Commission] for the Implementation of Compulsory Education for Children and Youth of the Floating Population in Beijing" *Beijingshi dui liudong renkou zhong shiling ertong shaonian shishi yiwu jiaoyu de zanxing banfa* | • All levels of government and relevant departments should create the conditions and adopt various measures to safeguard the right of children of the floating population to receive compulsory education [Article 1] <br>• Children of the floating population who have guardians in their place of household registration should return there to receive compulsory education; those who do not have guardians in their place of household registration and whose parents have lived in Beijing for over half a year and have a temporary residence permit (*zanzhuzheng*) can apply to attend a public primary or middle school in Beijing on a temporary basis [Article 1] <br>• Parents should apply for proof of household registration and present the required documents (e.g. parents' identification, temporary residence permits, and work permits) at the local street office, and a Beijing temporary schooling approval permit (*zai Jing jiedu pizhunshu*) will be issued if requirements are met; using the permit and proof of student status from their former school, children can contact nearby public schools, which will decide whether or not to accept them [Article 6] <br>• In districts with large floating populations, groups/individuals are allowed to create special schools for children of the floating population, as long as the schools meet the required standards and the district/county educational administrative departments approve; district/county educational administrative departments and educational supervision departments should increase their management and supervision of these schools, conduct regular inspections, and promptly shut down substandard schools that fail to make the necessary improvements by the given deadline (in these cases, the government should ensure that students are able to continue schooling) [Articles 10–11] |

*(Continued)*

Table 4.5 Continued

| Year | Document | Key content |
|---|---|---|
| 2004 | "Suggestions [of the Beijing Municipal Education Commission and Nine Other Departments] on Implementing the General Office of the State Council's Working Documents on Providing Better Compulsory Education to the Children of Migrant Workers in Cities" <br><br> *Guanyu guanche guowuyuan bangongting jinyibu zuohao jincheng wugong jiuye nongmin zinü yiwu jiaoyu gongzuo wenjian de yijian* | • Work done on migrant children's education is related to the healthy growth and overall development of these children and is significant in Beijing's efforts to promote socioeconomic development and safeguard social stability [Section 1] <br> • The work should be based on the principle of "government responsibility, joint administration, the central role of public schools, and regulation according to law" [Section 2] <br> • Migrant and local children should be treated equally (*yishi tongren*) in terms of the charging of fees [Section 3, Article 2] <br> • The clearing and rectification of unlicensed migrant schools should be continued [Section 5, Article 3] |
| 2005 | "Notice of the Beijing Municipal Education Commission on the Work of Strengthening the Management of Self-Run Migrant Schools" <br><br> *Beijingshi jiaoyu weiyuanhui guanyu jiaqiang liudong renkou ziban xuexiao guanli gongzuo de tongzhi* | • There are 269 migrant schools in Beijing, with about 99,000 students <br> • To strengthen the management of these schools as quickly as possible, district/county education commissions should adopt the following work strategy: (1) assist some schools; (2) examine and approve some schools; and (3) eliminate some schools (*fuchi yipi, shenpi yipi, taotai yipi*) [Section 2] |
| 2006 | "Notice of the General Office of the Beijing Municipal People's Government on the Work of Strengthening the Safety of Non-Approved Self-Run Migrant Schools" <br><br> *Beijingshi renmin zhengfu bangongting guanyu jinyibu jiaqiang weijing pizhun liudong renyuan ziban xuexiao anquan gongzuo de tongzhi* | • There are 239 remaining unlicensed migrant schools in Beijing, with over 95,000 students <br> • The majority of these schools pose safety and security risks <br> • To improve the school environment for children of the floating population and ensure the safety of teachers and students, local governments at all levels should increase their work on safety by "clearing up and rectifying" (*qingli zhengdun*) unlicensed migrant schools [Section 1] <br> • To clear up and rectify unlicensed migrant schools as quickly as possible, district/county governments should adopt the following work strategy: (1) distribute some students to public schools; (2) regulate some migrant schools; and (3) shut down migrant schools that do not meet the standards by the given deadline (*fenliu yipi, guifan yipi, qudi yipi*) [Section 2] |

| 2008 | "Suggestions of the General Office of the Beijing Municipal People's Government on Implementing the Spirit of the State Council's Working Documents on Waiving Tuition and Miscellaneous Fees for Compulsory School-Aged Children in Cities" <br><br> *Beijingshi renmin zhengfu bangongting guanyu guanche guowuyuan zuohao mianchu chengshi yiwu jiaoyu jieduan xuesheng xuezafei gongzuo wenjian jingshen de yijian* | • To date, temporary schooling and miscellaneous fees have been waived for migrant children in public schools who meet the requirements [Section 2] <br> • In waiving the tuition and miscellaneous fees for students in licensed self-run schools who possess the required documents and materials, the municipal government's finance department will cover the costs during the first year, but the municipal and district/county governments will each be responsible for 50 percent in subsequent years [Section 2, Articles 1 and 3] |
| 2008 | "Beijing Measures for Implementing the Compulsory Education Law (2008 Amendment)" <br><br> *Beijingshi shishi Zhonghua renmin gongheguo yiwu jiaoyufa banfa (2008 xiuding)* | • Municipal and district/county governments should ensure migrant children's access to compulsory education according to law [Article 13] |
| 2008 | "Suggestions of the Beijing Municipal Education Commission and Beijing Municipal Finance Bureau to Provide Better Compulsory Education to the Children of Migrant Workers in Beijing" <br><br> *Beijingshi jiaoyu weiyuanhui Beijingshi caizhengju guanyu jinyibu zuohao lai Jing wugong renyuan suiqian zinü zai Jing jieshou yiwu jiaoyu gongzuo de yijian* | • Migrant children's education should be incorporated into overall urban planning, urban population management, and plans for socioeconomic development; district/county governments should raise the quality of service and management [Section 3, Article 1] <br> • Based on the principle of territorial management, the primary role of the district/county governments should be strengthened; district/county governments should strengthen the safety management of unlicensed migrant schools (e.g. in areas like infrastructure and health and sanitation) and the regulation of how migrant schools are run [Section 3, Article 2] <br> • The municipal government's finance department will adopt a role of coordination and guidance and allocate special funds from the annual budget for districts/counties with large numbers of migrant children to encourage public schools to enroll migrant children [Section 3, Article 3] |

*(Continued)*

*Table 4.5* Continued

| Year | Document | Key content |
|------|----------|-------------|
| 2008 | "Notice of the Beijing Municipal Education Commission on Implementing Matters Concerning the Suggestions to Provide Better Compulsory Education to the Children of Migrant Workers in Beijing" *Beijingshi jiaoyu weiyuanhui guanyu luoshi jinyibu zuohao lai Jing wugong renyuan suiqian zinü zai Jing jieshou yiwu jiaoyu gongzuo yijian youguan shixiang de tongzhi* | • Based on current estimates of the number of self-run schools, district/county education commissions should "strengthen control" (*jiada guankong lidu*) [Section 3, Article 2] |

Source: Author's fieldwork (2009–10).

should not charge temporary schooling fees to migrant children who meet the standards. The final section also discusses the general duties of key departments. However, the approach towards migrant schools remains unchanged. The document's fifth section emphasizes once again the need to ensure that unlicensed migrant schools are shut down. It states that district and county governments should, in accordance with local conditions, set deadlines for migrant schools to reach the standards set for private (*minban*) schools, adding that the goal is for all migrant schools to reach these standards within three years.

The municipal government's attitude towards migrant schools was made more explicit in July 2006 with the promulgation of the "Notice of the General Office of the Beijing Municipal People's Government on the Work of Strengthening the Safety of Non-Approved Self-Run Migrant Schools," one of the city's most controversial moves. The document states that most unlicensed migrant schools offer poor quality education and pose security risks in areas like infrastructure, fire safety, and health and sanitation. It therefore proposes a three-part strategy: distributing some children to public schools (*fenliu*) and regulating a portion of the migrant schools (*guifan*) while shutting down the others (*qudi*). In terms of the third, district and county governments should set deadlines for improvement and shut down substandard schools by the end of September 2006. What followed was seen by many migrant school principals, NGOs, and others involved as an attempt to close down as many migrant schools as possible prior to the 2008 Beijing Olympics and generated widespread opposition, including criticism from principals, who appealed to influential figures and the media for support. In the end, even though a few district governments had already adopted measures to shut down schools in response, the municipal government eventually cancelled the decision. Still, the notice and the motives behind it are revealing in terms of the attitude towards migrant schools.

The municipal government has also been increasing the amount of responsibility given to district governments. The "Suggestions of the General Office of the Beijing Municipal People's Government on Implementing the Spirit of the State Council's Working Documents on Waiving Tuition and Miscellaneous Fees for Compulsory School-Aged Children in Cities" (2008) is one example. In addition to stating that tuition and miscellaneous fees (*xuezafei*) will be waived for students in licensed self-run schools who possess the required documents and materials, it gives 50 percent of the financial responsibility in covering these costs during subsequent years to the districts and counties (the other half being covered by the municipal government). In the same year, the "Suggestions of the Beijing Municipal Education Commission and Beijing Municipal Finance Bureau to Provide Better Compulsory Education to the Children of Migrant Workers in Beijing" was issued, calling for district and county governments to continue strengthening their primary role in the area in accordance with the "principle of territorial management" (*shudi guanli yuanze*). Such measures indicate efforts by the municipal government to reduce its share of the responsibility, potentially shedding light on the extent to which it sees migrant children's education as a policy priority.

There have been some positive developments in the city. At the end of 2008, the municipal government stated that it would provide a subsidy to students in licensed migrant schools of 80 RMB (about 12 USD) per student per term at the primary school level and 130 RMB (about 19 USD) per student per term at the middle school level. In 2009, it stated that it would provide new desks, chairs, podiums, and lights to licensed migrant schools (known as *sanxin yiliang*). However, while these two measures provide some support to licensed migrant schools and their students, they are relatively trivial in light of recent efforts in Shanghai. Perhaps of more significance is the decision in 2010 to include migrant children in the computerized lottery system (*diannao paiwei*) for enrollment in public middle schools (see Zhong and Yue 2010). At the time of fieldwork, though, it was unclear how the system would operate, whether or not students of licensed and unlicensed migrant schools would benefit equally, and whether or not implementation would vary across the districts. Conversations with key contacts during subsequent trips to Beijing in 2011 and 2013 revealed that knowledge about the extent to which the decision had been implemented – across both districts and schools – remained extremely limited. Still, the decision itself can be seen as an important step in moving towards more equal educational opportunities for migrant children in Beijing.

Despite such developments, the municipal government continues to adopt a more reserved attitude towards migrant schools. Of particular interest is the general absence of support for migrant schools in its policies. The Law on Promoting Private Education, adopted in December 2002 and effective as of September 2003, states that private (*minban*) schools and public schools share the same legal status. Yet, even though there have been calls for an increase in both the management of and support for migrant schools in central policies, Beijing municipal policies have largely omitted the latter, primarily calling for "management" (*guanli*), or in some cases "management and supervision" (*guanli he jiandu*), of the schools. One exception can be found in the "Notice of the Beijing Municipal Education Commission on the Work of Strengthening the Management of Self-Run Migrant Schools" (2005), which calls for a three-part strategy that includes assisting some schools (*fuchi yipi*). However, the strategy proposed less than a year later in the "Notice of the General Office of the Beijing Municipal People's Government on the Work of Strengthening the Safety of Non-Approved Self-Run Migrant Schools" (2006) omits any mention of support or assistance and calls instead for a three-part strategy involving distributing some migrant children to public schools, regulating some migrant schools, and shutting down others. The shift from a focus on managing migrant schools in the 2005 document to a focus on closing down unlicensed ones in the 2006 document is also noteworthy. So ultimately, even though the Beijing municipal policies reiterate many of the key sentiments expressed by the central government (including migrant children's right to education and the need to treat migrant and local children equally), the municipality has generally excluded discussion of support or assistance for migrant schools from its policies. What is more, the city's pursuit of urbanization has meant that frequent rounds of demolition also threaten the survival of these schools.

As a result, researchers, NGO staff, and principals in the sample discussed Beijing's approach as being more "conservative" (*baoshou*), "strict" (*yange*), and less supportive, especially when compared to Shanghai. As one principal in the sample asserted:

> [Migrant] children in Shanghai can just carry their backpacks and go to school. They don't have to pay. ... Beijing hasn't supplied the funds, so how are our schools supposed to be maintained? Children have all come to school carrying their backpacks, so what are we supposed to use to pay teachers' salaries? What are we supposed to use to pay rent? Shanghai has allocated funding, so [migrant] schools there have money to pay the rent and pay their teachers, and students can study for free. ... The Shanghai government has assumed its responsibility.
>
> (HL1P1)

Interviewees provided the following explanations for the municipal government's more cautious approach:

> [In terms of the reasoning behind Beijing's approach], my [conjecture] is that it has to do with Beijing's total population. ... Its current population has already surpassed Beijing's plans. Beijing's population last year or the year before already reached the urban planning population total for 2020. So Beijing has major population pressures ... so it wants to control the population. To control the population, it certainly cannot control the local Beijing population, can it? It must control the outside population [*wailai renkou*]. So these things will definitely impact policy implementation. ... Shanghai and Beijing are not the same. Shanghai is an economic center, while Beijing is a political center. Economic centers need labor. Beijing is a political center and doesn't necessarily [feel as great of a] need [for] these kind of people, these laborers.
>
> (A1)

> [Beijing's conservative approach is driven by the fear that] as soon as [the restrictions] are loosened, the city will become overcrowded ... . Beijing is particularly afraid of the emergence of elements of instability.
>
> (YOL4S1)

> The good thing is that Beijing has a relatively large amount of financial resources. That is, if it wanted to do it, it should be able to do it. It's not a simple issue of not having enough money. ... But, on the other hand, Beijing faces some of its own restrictions. It's the location of the CPC Central Committee and the State Council. ... [So] it's very difficult for it to be innovative. It cannot act very boldly like other parts of the country that are farther away. Those areas can experiment. When Beijing does these things, it has to be more cautious. ... This is its constraint. It cannot do anything about it.
>
> (YOF1S1)

In other words, Beijing's response to central policies on migrant children's education has been shaped to a large extent by social and political concerns regarding population growth and social instability. Its identity as the political center of China has greatly exacerbated these concerns. As L. Wang (2008: 692) summarizes:

> [T]here is anxiety that easing the situation will accelerate the growth of migrants and will increase pressure to make it easier to obtain urban social rights. The policy-makers are particularly concerned with the image of the capital and generally consider migrants as a disproportionate source of social and civic problems.

The result has been a policy environment in which barriers to the achievement of central-level policy ideals have emerged, with serious implications for the survival and development of migrant schools as a source of education for migrant children in the city.

## Towards a more comprehensive understanding of the effects of decentralization on migrant children's education in Beijing

In China, the dilemmas faced by the government in setting and implementing migration and educational policies often illustrate a basic tension between social and economic aspirations; that is, while migrant workers have made major contributions to urban development and economic growth, officials have frequently been driven by concerns about the socio-political ramifications of large-scale rural–urban migration (see Hannum 1999: 193; Guang 2001: 490–1). These concerns have contributed to the reality that policies intended to address the problems of migrant workers and their children are not necessarily translated into positive outcomes at the local level, illustrating the complexity of decentralized decision making. Though the recent experiences of a few cities, Shanghai in particular, do provide some evidence that decentralization through the policy of "two priorities" can have a positive impact on migrant children's education, the case of Beijing serves as an example of a municipality in which such concerns have heavily influenced the policy approach adopted. Indeed, the Beijing municipal government has adopted a conservative approach, a key aspect of which has been a general lack of support for migrant schools in its policies. In other words, central policies since the early 2000s have highlighted the importance of educational provision for migrant children, and yet Beijing – home to the central government – has been one of the most, if not the most, resistant cities in complying.

In the realm of migrant children's education, the emergence of such gaps between central-level policy ideals and the local reality could have serious consequences for rural–urban inequality and future trends in social stratification (see Chapter 2). As Wu (2001: 86) asserts: "With the increasing influx of migrant families, the frightening prospect is that a generation of uneducated, unemployed children may become a new urban underclass." Under such circumstances, it is crucial to evaluate whether or not central policies are leading to positive outcomes locally and why, including how far the issue goes beyond the *hukou* system. Yet ultimately missing from the discourse is an analysis of the process by which the policies are being implemented and the extent to which differential policy implementation extends to the district level. The latter is particularly relevant in the case of Beijing given efforts by the municipal government to increase the responsibilities of district and county governments in the policy area.

This discussion raises important questions that require further investigation. In light of the policy history evaluated above, what approaches are district governments in Beijing adopting and why? What are the consequences of the municipal and district policy approaches for the situations of migrant schools and their students? Given the gaps in knowledge regarding policy processes in China (especially urban China), what does such an analysis contribute to the understanding of decentralization and differential policy implementation and their potential long-term effects on trends in social stratification? These questions will be the focus of the remainder of this book.

## Notes

1 Recent exceptions include Qu and Wang (2008) and Han (2009), though their focus is primarily on central policies.
2 See http://english.people.com.cn/constitution/constitution.html (accessed February 8, 2012).
3 See www.edu.cn/20050114/3126820.shtml (accessed January 24, 2012).
4 See www.china.org.cn/english/education/184669.htm (accessed February 8, 2012).
5 For further reference to this outline, see Zhou (2004) and Yang (2005: 234).
6 See Appendix D for a list of the policy documents and legislation examined in this chapter.
7 Using 2003 documents as an example, Huang and Zhan (2005: 73–4) mention the goal of improving migrant children's education as a part of the central government's efforts to improve the treatment of migrant workers in cities during this period but do not explore this linkage in detail.
8 Qu and Wang (2008: 182–3, 192–3) make brief mentions of the inclusion of support for migrant schools in certain central policies.
9 See also Qu and Wang (2008: 184–7) for some additional information on the general situations in different cities.
10 Unless otherwise noted, US dollar amounts provided in this book are based on the average RMB/USD exchange rate of 6.77 in 2010.

## Bibliography

Beijing Migrant School Principals' Association. "Huiyi yiti" [Topics for Discussion]. Discussion notes prepared for a migrant school principals' forum, China Youth University for Political Sciences, Beijing, China, December 2009.

Beijing Municipal Statistics Bureau and National Bureau of Statistics Beijing Survey Team. *Beijing Area Statistical Yearbook 2008.* Beijing: Tongxin chubanshe [Tongxin Publishing House], 2008.

Beijing Municipal Statistics Bureau and National Bureau of Statistics Beijing Survey Team. "Beijingshi 2008 nian guomin jingji he shehui fazhan tongji gongbao" [Beijing National Economic and Social Development Statistical Bulletin for 2008]. 2009. www. china.com.cn/aboutchina/zhuanti/09dfgl/2009-02/25/content_17334846.htm (accessed March 5, 2012).

Blaikie, Piers and John Soussan. "Understanding Policy Processes." Livelihood-Policy Relationships in South Asia Working Paper No. 8, University of Leeds, Leeds, 2001. www. york.ac.uk/inst/sei/prp/pdfdocs/2_livelihoods.pdf (accessed May 10, 2009).

Chen, Huinan and Yaozong Li. "Renjun GDP tupo 1 wan meiyuan, Shanghai mairu zhongdeng fada jingjiti" [Per Capita GDP Surpasses 10,000 USD, Shanghai Joins the Economic System of Middle Income Countries]. *Dongfang zaobao* [*Oriental Morning Post*], January 20, 2009. http://news.xinhuanet.com/fortune/2009-01/20/content_10699613.htm (accessed March 5, 2012).

China Daily. "Shanghai Improves Education for Migrant Children." July 15, 2001. www. china.org.cn/english/China/36934.htm (accessed September 27, 2013).

China Labour Bulletin. "The Children of Migrant Workers in China." 2008. www.clb.org. hk/en/node/100316 (accessed December 3, 2008).

Dai, Yingmin. "Shanghai nongmingong zinü xuexiao jiang naru minban jiaoyu guanli" [Shanghai Migrant Schools to be Incorporated into Private Education Management]. *Xinmin wang* [*Xinmin Net*], January 21, 2008. http://news.sina.com.cn/c/2008-01-21/123714792321.shtml (accessed August 21, 2012).

Fan, Xianzuo and Pai Peng. "Educational Equity and Institutional Safeguards: An Analysis of Compulsory Education for Chinese Rural Migrant Workers' Children." *Frontiers of Education in China* 3, no. 3 (September 2008): 321–30.

Froissart, Chloé. "The Hazards of the Right to an Education: A Study of the Schooling of Migrant Worker Children in Chengdu." *China Perspectives* 48 (July–August 2003): 21–36. http://chinaperspectives.revues.org/document386.html (accessed November 16, 2007).

Gu, Bo and Deqing Wang. "Nongmingong zinü yiwu jiaoyu zhengce bianqian" [Policy Changes Concerning Compulsory Education for Migrant Children]. *Fuzhou dangxiao xuebao* [*Journal of the Party School of Fuzhou*] 3 (2008): 72–5.

Guang, Lei. "Reconstituting the Rural–Urban Divide: Peasant Migration and the Rise of 'Orderly Migration' in Contemporary China." *Journal of Contemporary China* 10, no. 28 (2001): 471–93.

Guangzhou Municipal Statistics Bureau and National Bureau of Statistics Guangzhou Survey Team. "2008 nian Guangzhoushi guomin jingji he shehui fazhan tongji gongbao" [Guangzhou National Economic and Social Development Statistical Bulletin for 2008]. 2009. www.gzstats.gov.cn/tjgb/qstjgb/200903/t20090326_8946.htm (accessed March 5, 2012).

Han, Jialing. "Beijingshi liudong ertong yiwu jiaoyu zhuangkuang diaocha baogao" [Report on the Investigation of the Compulsory Education Situation of Children of the Floating Population in Beijing]. *Qingnian yanjiu* [*Youth Studies*] 8 and 9 (2001): 1–7, 10–18.

Han, Jialing. "Beijingshi 'dagong zidi xuexiao' de xingcheng, fazhan yu weilai" [The Formation, Development, and Future of Migrant Schools in Beijing]. In *Zhongguo minban jiaoyu zuzhi yu zhidu yanjiu* [Research on the Organization and System of Private Education in China], ed. Xiaobing Sun. Beijing: Zhongguo qingnian chubanshe [China Youth Press], 2003, pp. 402–16.

Han, Jialing. "Education for Migrant Children in China." Paper commissioned for the *Education for All Global Monitoring Report 2010: Reaching the Marginalized*, 2009. http://unesdoc.unesco.org/images/0018/001865/186590e.pdf (accessed August 19, 2010).

Hannum, Emily. "Political Change and the Urban–Rural Gap in Basic Education in China, 1949–1990." *Comparative Education Review* 43, no. 2 (May 1999): 193–211.

Huang, Ping and Shaohua Zhan. "Internal Migration in China: Linking It to Development." In *Migration, Development and Poverty Reduction in Asia*, ed. International Organization for Migration. Geneva: International Organization for Migration, 2005, pp. 65–84. www.iom.int/jahia/webdav/site/myjahiasite/shared/shared/mainsite/published_docs/books/migration_development.pdf (accessed April 2, 2012).

Kwong, Julia. "Educating Migrant Children: Negotiations between the State and Civil Society." *The China Quarterly* 180 (December 2004): 1073–88.

Ming, Holly Ho. "Growing Up in the Urban Shadow: Realities and Dreams of Migrant Workers' Children in Beijing and Shanghai." PhD dissertation, Harvard University, 2009.

Mo, Honge. "Law to Ensure Migrant Workers' Children of Education Right." *Xinhua News Agency*, August 31, 2006. http://english.gov.cn/2006-08/31/content_374778.htm (accessed March 23, 2008).

Qu, Zhiyong and Li Wang. "Liudong ertong yiwu jiaoyu wenti he zhengce yingdui" [The Problem of Compulsory Education for Children of the Floating Population and Policy Responses]. In *Zhongguo jiaoyu fazhan yu zhengce 30 nian (1978–2008)* [*China's Education Development and Policy, 1978–2008*], ed. Xiulan Zhang. Beijing: Shehui kexue wenxian chubanshe [Social Sciences Academic Press], 2008, pp. 165–206.

Rural Education Action Project. "Education for Migrant Children." 2009. http://reap.stanford.edu/docs/education_for_migrant_children/ (accessed April 19, 2011).

Shanghai Municipal Statistics Bureau. *Shanghai Statistical Yearbook 2009*. Beijing: China Statistics Press, 2009.

Shanghai Municipal Statistics Bureau and National Bureau of Statistics Shanghai Survey Team. "2008 nian Shanghaishi guomin jingji he shehui fazhan tongji gongbao" [Shanghai National Economic and Social Development Statistical Bulletin for 2008]. 2009. www.shanghai.gov.cn/shanghai/node2314/node2319/node11494/node12335/userobject21ai351681.html (accessed March 5, 2012).

Wang, Hongyi. "Shanghai's Education 'Umbrella.'" *China Daily*, February 17, 2009. www.chinadaily.com.cn/cndy/2009-02/17/content_7482005.htm (accessed February 26, 2012).

Wang, Lu. "The Marginality of Migrant Children in the Urban Chinese Educational System." *British Journal of Sociology of Education* 29, no. 6 (November 2008): 691–703.

Wang, Xiaoyan. "Nongmingong zinü jiaoyu: wenti yu jianyi" ["Education for Children of Rural Migrant Workers: Problems and Suggestions"]. In *Shenru tuijin jiaoyu gongping (2008) (Jiaoyu lanpishu)* [*Promote Further Justice in Education (2008) (Blue Book of Education)*], ed. Dongping Yang. Beijing: Shehui kexue wenxian chubanshe [Social Sciences Academic Press], 2008, pp. 136–46.

Wen, Jiabao. "Opening Speech." Speech delivered at the Fifth High-Level Group Meeting on Education for All, Beijing, China, November 28–30, 2005. www.unesco.org/education/efa/global_co/policy_group/HLG5_presentations/Opening/china.doc (accessed December 9, 2010).

Wu, Weiping. "Labor Mobility in China: A Review of the Program Redressing Discrimination against Labor Migrants 1997–2001." In *Labor Mobility in China: A Review of Ford Foundation Grantmaking 1997–2001*, ed. Ford Foundation. Beijing: Ford Foundation, 2001, pp. 57–104.

Wuhan Municipal Statistics Bureau. *Wuhan Statistical Yearbook 2009*. Beijing: China Statistics Press, 2009. www.whtj.gov.cn/documents/tjnj2009/index.htm (accessed March 5, 2012).

Xiamen Municipal Government. "Zonghe shuju" [A Summary of the Data]. 2010. www.xm.gov.cn/zjxm/csjs/200708/t20070830_174453.htm (accessed March 5, 2012).

Xiamen Municipal Statistics Bureau and National Bureau of Statistics Xiamen Survey Team. "2008 nian Xiamenshi guomin jingji he shehui fazhan tongji gongbao" [Xiamen National Economic and Social Development Statistical Bulletin for 2008]. 2009. www.xm.gov.cn/zwgk/tqjj/tjgb/200905/t20090508_303349.htm (accessed March 5, 2012).

Xinhua News Agency. "Wuhanshi gong mianshou nongmingong zinü jiedufei 4400 duo wanyuan" [Wuhan Waives More than 44 Million Yuan in Temporary Schooling Fees for Migrant Workers' Children]. November 30, 2005. http://big5.gov.cn/gate/big5/www.gov.cn/gzdt/2005-11/30/content_113008.htm (accessed May 10, 2011).

Xinhua News Agency. "All Shanghai Migrant Workers' Children to Get Free Education This Year." February 24, 2010. http://english.peopledaily.com.cn/90001/90776/90882/6901632.html (accessed May 10, 2011).

Xinhua News Agency. "Chinese President Stresses Education Development." February 22, 2011. http://english.peopledaily.com.cn/90001/90776/90785/7296377.html (accessed June 20, 2011).

Yang, Dongping. "Zouxiang gongping: 2005 nian Zhongguo jiaoyu fazhan baogao" ["Towards Social Justice: Education in 2005"]. In *2006 nian: Zhongguo shehui xingshi fenxi yu yuce (Shehui lanpishu)* [*Analysis and Forecast on China's Social Development (2006) (Blue Book of China's Society)*], ed. Xin Ru, Xueyi Lu, and Peilin Li. Beijing: Shehui kexue wenxian chubanshe [Social Sciences Academic Press], 2005, pp. 234–47.

Ye, Kasi. "Guangzhou qunian GDP po 8000 yiyuan ju quanguo disan" [Guangzhou's GDP Surpassed 800 Billion Last Year, Ranking Third in the Country]. *Guangzhou ribao* [*Guangzhou Daily*], January 24, 2009. http://news.xinhuanet.com/local/2009-01/24/content_10711692.htm (accessed March 5, 2012).

Zhan, Lisheng. "Migrants Targeted as Population on the Rise." *China Daily*, March 7, 2007. www.chinadaily.com.cn/china/2007-03/07/content_821266.htm (accessed September 27, 2013).

Zhang, Wei. "Nongmingong zaisui wugong 3 nian yishang zinü jiedufei jiang jianmian" [Temporary Schooling Fees to be Waived for the Children of Migrant Workers Who Have Worked in Guangzhou for Over Three Years]. *Xinkuaibao* [*New Express Daily*], May 17, 2008. http://cn.chinagate.cn/education/2008-05/17/content_15284080.htm (accessed February 26, 2012).

Zheng, Xinrong *et al.* "Cujin nongmingong zinü yiwu jiaoyu xiangmu zongjie baogao" [Summary Report of the Program on Promoting Compulsory Education for Migrant Children]. Completion report prepared for the IDF program entitled Ensuring Access to Basic Education for Rural Migrant Children, under the aegis of the Department of Basic Education of the Ministry of Education, 2008. http://219.234.174.136/snxx/baogao/snxx_20081010092411_6154.html (accessed September 4, 2010).

Zhong, Yuwei and Borui Yue. "Beijing 2010 nian xiaoshengchu zhengce chutai, gongzuo shijianbiao gongbu" [Beijing Officially Launches 2010 Policy on Entry into Middle Schools, Announces Work Schedule]. *Fazhi wanbao* [*Legal Evening News*], April 15, 2010. http://edu.sina.com.cn/zhongkao/2010-04-15/1601243078.shtml (accessed March 16, 2012).

Zhou, Ji. "The Full Implementation of the 2003–2007 Action Plan for Invigorating Education." *China Education and Research Network*, March 24, 2004. www.edu.cn/20040324/3102182.shtml (accessed January 30, 2009).

Zhou, Wenting. "Shanghai Struggles with Growth." *China Daily*, July 11, 2013. http://usa.chinadaily.com.cn/china/2013-07/11/content_16759875.htm (accessed February 7, 2014).

Zhu, Junbo. "Xiamen liudong renkoushu bijin changzhu renkou, jingfang huyu qing jinkuai lai dengji" [The Size of Xiamen's Floating Population Approaching That of the Permanent Resident Population, Police Request Registration as Soon as Possible]. *Xiamen wanbao* [*Xiamen Evening News*], June 3, 2011. http://news.xmnn.cn/xmxw/201106/t20110603_1832792.htm (accessed March 5, 2012).

Zhu, Meihua. "The Education Problems of Migrant Children in Shanghai." *Child Welfare* 80, no. 5 (September–October 2001): 563–9.

# 5 Decentralization and migrant children's education in Beijing

## The significance of district policy approaches

"The views of the municipal and district leaders determine the fate of migrant workers' children. This is the fundamental issue."

(HU1P1)

Despite its potential benefits, decentralization is a highly complex phenomenon. It can create space for the emergence of different views and policy approaches that are shaped by the particular local context (Litvack *et al.* 1998: 4–9). Over the past few decades, decentralization in developing countries has often been associated with governance reform and increased accountability. Yet there is frequently a large gap between decentralization policy and reality in these countries, and "[t]he complexities and weaknesses within environments in which it is introduced produces outcomes that are not predicted by decentralisation policy" (Dunne *et al.* 2007: 7). Policy implementation can therefore be an extremely complex and political process (Thomas and Grindle 1990; Crosby 1996; Sutton 1999: 22; Little 2008: 14–17). Not only can it involve multiple levels of local government (as well as a range of actors within each level), but it can also be heavily influenced by local social, economic, political, and governance factors, with major consequences for the populations being targeted.

As demonstrated in Chapter 4, central policies have given municipal governments a degree of autonomy in adopting their own policy approaches towards migrant children's education. Policy document analysis shows that the Beijing municipal government has largely omitted support and assistance for migrant schools from its policies, creating a gap between central-level policy ideals and the local reality. Given the growing recognition in the policy processes literature of the complex effects of decentralization, as well as the tendency to focus on municipal-level situations when discussing migrant children's education in China, this chapter evaluates the potential importance of *district*-level policy responses for migrant schools and their students in Beijing and the role of local context in shaping these responses. That is, what attitudes and approaches have the selected district governments adopted towards migrant children's education and particularly migrant schools and why? What do these approaches reveal about the policy implementation process? Examining these questions will shed much needed light on the linkages between decentralization, local context, and policy implementation outlined in Figure 2.1 in Chapter 2, including the consequences of decentralization, the extent to which differential policy implementation extends to the district level, and the role of local social, economic, political, and governance factors. Ultimately, a stronger understanding of these district-level dynamics will allow for a more comprehensive analysis of the situations of migrant schools and their students.

The following exploration is based on interviews with district education commission officials, policy documents and materials acquired, and information from migrant school principals, researchers, and local organizations. The chapter starts by illustrating the increasing roles and responsibilities of the district governments – and district education commissions in particular – in the policy area and the subsequent importance of examining district policy approaches. This is followed by an analysis of the situations in three of Beijing's inner suburban districts: Shijingshan, Fengtai, and Haidian.

Evidence shows that, despite being constrained by municipal-level standards, the approaches do vary. Shijingshan has adopted an approach centered on the close regulation of its migrant schools, primarily in terms of safety and security. Fengtai has focused on minimizing the number of migrant schools and retaining full control. And Haidian has adopted a strategy of limited management towards migrant schools, in which it has neither been particularly aggressive nor supportive. Though decision making in the area continues to be a closed process, this chapter uses evidence from fieldwork to draw connections between the local context and the policy approach adopted in each district. It shows that several district-level factors – mainly the size of the district and its migrant population, the number of migrant schools, the district's financial situation, other policy interests and priorities, and external pressures – have had a substantial impact on the attitudes and approaches of these district governments. There is, however, variation among the districts in terms of which factors have been more influential, demonstrating that implementation does not operate in a systematic way.

## The role of district governments in migrant children's education

When asked to discuss the main problems surrounding educational provision for migrant children in Beijing, most researchers and migrant school principals interviewed expressed that policy implementation at the local levels is a serious problem (see Table 5.1). The fact that district governments must follow standards set by the municipal government might lead to the conclusion that the latter determines the situations of migrant schools. However, evidence shows that district governments are also given flexibility in their approaches, and they ultimately manage the situations in their localities. For example, though the Beijing municipal government may set the general guidelines for licensing migrant schools, district governments can interpret and implement the regulations. Districts are often responsible for deciding when to shut down or demolish migrant schools as well. In other words, district governments have a critical impact on two key aspects

*Table 5.1* The problem of implementation: views among interviewees

---

- According to one academic, the central policies cannot get any better in theory, but, in practice, the power to decide has been given to individuals. (A4)
- As one researcher asserted: "In China, a lot of factors are very individual factors. For example, this district chief or this bureau chief, what kinds of personal views they have, there is no way to determine." (A1)
- As one researcher described, the central policies merely put forth the principles, while the real policies are at the local levels. (GR1)
- As one academic argued, the Beijing municipal government simply tells the district governments what to do, and the district governments are the ones that actually manage their schools. (A5)
- According to one principal: "[Implementation] is an area of conflict. Sometimes the central and local governments vary in how they think. Local governments have local finances, and the central government has central finances. … Local governments can decide on their own how to spend the money that's in their hands. Sometimes the central government is not able to do anything about it." (HL1P1)
- As one principal described: "Our school will soon be demolished, and we still don't know what will happen. We don't know what will happen to these children and whether or not the education commission has a plan. The policies are, in principle, good. The idea of treating these children as though they are all under the same sun [*tongzai yige yangguang xia*] and ensuring that migrant children are able to benefit from a high quality education and learning environment, just as local children are, is a good idea. But why hasn't there been action, right? There hasn't been action." (HU2P1)

---

Source: Author's fieldwork (2009–10).

of migrant schools' existence: their legal status and their chances of survival. Moreover, according to a government-based researcher in the sample, much of the financial burden in the area is placed on the district governments, with only some support from the Beijing municipal government. They are also the main level of government that migrant schools interact with. Thus district-level approaches can have major consequences for migrant schools and their students.

This section identifies the district government actors involved in migrant children's education and their respective responsibilities, shedding light on the complexity attached to the policy area and motivating a deeper analysis of the district policy approaches. Since the introduction of the policy of "two priorities," migrant children's education has become a part of each district government's work on compulsory education. Within each district, the education commission has the main responsibility in terms of implementation. Based on documents collected, a key role of the district education commission in migrant children's education is to distribute the duties of accepting migrant children to all public primary and middle schools. It is also responsible for strengthening the management of and guidance for migrant schools (e.g. monitoring and regulating school conditions and how the schools are run, as well as providing substandard schools with deadlines for improvement).[1] Within each district education commission, responsibilities are spread across numerous sub-departments. As Table 5.2 shows, these responsibilities exhibit a strong focus on the management

*Table 5.2* Roles of key departments within the district education commissions

| Unit | Main responsibility in the area |
|---|---|
| School management with social resources section (*Shehui liliang banxue guanli ke*) | Generally responsible for work related to private (*minban*) schools and compulsory education for migrant children |
| Primary school education section, Middle school education section (*Xiaojiao ke, Zhongjiao ke*) | Responsible for providing guidance and services for licensed and unlicensed schools, coordinating the allocation and enrollment of migrant children into schools, and keeping track of the numbers of students |
| Private education section (*Minban jiaoyu ke*) | Responsible for doing the preliminary work when private schools apply for a license, as well as providing guidance and management for licensed and unlicensed schools and coordinating relevant departments and sections |
| Security section (*Baowei ke*) | Responsible for establishing safety systems and providing guidance for safety inspections at licensed and unlicensed schools |
| Health center (*Tiwei zhongxin*) | Responsible for doing work related to health and epidemic prevention at private schools, including strengthening inspection, guidance, and supervision |
| Housing management office (*Fangguan suo*) | Responsible for inspecting the safety of school buildings |
| Equipment department (*Zhuangbei chu*) | Responsible for improving the facilities of private schools |
| Personnel section (*Renshi ke*) | Responsible for doing work related to teacher training at private schools |
| Finance section (*Caiwu ke*) | Responsible for doing fund allocation and budgetary work, as well as reducing the temporary schooling fees and tuition and miscellaneous fees charged by licensed schools |
| Auditing section (*Shenji ke*) | Responsible for supervising, managing, and auditing the allocation and use of special funds, as well as reducing the temporary schooling fees and tuition and miscellaneous fees charged by licensed schools |
| Legal affairs section (*Fagui ke*) | Responsible for guiding the various departments in managing the schools, as well as guiding the implementation of relevant laws and regulations |

Source: Author's fieldwork (2009–10) and district-level documents collected.

and supervision of migrant schools (including safety and health regulation), reflecting the municipal-level perception of migrant children's education as a policy area closely linked to issues of public security and social stability.

A range of other district-level organs have also become involved (see Table 5.3). For example, the health bureaus and public security sub-bureaus (or sometimes local police stations) play a key role in conducting regular inspections; aside from the district education commission, migrant schools generally have the most interaction with these two organs. The participation of such actors provides

*Table 5.3* Roles of other key organs at the district and sub-district levels

| Unit | Main responsibility in the area |
| --- | --- |
| District public security sub-bureau (*Qu gongan fenju*) | Responsible for carrying out safety inspections and strengthening the security management of schools accepting migrant children, protecting the safety and stability of the school environment, and cooperating with other departments in carrying out safety regulation and shutting down unlicensed schools |
| District health bureau (*Qu weisheng ju*) | Responsible for carrying out health inspections at schools, including work related to health and epidemic prevention and food safety |
| District construction commission (*Qu jianshe weiyuanhui*) | Responsible for regulating and inspecting the safety of school buildings |
| District fire brigade (*Qu xiaofang zhidui*) | Responsible for inspecting, supervising, and managing fire safety in schools |
| District finance bureau (*Qu caizheng ju*) | Responsible for allocating and monitoring the use of special funds for migrant children's education |
| District development and reform commission (*Qu fazhan he gaige weiyuanhui*) | Responsible for managing and supervising schools in terms of charging and refunding fees |
| District city administration and law enforcement bureau (*Qu chengshi guanli zonghe xingzheng zhifa jiancha ju*) | Responsible for assisting the various departments in conducting relevant inspections |
| District floating population and rental housing management commission office (*Qu liudong renkou he chuzu fangwu guanli weiyuanhui bangongshi*) | Responsible for providing relevant services and guidance and playing a coordinating role |
| District civil affairs bureau (*Qu minzheng ju*) | Responsible for organizing and coordinating implementation |
| District social work commission (*Qu shegong weiyuanhui*) | Responsible for urging all relevant commissions, offices, village and township-level units, and street-level units to implement policies and decisions |
| District commission of rural affairs (*Qu nongcun gongzuo weiyuanhui*) | Responsible for guiding, coordinating, and encouraging relevant work at the village and township level |
| District education supervision office (*Qu jiaoyu dudao shi*) | Responsible for including all relevant work done by the departments and schools into its work scope and carrying out regular supervision |
| All related village and township governments (*xiangzhen zhengfu*) and street offices (*jiedao banshichu*) | Responsible for supervising, managing, and inspecting migrant children's education and reporting their situations to the district education commission, as well as issuing Beijing temporary schooling approval permits to migrant children who meet the conditions |

Source: Author's fieldwork (2009–10) and district-level documents collected.

further evidence that migrant children's education is not simply a matter of education and is seen as a complex policy area that involves a variety of issues like public security, sanitation, food safety, and housing and rent. As one education expert summarized:

> Aside from those doing work related to education, [the policy area also involves government actors working in areas like] public security, city management, housing management, health and sanitation, and trade and commerce. These people do not work in education, but it is their participation that makes this education possible.
>
> (YOF1S1)

Ultimately, the education commission retains the primary responsibility for coordinating these various organs in regulating migrant schools and plays a leading role in the implementation process.

Thus district governments – and district education commissions in particular – have acquired critical roles and responsibilities in migrant children's education, creating the potential for variation among policy approaches and making a closer exploration of the district-level dynamics crucial. The rest of this chapter examines the approaches adopted in Shijingshan, Fengtai, and Haidian, primarily from the perspective of the district education commissions. It shows that decentralization has generated space for differential policy implementation at the district level, and different local factors have shaped the policy response in each district.

## The cases of Shijingshan, Fengtai, and Haidian

The above discussion raises critical questions surrounding the extent to which variations have emerged among district policy approaches, particularly in terms of the level of attention and support given to migrant schools and the approaches towards licensing, closures, and demolition. A common perception among many local academics I spoke with was that, since local policies and standards are set at the municipal level, any variation among the districts would be small and inconsequential. Yet, based on interviews with other researchers, migrant school principals, and NGO staff, there is increasing acknowledgement of differences among district governments' approaches. Among those with some knowledge about the districts, it was often stated that Chaoyang and to a lesser extent Changping and Tongzhou have stronger reputations in terms of their support for migrant schools and their students, and Fengtai has the worst. Districts including Shijingshan, Haidian, and Daxing fall somewhere in between. However, while such general reputations exist, there has been a lack of detailed exploration of the actual attitudes and approaches adopted. The question then arises: what is driving these different reputations?

As Table 5.4 shows, the four inner suburban districts vary not only in area, but also in terms of population size, economic indicators like GDP and average incomes, and the size of their public school systems. Shijingshan is the smallest

Table 5.4 Basic information on Beijing's inner suburban districts

| | | Shijingshan | Fengtai | Haidian | Chaoyang | BEIJING |
|---|---|---|---|---|---|---|
| Area (km²) | | 84.32 | 305.80 | 430.73 | 455.08 | 16,410.54 |
| **POPULATION*** | | | | | | |
| Total population (2000 census) | | 489,439 | 1,369,480 | 2,240,124 | 2,289,756 | 13,569,194 |
| Total population (2010 census) | | 616,000 | 2,112,000 | 3,281,000 | 3,545,000 | 19,612,368 |
| Permanent resident population | | 546,000 | 1,693,000 | 2,814,000 | 3,001,000 | 16,330,000 |
| (changzhu renkou) | | | | | | |
| Registered population | | 354,000 | 1,017,000 | 2,039,000 | 1,784,000 | 12,133,000 |
| (huji renkou) | | | | | | |
| % of permanent resident population | | 64.84 | 60.07 | 72.46 | 59.45 | 74.30 |
| Outside population | | 167,000 | 447,000 | 848,000 | 963,000 | 4,197,000 |
| (wailai renkou) | | | | | | |
| % of permanent resident population | | 30.59 | 26.40 | 30.14 | 32.09 | 25.70 |
| Temporary resident population | | 174,000 | 858,000 | 1,037,000 | 1,353,000 | 5,549,000 |
| (zanzhu renkou) | | | | | | |
| **ECONOMIC SITUATION**** | | | | | | |
| GDP | RMB (billion) | 22.64 | 46.32 | 182.88 | 169.74 | 935.33 |
| | USD (billion) | 2.98 | 6.09 | 24.03 | 22.31 | 122.91 |
| Local financial revenue | RMB (billion) | 1.38 | 3.03 | 11.57 | 14.15 | 188.20 |
| | USD (million) | 180.85 | 398.56 | 1,520.09 | 1,860.02 | 24,731.15 |

| | | | | | | |
|---|---|---|---|---|---|---|
| Local financial expenditure | RMB (billion) | 2.41 | 6.20 | 14.94 | 13.06 | 206.77 |
| | USD (million) | 316.31 | 815.00 | 1,963.29 | 1,716.52 | 27,170.22 |
| Average annual wage of staff and workers in urban units | RMB/year | 40,841 | 35,484 | 51,841 | 53,768 | 46,507 |
| | USD/year | 5,367 | 4,663 | 6,812 | 7,065 | 6,111 |
| Per capita annual disposable income of urban households | RMB/year | 20,745 | 20,574 | 25,312 | 22,377 | 21,989 |
| | USD/year | 2,726 | 2,704 | 3,326 | 2,940 | 2,889 |
| **EDUCATIONAL SITUATION** | | | | | | |
| Number of primary schools | | 32 | 94 | 109 | 149 | 1,235 |
| Number of general secondary schools | | 22 | 49 | 83 | 78 | 689 |

Source: Beijing Municipal Statistics Bureau and National Bureau of Statistics Beijing Survey Team (2008). Figures for the total population from the 2000 and 2010 censuses came from National Bureau of Statistics of China (2000, 2011); Sixth National Census Leading Group Office of Beijing Municipality, Beijing Municipal Statistics Bureau, and National Bureau of Statistics Beijing Survey Team (2011).

* The *permanent resident population* is usually defined as including the *registered population* (those with registered permanent residence in the locality) and the *outside population* (those who have lived in the locality for over half a year but lack local permanent residence status). The *temporary resident population* refers to those who have stayed in the locality for over three days but lack local permanent residence status. The sources of these figures can vary; in this table, figures for the registered and temporary resident populations were determined by Beijing's public security bureau, while figures for the permanent resident and outside populations were based on a 2007 sample survey on population change. The percentages calculated here based on these figures should therefore be seen as rough estimates.

** The figures presented here for GDP, local financial revenue, and local financial expenditure are rounded to the nearest ten million RMB. The USD amounts were calculated using the average RMB/USD exchange rate of 7.61 in 2007.

of the four in terms of area, total population, and GDP. Fengtai, the second smallest in area and total population, has the lowest GDP per capita of the four districts. Haidian, which is only slightly smaller than Chaoyang in area and total population, has the highest GDP and local financial expenditure in the entire city (see also Chapter 3).

Given the stronger reputation of Chaoyang, the largest of the four in area and the largest of all the districts and counties in total population, it is useful to briefly discuss its situation before moving on. Though usually associated with being home to most of the city's embassies, foreign businesses, and international agencies, Chaoyang is also home to Beijing's largest migrant population and, based on data from 2009, nearly 95,000 compulsory school-aged migrant children (Ni and Zhao 2010). According to a long-time principal in the district, its earliest migrant schools were established around 1996–7, and it had over 100 at its peak. At the time of fieldwork, it had 14 licensed migrant schools and an estimated 60–70 unlicensed ones (see Table 5.5).

Interviewees frequently discussed Chaoyang as being more supportive of migrant schools. Based on conversations with principals, migrant schools have been incorporated into the district's educational work and planning to a greater extent than in many other districts. For example, principals of licensed and unlicensed migrant schools may regularly attend meetings held by the education commission together, whereas it is common for other districts to only include the principals of unlicensed migrant schools in a small number of safety-related meetings.[2] It has also allowed the largest number of migrant schools to exist over the years and has the second highest number of licensed ones.

Two of the outer suburban districts, Changping and Tongzhou, have also acquired relatively positive reputations. Changping has not only licensed the largest number of migrant schools, but it has also "never once forcefully clamped down [on migrant schools]" (HL1P1). According to principals, Tongzhou has been more open-minded in its approach towards the schools as well; for example, it was the first district in Beijing to license migrant schools and licensed five in 2001 alone. As of late 2011, both districts were still allowing the establishment of new migrant schools (e.g. post-demolition). As one principal highlighted: "[In Changping and Tongzhou], you can still open some new [migrant] schools. If you go to other districts you can't. [They] won't let you" (YL1P1). Though the experiences of these two districts may differ from those in the inner suburban areas in terms of migration patterns and the attitudes towards migrants, such examples provide additional evidence of positive steps taken towards migrant schools at the district level.

In light of the above, the rest of the chapter examines the situations in Shijingshan, Fengtai, and Haidian districts, with a focus on the approaches adopted towards migrant schools and the factors driving them. While the depth of analysis is ultimately limited by the closed nature of internal policy deliberations and decision making, the discussion uses information from interviews and evidence from policy documents and materials to explore the three trajectories followed.

*Table 5.5* Number of migrant schools in Beijing by district/county

| District/county | Outside population (wailai renkou) (10,000 persons) | Total number of migrant schools (estimated) | Number of licensed migrant schools |
|---|---|---|---|
| **City proper** | | | |
| Dongcheng | 10.1 | 0 | 0 |
| Xicheng | 11.0 | 0 | 0 |
| Chongwen | 5.5 | 0 | 0 |
| Xuanwu | 10.9 | 1 | 1 |
| **Inner suburbs** | | | |
| Chaoyang | 96.3 | >80 | 14 |
| Fengtai | 44.7 | 9 | 3 |
| Shijingshan | 16.7 | 9 | 3 |
| Haidian | 84.8 | 21 | 2 |
| **Outer suburbs** | | | |
| Mentougou | 3.2 | 0 | 0 |
| Fangshan | 13.0 | <10 | 3 |
| Tongzhou | 27.8 | 40–50 | 11 |
| Shunyi | 17.3 | 10–20 | 0 |
| Changping | 30.5 | 50–60 | 16 |
| Daxing | 33.7 | 50–60 | 12 |
| Huairou | 4.5 | 2 | 0 |
| Pinggu | 3.2 | 0 | 0 |
| Miyun | 4.0 | 0 | 0 |
| Yanqing | 2.5 | 1 | 1 |
| **Total (Beijing)** | **419.7** | **>300** | **66** |

Source: Figures for the outside population came from Beijing Municipal Statistics Bureau and National Bureau of Statistics Beijing Survey Team (2008). Figures for the numbers of migrant schools were mainly provided by a prominent principal during fieldwork, and estimates for the total number of schools in each district/county should be seen as rough. Moreover, the numbers of schools may have since declined because of demolitions and closures.

## Shijingshan district

As shown in Table 5.4, Shijingshan is the smallest of the four inner suburban districts. At only 84.32 square kilometers, it is less than one-fifth the size of Chaoyang. By 2007, the district's permanent resident population was 546,000, while its outside population was 167,000. Based on figures in the education commission's "Shijingshan District's Situation Report on the Regulation of Self-Run Migrant Schools" (2009) (hereafter, "Shijingshan Report" (2009)),[3] there were over 16,000 compulsory school-aged migrant children in the district by late 2009, the lowest among the inner suburban districts (see Table 5.6). The report also stated that, at its peak, Shijingshan had 18 migrant schools with over 14,000 students in 2000. By late 2009, it had about nine migrant schools, three of which were licensed.

Shijingshan's district government started to pay attention to the provision of education for migrant children around 2000 and has since made some notable achievements. As discussed in the "Shijingshan Report" (2009), for example, it

*Table 5.6* Official estimates of the numbers of migrant children and migrant schools in the selected districts

|  | *Shijingshan* | *Fengtai* | *Haidian* |
|---|---|---|---|
| Estimated number of compulsory school-aged migrant children | > 16,000 | > 55,100 | > 62,000 |
| Total number of migrant schools | 9 | 9 | 21 |
| Number of licensed migrant schools | 3 | 3 | 2 |
| Number of unlicensed migrant schools | 6 | 6 | 19 |
| Number of children in licensed migrant schools | ≈ 4,000 | > 3,600 | > 1,500 |
| Number of children in unlicensed migrant schools | > 2,000 | > 4,800 | > 9,400 |

Source: Author's fieldwork (2009–10) and district-level documents collected. These estimates should be seen as extremely rough. As will be discussed in Chapter 6, there may be a number of unlicensed migrant schools and migrant children that are not included in these figures. Also, estimates for the migrant children's population may refer to "children of the floating population" rather than "migrant workers' children."

converted a vocational high school into a migrant school in 2000, becoming Beijing's first public school for the children of migrants. It also chose two public primary schools and two public middle schools to primarily accept children of the floating population. According to the report, over 10,000 children of the floating population were attending its public schools by 2009. Moreover, the district government has received recognition from higher-level leadership. In 2003, for instance, Shijingshan was chosen to represent Beijing at a seminar on education for children of the floating population held by UNESCO. In addition, on Teachers' Day in 2003, then Premier Wen Jiabao visited one of the district's public schools set aside for migrant children. Not only did he commend the district for its progress in the area, but he also wrote on a blackboard at the school the now famous words: "Under the same blue sky, grow up and progress together" (*tongzai lantian xia, gongtong chengzhang jinbu*).

### Shijingshan's focus on close regulation and safety management

According to the official interviewed, the district education commission has adopted a three-pronged strategy in the area: to distribute some migrant children to public schools (*fenliu*) and to regulate a portion of its migrant schools (*guifan*), while shutting down the others (*qudi*).[4] Since 2000, it has evaluated the performance of its migrant schools with a focus on safety, health and sanitation, and teacher certification, though the official emphasized that safety regulation is a particular concern.

An example of the focus on safety can be seen in the decision to prohibit migrant schools in the district from using school buses (a decision that only one other district, Chaoyang, has made).[5] As described by the official, in 2009, after observing school bus activity among its migrant schools, the education commission decided to prohibit the use of these buses in order to ensure the safety of the students, prevent migrant schools from enrolling students from neighboring districts, and ensure that students attend schools close to their homes.

The district's emphasis on safety-related issues can also be seen in its 2006 decision to shut down several unlicensed migrant schools. In the period leading up to the 2008 Beijing Olympics, the "Notice of the General Office of the Beijing Municipal People's Government on the Work of Strengthening the Safety of Non-Approved Self-Run Migrant Schools" (2006) called for the "clearing up and rectification" (*qingli zhengdun*) of unapproved migrant schools. As mentioned in Chapter 4, the notice generated widespread opposition, and the decision was eventually cancelled. Still, conversations with principals revealed that, by that time, Shijingshan – one of the few districts to adopt measures in response – had already closed down about eight schools it considered to be unsafe.

What, then, has this approach meant for the district's migrant schools? The education commission claims to be supportive of *public* schools that accept migrant children. As discussed in the "Shijingshan Report" (2009), it has assisted these schools in areas like funding and the treatment of teachers. In addition, given the high mobility of migrant children, it has adopted a public school management system based on the notion of registration, enrollment, and transfer at any time. However, the focus of its approach towards migrant schools has predominantly been on safety and health regulation, rather than measures more directly related to the quality of education. In other words, migrant schools receive considerably less support than the district's public schools, both financially and otherwise. During fieldwork, I visited four of the five remaining unlicensed migrant schools in Shijingshan and was told each time that their relationship with the district government revolves primarily around health and safety inspections, as well as safety meetings at least once or twice per school term. Principals described that, while the education commission does a lot of regulation, it has not given them much assistance (see Table 5.7).

## The impact of local factors

Ultimately, the size of the district and its migrant population has played a central role in shaping Shijingshan's approach. Its outside population is only about three-eighths the size of Fengtai's and about one-fifth the size of Haidian's, while the estimated number of migrant children is about three-tenths the size of Fengtai's and about one-fourth the size of Haidian's. According to the official interviewed, Shijingshan's situation is unique in that, with fewer than ten migrant schools, the education commission can closely monitor and regulate the schools – as called for in Beijing municipal policies – more easily than other districts. For instance, as spelled out in the "Shijingshan District Education Commission's Trial Suggestions for Strengthening the Management of School Conduct among Private Educational Institutions" (2003), Shijingshan introduced a points system to regulate the daily behavior of its private schools. Under this system, each school would begin with 30 points, and points would subsequently be added or deducted based on behavior.[6] Such a system required that the district education

*Table 5.7* Shijingshan's approach: views of principals in the sample

| Approach | Examples |
|---|---|
| Close management but general lack of support | • "Some districts are really supportive of migrant schools. Some districts discriminate against them or don't manage them. Shijingshan is average." (SU3P1)<br>• "I think Shijingshan says a lot and manages a lot but, in terms of real help, it hasn't been implemented. ... For example, around the time of the [2008 Beijing] Olympics, they basically required us to attend meetings every day. If today there was a meeting with the education commission, then tomorrow it would be with the safety departments, and then the day after it would be with the health departments. ... Every department contacted us to attend meetings. But in the end none of the problems were resolved. ... Maybe from their point of view [all of the regulation] is for our own good, for our own safety. We can understand that." (SU2P1)<br>• "There is no support [from the government]. They have never given us a penny. The treatment is just not the same [as that given to public schools]." (SU4P1) |

Source: Author's fieldwork (2009–10).

commission and other relevant departments keep extremely close watch over the schools, and its introduction was possible largely because of the district's small size. As the official maintained, Shijingshan's education commission is able to be very familiar with its migrant schools, whereas it is common for education commission section chiefs in Haidian, a district with a much larger number of schools, to have never met with the principals of migrant schools.

The official further highlighted the link between the district's size and its ability to closely monitor migrant schools by pointing to its response to the sudden closing of an unlicensed migrant school in 2009. As described in the "Shijingshan Report" (2009), because of the decision to prohibit the use of school buses, this particular school's student body declined from over 600 students at its peak to around 170. As a result, the principal began to face difficulties paying rent and other expenses. In addition, the principal's spouse had fallen ill and had to return to their home province for medical treatment. Under these circumstances, the principal decided to close the school, leaving the students without a school to attend. The incident attracted attention from the local media and society. Aware of the situation, the district education commission immediately adopted measures to maintain stability. First, it placed over 80 students into four nearby public schools, while the remaining students were placed into a nearby migrant school. Second, it made sure that the principal refunded all of the fees parents had paid during the preceding period. And third, officials went to the school to assess the scene and resolve any remaining issues. The day after the school's closure, they met with the principals of the four public schools and introduced principles to guide them in their enrollment of the children.[7] Thus, because of the district's small size and its ability to closely observe its migrant schools, the education commission was able to adopt a rapid response.

In sum, largely in line with the Beijing municipal policies, Shijingshan's approach towards migrant schools has been one centered on regulation, primarily in relation to safety and public security. According to the official interviewed, the main factor shaping its approach has been the small size of the district and its migrant population and the small number of migrant schools, making close regulation more manageable. Shijingshan has received recognition from higher-level officials, and its reputation among researchers and principals interviewed remains relatively uncontroversial. However, unlike some of the efforts made by Chaoyang, Changping, and Tongzhou discussed earlier, it has not strayed far from municipal-level attitudes in terms of the level of support given to migrant schools.

### Fengtai district

Fengtai is one of Beijing's key rural–urban transition areas and industrial districts. At 305.80 square kilometers, it is about two-thirds the size of Chaoyang. By 2007, the district's permanent resident population was 1,693,000, and its outside population was 447,000 (see Table 5.4). As stated in the education commission's "Situation Report on Resolving Compulsory Education for Migrant Children" (hereafter, "Fengtai Report" (2004)) and "Fengtai District's Work Report on Education for Children of the Floating Population" (hereafter, "Fengtai Report" (2007)), its floating population in 2004 was close to 400,000, including over 34,000 school-aged children, and it grew to nearly 816,000 by 2007, including over 48,000 school-aged children. In addition, based on figures in the education commission's "Fengtai District's Work Plan on Guaranteeing Compulsory Education for Migrant Children" (2009), it had over 55,100 compulsory school-aged migrant children by 2009. That is, even though Fengtai is only about 70 percent the size of Haidian in area, the estimated number of school-aged migrant children is nearly 90 percent of that in Haidian. Yet, as of late 2009, Fengtai only had about nine migrant schools, including three licensed ones.

Fengtai was chosen as one of six pilot sites for the State Education Commission's "Trial Measures for the Schooling of Children and Youth among the Floating Population in Cities and Towns" (1996). The other sites selected were Hebei district in Tianjin, Xuhui district in Shanghai, Luohu district in Shenzhen, Yiwu city in Zhejiang province, and Langfang city in Hebei province. As explained by a government-based researcher, Fengtai was chosen mainly because of the large size of its floating population and migrant workforce. However, understanding of what measures it adopted at the time and what the outcomes were remains extremely limited, and both officials interviewed expressed a lack of knowledge about the district's early role in the area. While it was difficult to acquire information about Fengtai during this period, another government-based researcher did recall the establishment of a special public school for migrant children in the district at the time. The school, though, was closed within a year or so, most likely because of issues concerning expensive fees like the temporary schooling fee and discrimination by teachers.

According to the officials, the district government began paying attention to migrant children's education around 2001, after coming across some migrant schools while doing public security work.[8] They discovered that these schools – often referred to as "simple schools" (*jianyi xuexiao*) – posed serious public safety and security risks. Several areas of concern were highlighted in the "Fengtai Report" (2004). One was the poor quality of education and teaching. Another involved the use of illegal school buses; they found that schools were using 17-seater buses, most of which were old and in poor condition, to carry close to 50 students at a time. Moreover, schools were expanding in a disorderly manner; at one school, for instance, the size of the student body grew from 600 to over 1,200 within one year. Most of the school canteens were also not certified, and schools were not taking proper precautions in terms of disease prevention. Such findings and subsequent fears about public security and stability would play a central role in shaping the district government's approach.

### *Fengtai's pursuit of "total control" and the elimination of migrant schools*

The primary goal of the district government's work in the area has, in principle, been to ensure that migrant children receive compulsory education. However, the approach adopted has been extreme compared to other districts. Based on the "Fengtai Report" (2004), the education commission's core strategy revolved around two key ideas. One was a focus on the central role of public schools and the use of multiple channels to ensure this. The other, and the one that ultimately set the district apart, involved a combination of the two concepts of *shu* and *du* (*shu du jiehe*). Formulated to ensure the right of children of the floating population to life, education, and health, the notion of *shu* (literally to clear away an obstruction) refers to the goal of allocating these children to public schools rather than migrant schools, while that of *du* (literally to block or stop) refers to shutting down migrant schools with security risks.

This line of thinking – evident in the use of terms like "strengthening management" (*jiaqiang guanli*) and "total control" (*zongliang kongzhi*) in district-level documents – materialized into an effort to close down all of the district's migrant schools within a short amount of time. As stated in the "Fengtai Report" (2007), the conditions and behavior of these schools were in violation of the Compulsory Education Law (1986) and the Law on Promoting Private Education (2002). A process of rectification and clearing up (*zhengdun qingli*) was therefore initiated to ensure that substandard migrant schools were not allowed to exist.[9]

The result of this approach – and what has given the district government its poor reputation in the policy area – was that Fengtai was essentially left with no migrant schools for a period of time, leading many principals and researchers to refer to it as a *yidaoqie* (literally "to cut down completely with a single stroke") approach. Under the premise of protecting the right of children of the floating population legally residing in the district to life, education, and health, the education commission wrote in one of its reports that 89 unlicensed migrant schools were shut down between 2001 and 2007.

The primary reason for which this became so controversial was its impact on the students of these schools (see Table 5.8). These children basically had four options: they could look for schools in other districts, move with their migrant school to another district (if their principal decided to relocate the school), enroll in a public school in Fengtai, or return to their hometowns. The "Fengtai Report" (2004) and the "Fengtai Report" (2007) claimed that public schools had absorbed the majority of the compulsory school-aged children in the district's floating population. But principals in the sample said otherwise, stating that most children affected had to either attend migrant schools in other districts like Daxing or return to their hometowns for further schooling. Indeed, principals of the licensed migrant schools visited in Fengtai maintained that, unlike Shijingshan and Haidian, there are no public schools in the district that primarily accept migrant children. As a result, while some students were able to continue their schooling in Fengtai, others had to go to other districts or return to their hometowns. Only a small proportion of them were placed into public schools. Though the officials interviewed admitted that no reliable figures exist, one district-level document obtained cited the estimate that, by the mid-2000s, about 10,000 migrant children whose parents worked in Fengtai were attending schools in other districts.

*Table 5.8* Fengtai's approach: views of principals in the sample

| Approach | Examples |
| --- | --- |
| A pursuit of "total control" and the elimination of migrant schools | • As one principal argued: "Fengtai is the worst of the districts. Within a three-year period, it strove to exterminate all migrant schools, not leaving a single one. As a result, large numbers of children were left on the streets and had to go to other districts like Haidian, Chaoyang, and Daxing to find schools." (HU1P1) <br> • One principal stated that, as a result of government intervention, Fengtai had become an "empty district" (*kong qu*) by the mid-2000s. Under such circumstances, he saw an opportunity and a need to open his own migrant school in the district. (FU1P1) <br> • As one principal explained, one of the reasons that Daxing district has such a large migrant population is that a lot of migrant families moved to Daxing from other districts because of demolitions and school closures, including the closures in Fengtai. (XU1P1) |

Source: Author's fieldwork (2009–10).

Since the mid-2000s, migrant schools have begun to appear in the district again, albeit on a much smaller scale. As previously stated, Fengtai only had about nine migrant schools at the time of fieldwork. In addition to being required to attend one to three safety meetings held by the district education commission every school term, unlicensed schools are subject to regular inspections. They also continue to be in danger of being shut down, with consequences for their stability. One unlicensed school in the sample, for instance, had already moved three times since its establishment in 2005. While Fengtai's licensed schools receive some governmental support (e.g. in terms of equipment and facilities), principals of the unlicensed schools stated that they remain largely unsupported. As described by the principal of the school just mentioned, they have not yet been "pushed out" (*paiji*) by the district government, but they have not received much support or assistance either (FU1P1).

Thus, even though Fengtai has allowed the reemergence of a small number of schools, the objective to keep their number at a minimum remains. For example, recommendations made in district-level documents obtained called for strengthening the management of unlicensed migrant schools and called on the Beijing Municipal People's Congress, the municipal government, the media, and society to help the district government by supporting the work of clearing up the unlicensed schools. In addition, given the difficulties faced in shutting down migrant schools, village and township governments and street offices should prevent the renting of buildings to the individuals who run schools illegally.

## The impact of local factors

Given the district government's controversial approach, it is necessary to explore the reasons underlying its attitude towards migrant children and migrant schools. Though the documents discussed above emphasize that the strategy adopted was largely driven by the goal of protecting the rights of children of the floating population, a closer analysis of the documents and views expressed by the officials interviewed suggests a more complex picture. First, compared to other districts, the officials asserted that the scale of the problem is larger in Fengtai; not only does it have one of the largest migrant populations, but migrant workers' children make up 98 percent of the children in its floating population. The officials also pointed to the low status of migrant workers in the district, maintaining that there are too many "low-level parents" (*dicengci de jiazhang*), as opposed to those, for example, in Haidian (which is generally seen as a more "civilized" district). All of this has led them to view migrant children's education as an extremely difficult area that requires "controlling."

Second, as highlighted earlier, much of the financial responsibility in the provision of education for migrant children has been given to the district governments. This has been a particular problem for Fengtai, one of Beijing's poorer districts. Not only does it have the lowest GDP per capita among the four inner suburban districts, but, as shown in Table 5.4, its local financial revenue is only about one-quarter of that in Haidian. In other words, Fengtai lacked the financial capacity to manage such a large number of informal schools, and this directly impacted its early decision to shut all of them down. In the "Fengtai Report" (2007), extreme financial stringency was first in a list of key problems faced by the district government in the area. It was further expressed that the financial pressure on Fengtai has substantially increased since the municipal government's decision to eliminate the temporary schooling fee for migrant children in public schools. In addition, the report's first recommendation was that, since Fengtai's economy is underdeveloped and the district is facing a great deal of financial pressure, the Beijing municipal government should allocate special funds to support public schools in educating children of the floating population. Thus, as one academic in the sample asserted, whereas Chaoyang has the money and can afford to adopt a more supportive approach, Fengtai is simply too poor.

These two factors have contributed to a heightened sense of concern within the district government about the increased flow of migrants into Beijing and particularly into Fengtai. The officials emphasized that the central and municipal policies on migrant children's education are becoming more relaxed, which has increased the number of migrant workers in the city. The resulting increase in the number of migrant children trying to attend school in Beijing has become a major concern. According to the officials, this has not only been a problem for the district education commission, but it has also required an excessive use of the city's educational resources, while the resources of sending governments have not been fully utilized. In other words, Fengtai adopted the strategy it did because of fears about public security issues and social instability, as well as the belief that eliminating migrant schools and relying solely on public schools would be the right thing to do. The large size of Fengtai's migrant population – along with the fact that it has a smaller amount of financial resources to draw from than wealthier districts like Chaoyang – played a critical role in motivating these concerns and its pursuit of "total control."

In sum, Fengtai has adopted a strict policy based on minimizing the number of migrant schools and maintaining control. During the early to mid-2000s, this involved efforts to eliminate the schools altogether. As expressed in the "Fengtai Report" (2007), the outcomes of closing down unlicensed migrant schools have not been ideal, but the district government is ultimately unable to resolve the roots of the problems. Since the reemergence of a small number of migrant schools in the mid- to late 2000s, the district education commission's aim has been to keep the number of these schools at a minimum and ensure that they are subject to regular inspections. Thus Fengtai's reputation remains controversial; the impact of its approach in the early 2000s is still apparent, and, as of mid-2010, the number of migrant schools in the district was comparable to that in Shijingshan, even though Fengtai is more than three and a half times larger in area and has a compulsory school-aged migrant children population estimated to be almost three and a half times the size of Shijingshan's.

## Haidian district

At 430.73 square kilometers, Haidian is the second largest inner suburban district and is only about 24 square kilometers smaller than Chaoyang. By 2007, it had a permanent resident population of 2,814,000 and an outside population of 848,000 (see Table 5.4). According to figures provided by the official interviewed, by late 2009, the district had over 62,000 compulsory school-aged migrant children (almost quadruple that in Shijingshan), as well as about 21 migrant schools, including two licensed ones.

Beijing's earliest migrant schools were in Haidian. As pointed out by a long-time principal in the district, the city's first three migrant schools emerged in Haidian within a one-year period between 1993 and 1994, and, according to the official, the district had roughly 61 migrant schools by 2001. It therefore has an important place in the history of migrant schools in Beijing. As the principal of one of the first migrant schools remarked: "If the earliest migrant schools in Beijing had been in Fengtai, then the over 300 migrant schools that subsequently emerged would not exist today. Haidian did not shut down our school, whereas Fengtai did not leave a single one" (HL1P1).

The district government became aware about the existence of migrant schools early on. As mentioned in Chapter 3, the discovery of migrant schools in Beijing during the mid-1990s is usually attributed to local researcher Zhao Shukai, who then brought the issue to the attention of the media and the government. These first schools to be discovered were located in Haidian. Indeed, the official stated that the education commission started paying attention to migrant children's education around 1996 and even conducted some early research on the subject. Yet it did not adopt any measures in response at the time, as its priority was to provide education to children with Beijing *hukou*. Indeed, it only began to pay more attention to migrant children's education in the early 2000s, at a time when the municipal government and many other district governments were beginning to adopt responses. Since then, its primary goal has been to increase the number of migrant children in public schools.

Like Shijingshan, Haidian has also seen some positive developments. The official emphasized two achievements in particular. First, in 2008, students from one of the district's licensed migrant schools were invited to perform in the CCTV New Year's Gala, China's most widely watched television program of the year. Second, in 2009, then President Hu Jintao and other key government figures, including Zhou Ji (Minister of Education, 2003–9), made a special visit to a Haidian public primary school at which migrant children made up 90 percent of the student body.[10] According to a district-level document obtained, this particular school has received attention from central and municipal leaders and was also named Beijing's "model school for moral education" (*deyu gongzuo shifan xuexiao*).

In addition, given Haidian's high concentration of academic and research institutions, a distinctive aspect of the district government's early approach was the creation in 2004 of a research center dedicated entirely to compulsory education for migrant children. As stated in the document just mentioned, under the support of the central and municipal government, research results produced by the center would be applied to education and teaching practices in the district.

## Haidian's strategy of limited management

Despite such efforts, Haidian has been more ambivalent than Shijingshan and Chaoyang in its approach towards migrant children's education. The official interviewed listed several difficulties encountered by the education commission, especially in terms of placing migrant children into public schools. First, public schools are primarily created for the permanent resident population and often cannot accommodate migrant workers' needs; for instance, migrant parents usually go to work early in the morning and may need to drop off their children as early as 5 a.m., creating serious safety risks. Second, if public schools continue admitting migrant children, more and more local children (and their parents) may want to change schools, causing transportation problems for the district. Third, all of the district's public schools are basically full.

It was further expressed that the high mobility of the migrant population has made it difficult for the district education commission to formulate any long-term work plan. The official explained that if the number of migrant children in the district were to increase during one period, the education commission might respond by increasing the number of public school teachers. But if the number of migrant children then declined, there would be a surplus of teachers. Moreover, since migrant children come from different regions across China, there is considerable variation in their educational levels, performance, and needs, and public school teachers may not be able to handle such a wide range of students.

Such factors have made the district's education commission less willing to invest a significant amount of resources and energy into migrant children's education, with major consequences for its approach. For example, as one researcher revealed, the research center on migrant children's education created in 2004 was initially meant to demonstrate that Haidian, as the country's leading district in education, recognized the importance of the policy area; it was hoped that the center would further boost its reputation. This, however, did not happen. Though the education commission had taken the time to appoint a public school principal as the center's director and to recruit local academics and researchers to contribute to research efforts, the center faded away after a few meetings and events and has essentially become an empty structure. Furthermore, while officials from Fengtai and to a lesser extent Shijingshan mentioned shortages of funding as an issue, the Haidian official expressed a degree of hesitation about investing the district's resources into what they see as a difficult, unstable policy area, despite the fact that its financial revenue is nearly four times that of Fengtai and more than eight times that of Shijingshan (see Table 5.4).

How, then, has this affected Haidian's migrant schools? Given the concerns about continuing to place migrant children into public schools, has more emphasis been placed on migrant schools instead? The official did emphasize that the district government sees its migrant workers and their children as "Haidian's new citizens" (*Haidianqu de xinqumin*) and acknowledged that many migrant children are born and/or raised in Beijing and do not feel a connection to their hometowns. Yet, when it came to discussing migrant schools, the official expressed the view that many of them are run for profit-seeking purposes. Thus, while the education commission has been relatively supportive of the two licensed migrant schools (e.g. in terms of assisting with supplies and facilities), principals of unlicensed migrant schools in the sample stated that it has not given them much support at all.

Particularly in the early to mid-2000s, migrant schools did not receive much attention from the district government. Haidian's current approach towards unlicensed migrant schools continues to be one of limited management. This was certainly the opinion of many principals in the sample (see Table 5.9). For example, as previously mentioned, unlicensed migrant schools in Shijingshan and Fengtai must attend district-level safety meetings at least once or twice per school term. In contrast, principals of unlicensed schools visited in Haidian stated that they are asked to attend such meetings as little as once a year. One principal even said that his school, which was established in 1994, had never been notified by the education commission to attend meetings and that the only interaction he had with the district education commission was when someone from the commission called about once a year to ask general questions about the school. As this principal described, the education commission keeps track of the school's situation, but "it has never once asked what the school needs" (HU4P1).

The district education commission has also been reluctant to license migrant schools. Even though it has more than triple the number of unlicensed schools than Shijingshan and Fengtai, both of which have licensed three, Haidian only has two licensed migrant schools. Moreover, one of these two schools had three branches at the time of fieldwork, but only one of the three branches was given a license when, according to the principal, there were no significant differences between them. When asked why this was the case, the principal asserted that "only the education commission knows," adding that Haidian is simply "not willing to license too many [migrant schools]" (HL1P1).

### The impact of local factors

Haidian's approach has largely been driven by two interrelated factors: attention from external actors and a focus on local schools and institutes of higher education. Given the district's strong reputation in education, as well as the fact that migrant schools in Beijing have had the longest presence in Haidian, the district government's work on migrant children's education has attracted much attention from actors like the media, which is one of the reasons why Haidian has not been as extreme as Fengtai in shutting down migrant schools. As the official described, many migrant school principals are driven by self-interests and their schools are substandard, but it is ultimately difficult for the district government to close the schools because of external pressure.

*Table 5.9* Haidian's approach: views of principals in the sample

| Approach | Examples |
| --- | --- |
| Limited management and support | • At one of the district's earliest migrant schools, the principal maintained: "The attitude that Haidian has adopted towards its migrant schools has been one in which there haven't been too many restrictions but there also hasn't been too much support. ... It is unlike Chaoyang, [where migrant schools have been] brought into the district government's planning, given reasonable support, and integrated in a fair way. It is also unlike Fengtai, where the aggressive approach did not leave a single school." (HU1P1) |
|  | • At one school that was located in Haidian during the early 2000s, the principal recalled: "During the four years that our school was in Haidian, there was basically no regulation [from the district government] and no one asked questions. ... For example, in terms of school buses, in Haidian, and perhaps this is because Haidian is relatively large, ... we had school buses during those four years but did not run into the police a single time. But as soon as we moved to Shijingshan, the local police came to our doors to inspect the buses." (SU2P1) |
|  | • At one school that had spent time in Fengtai, Haidian, and Shijingshan, the principal asserted: "In terms of Haidian's approach towards migrant schools, you could say that it couldn't handle the situation, you could also say that it didn't have time to deal with us, or you could even say that it didn't want to provoke any trouble, but those two years [in Haidian] were our most uneventful and quietest years, with the least amount of intervention [from the government]." (SU1P1) |

Source: Author's fieldwork (2009–10).

This was most apparent in 2006 when – in the context of policies such as the "Notice of the Beijing Municipal Education Commission on the Work of Strengthening the Management of Self-Run Migrant Schools" (2005) and the "Notice of the General Office of the Beijing Municipal People's Government on the Work of Strengthening the Safety of Non-Approved Self-Run Migrant Schools" (2006) – Haidian made efforts to shut down a large number of unlicensed schools. As described in a district-level document obtained, that year, 12 government agencies in Haidian, including the education commission and the office for comprehensive management of public security, organized ten joint inspection units and conducted inspections of 39 unlicensed migrant schools. The results of the inspections showed serious safety risks in areas like the use of electricity and food safety. Thirty-seven of the schools were issued deadlines for improvement and later issued orders to close.[11] According to principals in the sample, however, the education commission encountered several problems while trying to distribute the children to public schools; for example, it could not find enough space for the students, and many public schools were located too far away from migrant communities. This attracted a great deal of societal attention, including criticism from the principals themselves and other actors like the media. In the end, the education commission retracted the order to close the schools, allowing many to continue operation.

This decision signifies a fundamental difference between the approaches adopted in Haidian and Fengtai. It is interesting, though, that despite this difference, there remain similarities between their attitudes. Indeed, when asked about Haidian's approach compared to other districts, the Haidian official expressed that Fengtai's district government has performed well in the area, as the district basically has no migrant schools left. Ultimately, while its approach has not been nearly as controversial as Fengtai's, the reality is that the Haidian education commission's focus is on local schools and higher education and science and technology, where its reputation is strongest. This focus, combined with the fact that the district has a much larger number of schools to manage than neighboring districts like Shijingshan, has taken much of its attention away from migrant children and made it less willing to invest its resources into migrant children's education and migrant schools. The fading away of its research center on migrant children's education is a case in point.

In sum, Haidian has adopted an approach in which it has not been particularly aggressive towards migrant schools, but it has also not been particularly supportive, especially of the unlicensed schools. While attention and pressure from external actors like the media have been important in driving its progress and achievements in the area, its ultimate focus on local schools and issues concerning higher education has affected its willingness to invest time and resources into what it sees as an unstable area. Thus, even though the official interviewed did express feeling sympathetic towards migrant schools and their students, the district education commission has been ambivalent in its approach, and the district has acquired somewhat of a mixed reputation in the area.

## The importance of district-level approaches

In the case of migrant children's education, the overarching problem of differential policy implementation at the municipal level has been made even more complicated because of district-level variations that have developed, especially since the introduction of the policy of "two priorities." As shown in Tables 5.2 and 5.3, district governments – and district education commissions in particular – have acquired a critical role and important responsibilities in migrant children's education. This decentralization, along with the fundamental complexity of the policy area itself (evidenced by the range of responsibilities and departments involved), has created space for differing policy approaches at the district level. Using evidence from fieldwork, this chapter identifies three trajectories that illustrate significant differences among the district-level approaches towards migrant children's education and specifically migrant schools, the most extreme case being Fengtai.

Although the officials interviewed each expressed a hope for all migrant children to attain an education, the complex nature of educational provision for migrant children has meant that some district governments are less able or equipped, or sometimes less willing, than others to address the policy area. District-level factors – mainly the size of the district and its migrant population, the number of migrant schools, the district's financial situation, other policy interests and priorities, and external pressures – have led to differences among the district education commissions in terms of what they view as the main issue or problem, the degree of importance or urgency attached to that problem, and the approaches adopted in response. Evidence from interviews and policy documents shows that there is variation in terms of which local factors play a larger role in shaping the different attitudes and approaches. In Shijingshan, the small size of the district and its migrant population and the small number of migrant schools have allowed the district to adopt an approach centered on the close management of the schools (largely in line with the municipal policies). In Fengtai, the large size of the migrant population and a tight financial situation have been especially influential in shaping the district's efforts to eliminate and later minimize the number of migrant schools. In Haidian, external pressures (e.g. from the media) resulting from its strong reputation in the educational arena, combined with a prioritization of issues concerning local schools and higher education, have contributed to an approach of limited management in which the district has neither been too aggressive towards nor too supportive of migrant schools.

The municipal and district-level attitudes and approaches can also interact and overlap in important ways, further illustrating the complexity of the implementation process. Here, the case of Fengtai is particularly relevant. As pointed out by a principal in the sample, the deputy director of Beijing's education commission at the time of fieldwork had previously held several key posts in Fengtai's district government, including director of the district's education commission and deputy district chief, during the late 1990s and early 2000s, at the height of the district government's efforts to shut down all of its migrant schools. The fact that an influential figure in Fengtai during that period subsequently assumed a high-ranking post in Beijing's education commission provides major insight into the municipal-level concerns about the potential implications of migrant children's education for social stability, as well as the general lack of support for migrant schools and their students in municipal policies.

This chapter therefore sheds substantial light on the complex effects of decentralization, the importance of district-level dynamics, and the differing ways in which local factors can shape policy implementation. In doing so, it demonstrates that the linkages between decentralization, local context, and policy implementation proposed in Figure 2.1 in Chapter 2 are close but complicated. These findings are significant; not only do they show that the implementation process does not operate in a systematic way, but, as will be illustrated in the following two chapters, they also have serious implications for the situations of migrant schools and their students, including the amount of assistance they receive from civil society.

In view of the limited amount of support given to migrant schools at the Beijing municipal level and the variation among district-level approaches, it becomes necessary to examine questions regarding the consequences of both for the situations of migrant schools and their students. What are the key problems these schools face, and how have the policy approaches adopted at both levels affected them? What implications does this have for the quality of migrant schools compared to public schools and for the situations of their principals, teachers, and students? And, perhaps most importantly, given the continued policy focus on the primary role of public schools in this area, are such questions increasingly irrelevant?

## Notes

1 See, for example, the "Haidian District's Measures for the Implementation of Providing Compulsory Education to School-Aged Children and Youth of the Floating Population," issued by the Haidian district government in 2002, and the "Suggestions on Implementing the Provision of Compulsory Education to School-Aged Children and Youth of the Floating Population," issued by Fengtai's education commission, agriculture commission, civil affairs bureau, public security sub-bureau, and education supervision office in 2003.
2 Since licensed migrant schools are considered to be private (*minban*) schools, they usually attend the district government's meetings on a range of topics, while unlicensed ones often only attend a few safety meetings each year. Ultimately, which schools attend which meetings will vary from district to district.
3 As these materials were obtained during fieldwork, I shall not burden the reader with the Chinese (pinyin) titles.
4 These were goals described in the "Notice of the General Office of the Beijing Municipal People's Government on the Work of Strengthening the Safety of Non-Approved Self-Run Migrant Schools" (2006) (see Chapter 4).
5 The seven schools visited in Shijingshan each had two to six buses prior to this decision. As will be discussed in Chapter 6, the conditions of the buses used by migrant schools tend to be poor.
6 Points could be awarded if, for instance, a large sum of money was invested into improving the school's quality. Points could be deducted as a result of improper behaviors, such as failing to submit relevant materials and forms to higher authorities. If the overall deduction of points exceeded a certain number, the principal would be required to go to the education commission for training and would be given a deadline for improvement.
7 These principles included accepting all of the migrant children without entrance examinations and waiving tuition and miscellaneous fees. In addition, to reduce the financial burden on migrant parents, the education commission would cover the costs of new teaching materials for the children.
8 According to a principal whose school was located in Fengtai during the late 1990s but later moved to another district, Fengtai's district government knew about the existence of migrant schools at the time, but there was very little regulation or interaction with them.
9 See also, for example, the "Suggestions [of the Fengtai District Education Commission and Four Other Departments] on Implementing the Provision of Compulsory Education to School-Aged Children and Youth of the Floating Population" (2003).

10 Similar to Shijingshan, Haidian also has a small number of public schools attended primarily by migrant children. The exact number of such schools, however, is unclear.
11 For a more detailed account, see Han (2007).

## Bibliography

Beijing Municipal Statistics Bureau and National Bureau of Statistics Beijing Survey Team. *Beijing Area Statistical Yearbook 2008*. Beijing: Tongxin chubanshe [Tongxin Publishing House], 2008.

Crosby, Benjamin L. "Policy Implementation: The Organizational Challenge." *World Development* 24, no. 9 (September 1996): 1403–15.

Dunne, Máiréad, Kwame Akyeampong, and Sara Humphreys. *School Processes, Local Governance and Community Participation: Understanding Access*. CREATE Pathways to Access Research Monograph No. 6. Brighton: University of Sussex, Centre for International Education, 2007. www.create-rpc.org/pdf_documents/PTA6.pdf (accessed May 21, 2009).

Han, Jialing. "Luoshi liudong ertong yiwu jiaoyu zhengce de zhidu chongtu" ["System Conflicts of Implementing Floating Children's Compulsory Educational Policy"]. In *2006 nian: Zhongguo jiaoyu de zhuanxing yu fazhan (Jiaoyu lanpishu)* [*Transformation and Development of China's Education (2006) (Blue Book of Education)*], ed. Dongping Yang. Beijing: Shehui kexue wenxian chubanshe [Social Sciences Academic Press], 2007, pp. 237–50.

Little, Angela W. *EFA Politics, Policies and Progress*. CREATE Pathways to Access Research Monograph No. 13. London: University of London, Institute of Education, 2008. http://sro.sussex.ac.uk/1861/1/PTA13.pdf (accessed June 18, 2011).

Litvack, Jennie, Junaid Ahmad, and Richard Bird. *Rethinking Decentralization in Developing Countries*. Washington, DC: World Bank, 1998. www1.worldbank.org/publicsector/decentralization/Rethinking%20Decentralization.pdf (accessed May 6, 2011).

National Bureau of Statistics of China. "Biao 1: Zong renkou, huji renkou, shaoshuminzu renkou bizhong, feinongye hukou renkou bizhong, chengxiang renkou, jiatinghu renkou, jiatinghu leibie (quanbu shuju)" [Table 1: Total Population, Registered Population, National Minority Population as a Percentage, Agricultural Population as a Percentage, City and Countryside Population, Household Population, Household Type (Complete Data)]. 2000. www.stats.gov.cn/tjsj/ndsj/renkoupucha/2000fenxian/htm/table1.htm (accessed March 29, 2012).

National Bureau of Statistics of China. "2010 nian diliuci quanguo renkou pucha zhuyao shuju gongbao (di er hao)" [Bulletin of Key Data from the Sixth National Population Census of 2010 (No. 2)]. 2011. www.stats.gov.cn/tjgb/rkpcgb/qgrkpcgb/t20110429_402722510.htm (accessed March 29, 2012).

Ni, Guanghui and Yuanyuan Zhao. "Jing: 30 duo suo dagong zidi xuexiao chaiqian, shu qianming haizi ruxue nan" [Beijing: The Demolition of Over 30 Migrant Schools, Thousands of Children Face Difficulties Enrolling in School]. *Renmin ribao* [*People's Daily*], March 1, 2010. http://news.xinhuanet.com/employment/2010-03/01/content_13072448.htm (accessed April 22, 2010).

Sixth National Census Leading Group Office of Beijing Municipality, Beijing Municipal Statistics Bureau, and National Bureau of Statistics Beijing Survey Team. "Beijingshi 2010 nian diliuci quanguo renkou pucha zhuyao shuju gongbao" [Bulletin of Key Data on Beijing from the Sixth National Population Census of 2010]. 2011. www.bjstats.gov. cn/xwgb/tjgb/pcgb/201105/t20110504_201363.htm (accessed March 29, 2012).

Sutton, Rebecca. "The Policy Process: An Overview." ODI Working Paper No. 118, Overseas Development Institute, London, 1999. www.odi.org.uk/resources/odi-publications/working-papers/118-policy-process.pdf (accessed November 2, 2008).

Thomas, John W. and Merilee S. Grindle. "After the Decision: Implementing Policy Reforms in Developing Countries." *World Development* 18, no. 8 (August 1990): 1163–81.

# 6 The survival and development of migrant schools in Beijing
## Impacts of the municipal and district policy approaches

"When I got to the school, I stared blankly at the sight in front of me – a low enclosing wall, a few unbearably disorderly classrooms, an extremely small sports area. Could this really be a school? Feeling astonished, puzzled, and helpless, I took my first step into a migrant school."

(A migrant school teacher in Beijing[1])

Although decentralization can potentially increase the efficiency of service delivery, "in itself it is, in the end, merely a mechanism" (Davies *et al.* 2003: 139), and it can ultimately have serious implications for issues of social development and inequality (Litvack *et al.* 1998: 1). The previous two chapters established that the decentralization of responsibility to local governments and public schools through the policy of "two priorities" has not only created space for the Beijing municipal government to adopt a conservative approach towards migrant children's education, including a general lack of support for migrant schools, but it has also allowed district governments to adopt different policy approaches based on local factors.

This chapter examines the impact of the municipal *and* district policy approaches on the survival and development of migrant schools in Beijing, shedding light on the extent to which central-level policy ideals are being realized and why. Two sets of questions are evaluated. First, how have the municipal and district policy attitudes and approaches affected the situations of migrant schools in Beijing? What impact has this had on the principals, teachers, and students, as well as the quality of the schools compared to public schools? Second, given the policy of "two priorities" and its focus on the role of public schools, are migrant schools increasingly unimportant in the provision of education for migrant children in Beijing and why?

The first section of this chapter argues that, because of the general lack of support for migrant schools in Beijing municipal policies, migrant schools in the city – licensed and unlicensed – face many of the same fundamental problems as they did during the 1990s. However, the extent to which they experience these problems has also been influenced by the district-level dynamics discussed in Chapter 5, illustrating the important impacts of municipal *and* district-level policy implementation on their situations. Despite the continued existence of these problems, as well as the policy focus on the role of public schools and increased efforts to shut down or demolish migrant schools, the rest of the chapter shows that migrant schools remain a necessary source of education for many migrant children in Beijing, making an understanding of the effects of decentralization on these schools and, ultimately, trends in social stratification all the more critical.

## The continued problems of migrant schools in Beijing

Migrant schools in Beijing remain, on the whole, poor in quality and still lag behind public schools (Duan and Liang 2005: 16; Wang 2008: 702). This section illustrates that, despite calls for the increased support of migrant schools in central policies, these schools face some of the same problems as they faced in the 1990s. Based on fieldwork, the main problem areas that continue to define the situations of migrant schools in Beijing are a general lack of resources and poor physical conditions, a low quality of teaching, instability, and difficulties acquiring licenses (see Table 6.1). The discussion below evaluates how the overall lack of assistance from the municipal government and differing district-level approaches have affected migrant schools in these four interrelated areas and the implications for the principals, teachers, and families, contributing a more nuanced understanding of their current situations.

### *A general lack of resources and poor physical conditions*

Migrant schools are self-funded and, without government assistance, lack the physical and financial resources to provide a learning environment on a par with that in public schools. During the 1990s, the physical conditions of migrant schools were very poor. The schools were typically housed in simple and crude single-storey rooms or houses or temporary classrooms converted from warehouses. The classrooms would often lack ventilation and be overcrowded. Wooden boards and bricks would frequently be used to create desks and chairs. Most of the schools did not provide drinking water (Han 2001: 6).

While conditions have since improved, there was agreement among interviewees that the overall physical conditions of migrant schools in Beijing still lag far behind public schools.[2] As one principal stated: "We cannot be compared to public schools. Our facilities are just one-tenth or one-twentieth, even one-hundredth of theirs [in quality]. It cannot be compared" (HL1P1). Most schools visited did not have enough computers, and the computers they had were usually second-hand and outdated. According to one principal, if they were to sell their computers, they would get less than 200 RMB for each one (FL2P1). One unlicensed school in the sample not only did not have any computers or telephones, but it also did not have a library, sports area, or heating. As the principal described:

> One of the biggest problems we face is that our school is not in a stable situation. ... In terms of equipment, we don't have anything. We don't have computers. We used to have a computer class, but our second-hand computers

*Table 6.1* Key problems of migrant schools in Beijing over time

| Key problems (based on fieldwork) | Lü (2007) | Han (2001) |
|---|---|---|
| General lack of resources and poor physical conditions | • School conditions were extremely simple and crude (*jianlou*)<br>• Schools frequently lacked basic equipment and teaching materials | • Most school buildings were simple and crude, and supplies and equipment were very limited |
| Low quality of teaching | • Many teachers lacked basic training and experience<br>• Teacher turnover rates were high; many teachers would leave for higher-paying jobs, as the average salary of migrant school teachers was only 400–500 RMB per month | • The quality of teaching was far behind that in proper (*zhenggui*) schools<br>• Most teachers were uncertified<br>• Teacher mobility was high because of factors including the low pay, heavy workloads, and difficult living conditions |
| Instability | • One or two districts/counties (e.g. Fengtai) adopted measures to completely clamp down on migrant schools, with serious consequences for their stability | • Since migrant schools were often in danger of being shut down or demolished, principals were reluctant to make long-term investments in their schools |
| Difficulties acquiring licenses | • No migrant schools were licensed<br>• Because of reasons like the lack of comprehensive policies and a lack of organizations to provide social services for the floating population, migrant schools were essentially "underground" schools | • No migrant schools were licensed<br>• The government saw migrant schools as "underground" schools and knowledge about them was limited |

Source: Han (2001: 2, 5–6, 10–13); Lü (2007: 225–6, 228–9, 233, 238). Lü's discussion of migrant schools is based on research conducted in 1999–2000. Han's research was conducted in late 2000.

broke down, so then we stopped. ... We don't even have a telephone. ... It would be great if we had our own telephone and could contact students' parents at any time. ... There is a telephone outside, but it can only receive calls. ... If our teachers need to contact students' parents, they have to use their own cell phones.

(HU2P1)

In addition, because of financial constraints, school buses used are generally poor in condition and are often used to carry more students than there are seats. At the school just mentioned, for instance, the principal stated: "I cannot tell you [how many children are in each bus]. If we followed the [government] standards, then we'd be picking up and dropping off children all day, and there would be no class" (HU2P1). As described by a parent from another school: "Basically, one child sits down and holds on to another child. It is very crowded and unsafe" (FU2F2).

Moreover, the few government efforts to improve the conditions of migrant schools have ultimately had little impact. The municipal government's "Hand-in-Hand" (*shou la shou*) program is a case in point. According to principals and teachers, the program, which pairs up migrant schools with local public schools, is primarily focused on passing second-hand supplies and equipment no longer required by public schools to migrant schools. However, of the 22 schools in the sample, principals at 12 of the schools (including eight unlicensed ones) expressed that they had had little to no contact with public schools, and some had not even heard of the program. Among the remaining ten schools (including five licensed ones), interaction with public schools was limited and irregular, and the general view was that the program is essentially too little, too late.

An additional outcome of the lack of resources is the limited capacity of migrant schools to offer middle school education. According to principals, most migrant schools in Beijing, particularly unlicensed ones, are primary schools and do not offer the full three years of middle school education given the difficulties of maintaining additional grade levels (e.g. having to hire additional teachers and find classroom space).[3] Schools that try offering middle school may give up after a few years, as was the case with two of the 17 schools visited in Haidian, Shijingshan, and Fengtai. District approaches can also affect the number of schools that offer middle school education, as well as the proportion of cases in which the middle school level is licensed (for licensed migrant schools offering both, it is frequently only the primary school levels that are licensed). In Shijingshan, all three licensed migrant schools (and one of the four unlicensed schools visited) offered middle school; at all three licensed schools, both levels were licensed. In Haidian, however, only one licensed school and one of the unlicensed schools I came across were able to offer middle school education; at the former, only the primary school level was licensed, meaning that there are no licensed migrant middle schools in the district. Interestingly, the two schools mentioned above that gave up offering middle school classes were both in Haidian. Of the Fengtai schools visited, only one was able to offer the full three years of middle school, though it was given a license.[4]

The lack of resources has created serious challenges for migrant school principals and, subsequently, the teachers and students. Using limited resources, principals must ensure that they have sufficient funds to pay rent and other fees to maintain their schools.[5] One result is that they often cannot afford to raise their teachers' salaries. The average salary of migrant school teachers in Beijing is around 800–1,000 RMB (roughly 120–150 USD) per month, compared to 400–500 RMB in the late 1990s (Lü 2007: 229; Zhang 2010). While migrant workers' salaries have increased over time, the average salary of migrant school teachers in Beijing remains low; according to Zhang (2010), it is often only about a quarter of the average salary of public school teachers, which is about 4,000

RMB. Among the 17 schools visited in the three selected districts, teachers' salaries ranged from 750 to 1,300 RMB per month, which was lower than the salaries of most migrant parents interviewed.[6] As shown in Table 6.2, there was little variation between the average salaries of primary school teachers at licensed and unlicensed migrant schools, indicating that teachers at licensed and unlicensed migrant schools in Beijing frequently face similar circumstances and treatment.[7] However, there was some slight variation across districts; the average salary of teachers at the primary school level was highest in Haidian (around 975 RMB), followed by Shijingshan (about 950 RMB), and then Fengtai (about 900 RMB), the potential consequences of which will be discussed later.

In addition, whereas public school teachers are provided insurance, migrant school teachers are generally not.[8] As one teacher stated:

> There are no migrant schools in Beijing that give their teachers insurance. A few schools might simply provide accident insurance. The personal safety of these teachers is not even fully protected. Medical insurance, work-related injury insurance, and unemployment insurance are currently treated as nothing more than unreasonable requests!

> (Zhang 2010)

*Table 6.2* Teachers' salaries at migrant schools in the sample

| District | Legal status | Teachers' salaries (RMB/month) | |
| --- | --- | --- | --- |
| | | Primary school | Middle school |
| Haidian | Licensed (unlicensed branch) | 1,000–1,200 | NA |
| | Licensed | 800–1,300 | 800–1,300 |
| | Unlicensed | ≈1,000 | NA |
| | Unlicensed | 800–>1,000 | NA |
| | Unlicensed | >900 | >900 |
| | Unlicensed | ≈900 | NA |
| Shijingshan | Licensed | ≈850 | ≈950 |
| | Licensed | 800–1,000 | 800–1,000 |
| | Licensed | ≈1,000 | >1,000 |
| | Unlicensed | ≈1,000 | ≈1,000 |
| | Unlicensed | ≥850 | NA |
| | Unlicensed | 900–1,200 | NA |
| | Unlicensed | ≈1,000 | NA |
| Fengtai | Licensed | 1,000–1,050 | 1,000–1,050 |
| | Licensed | 750–800 | NA |
| | Unlicensed | 1,000 | 1,000 |
| | Unlicensed | 800 | NA |
| Chaoyang | Licensed | ≥1,000 | ≥1,000 |
| | Licensed | 1,400 | NA |
| Changping | Licensed | >1,000 | >1,000 |
| | Unlicensed | 800–1,000 | 800–1,000 |
| Daxing | Unlicensed | 1,000 | NA |

Source: Author's fieldwork (2009–10).

Only about five schools in the sample provided some insurance for their teachers. In two of those cases, the schools – in Haidian and Shijingshan – were licensed, and insurance was subsidized by an NGO.[9] Ultimately, most principals expressed that they cannot afford to increase teachers' salaries or provide insurance, making the job less attractive.[10] As will be shown later, the resulting high teacher mobility has had major consequences for the quality of teaching.

Another result of the lack of resources is that principals charge their students tuition and other fees. As mentioned in Chapters 1 and 2, the Compulsory Education Law (1986) stipulated that primary and middle school education in China would be provided free of tuition. However, as one principal emphasized: "In China, there are two groups that still pay for it: students in private aristocratic [*guizu*] schools and migrant workers' children in cities. One of these groups is poor, … [and] one is wealthy" (HL1P1). Within the sample, tuition ranged from 400 to 700 RMB (about 60–100 USD) per term for primary school students and 500 to a little over 1,000 RMB (about 70–150 USD) per term for middle school students (see Table 6.3).[11] Overall, the average tuition fees were slightly higher at licensed migrant schools, but the difference was relatively marginal, and the fees at certain unlicensed schools were even higher than at some of the licensed ones, providing further evidence that there is often no substantial difference between licensed and unlicensed migrant schools in the city.

*Table 6.3* Tuition fees at migrant schools in the sample

| District | Legal status | Tuition (RMB/school term) | |
|---|---|---|---|
| | | Primary school | Middle school |
| Haidian | Licensed (unlicensed branch) | 600 | NA |
| | Licensed | 500 | 500 |
| | Unlicensed | 400 | NA |
| | Unlicensed | 400 | NA |
| | Unlicensed | 700 | 900 |
| | Unlicensed | 550 | NA |
| Shijingshan | Licensed | 600 | 1,000 |
| | Licensed | 400 | 800 |
| | Licensed | 600 | 1,000 |
| | Unlicensed | 520 | 700 |
| | Unlicensed | 550 | NA |
| | Unlicensed | 550 | NA |
| | Unlicensed | 400 | NA |
| Fengtai | Licensed | 620 | 1,070 |
| | Licensed | 600 | NA |
| | Unlicensed | 500 | 800 |
| | Unlicensed | 600 | NA |
| Chaoyang | Licensed | 600 | 1,000 |
| | Licensed | 470 | NA |
| Changping | Licensed | 570 | 1,000 |
| | Unlicensed | 500 | 800 |
| Daxing | Unlicensed | 600 | NA |

Source: Author's fieldwork (2009–10).

Besides tuition, migrant schools may also charge a range of additional fees. Based on the sample, these can include book fees of 80–150 RMB per term; lunch fees of 80–130 RMB per month; heating fees, which can cost about 100 RMB per winter; water fees, which can cost around 30 RMB per term; school bus fees of 150–200 RMB per term; summer and winter uniform fees, around 25–80 RMB per set; summer homework fees of about 20 RMB; and fees for school outings, which can cost 50–100 RMB per trip. As a result, parents may be required to pay a total of over 1,000 RMB per term in school-related fees.

As will be discussed later in the chapter, the fees described above are lower than what is frequently required for migrant children to attend public schools. Still, migrant school fees can be an issue for migrant families. According to a government-based researcher, the average monthly income of migrant families around the late 1990s was 1,000–1,300 RMB.[12] Though most migrant workers are now able to make at least 1,000 RMB (about 150 USD) per month per person, the monthly household income among these families remains low.[13] For example, over 40 percent of the families in the sample who had children in migrant schools and were willing to disclose their household incomes made less than 3,000 RMB per month (see Table 6.4).[14] Though some families make several thousand RMB per month doing work in areas like business or sales, most do lower-paying jobs like selling fruit and vegetables, cleaning, working in factories, doing small business, making clothes, washing dishes, working on construction sites, moving bricks, and collecting garbage to name a few. The work they do is frequently described as being "dirty, tiring, arduous, and dangerous" (*zang lei ku xian*). As shown in Appendix B, the average income among parents tended to be higher in Haidian, followed by Shijingshan, and finally Fengtai, consistent with the economic situations of the districts (see Chapter 5).[15] Yet there was no observable correlation between parents' educational background, household income, and the type of migrant school their children were attending (licensed or unlicensed), reflecting the reality that migrant workers often simply send their children to schools closest to where they live.[16]

Furthermore, while there are no accurate statistics, principals stated that at least 50–60 percent of migrant families in Beijing have more than one child, increasing the costs of school-related fees. Within the sample of 40 families, only 12 had one

*Table 6.4* Incomes of families in the sample with children in migrant schools

| Household income (RMB/month) | Number of families |
| --- | --- |
| <1,000 | 1 |
| 1,000–1,999 | 2 |
| 2,000–2,999 | 13 |
| 3,000–3,999 | 8 |
| 4,000–4,999 | 5 |
| 5,000–5,999 | 2 |
| >6,000 | 3 |
| Not willing to disclose | 3 |

Source: Author's fieldwork (2009–10).

child, while 15 had two children, nine had three children, three had four children, and one had five children. Of the 28 families with more than one child, there were 18 families in which all of the children were living in Beijing with their parents (see Appendix B). In addition, with only four exceptions, all of the families with children in either primary or middle school had them attending school in Beijing rather than in their home provinces. Though some migrant schools give discounts to families with more than one child enrolled, this is not always the case. Indeed, in one of the families in the sample, all four children were attending the same migrant school, and the parents were paying full tuition for all of them (SU1F3). Thus school fees, even those charged by migrant schools, can be an issue.

What is more, some migrant families face difficult circumstances that result in even tighter financial situations. There were numerous such cases within the sample. For example, in one family, a single parent, who worked 13 hours per day washing dishes, was raising two school-aged children on a monthly salary of 900 RMB (HU2F3). In one family with two children to support (including one who was still in school), the father was injured while working on a construction site and the mother had to quit her own job to take care of him (SU1F1). In one family with two school-aged children, the parents made a total of about 2,700 RMB per month, sometimes less, but one of the children had a medical condition that required over 2,000 RMB per month to treat (HU2F2). In one family with four school-aged children, the eldest child had been suffering from a rare health condition since the age of four. After going to several hospitals in their home province and Beijing, the parents found that the only hospital able to treat the condition was in Beijing, and the average cost of each hospital visit was often over 10,000 RMB. The family also had to send an additional 10,000–20,000 RMB in remittances each year to one of the father's parents, who was in poor health (FU2F2). Such examples illustrate that school fees can be a source of concern and, out of the 37 families in the sample with children in migrant schools, 22 (from across the three districts) stated that tuition was one of the key problems they faced in terms of education.

Besides tuition, the limited capacity of migrant schools to offer middle school education has important consequences for migrant children's post-primary school options, a top concern among families in the sample. For middle school, migrant children in Beijing generally have three options. The first is to attend a migrant school offering middle school classes.[17] Most migrant schools in Beijing are unable to offer both primary and middle school education because of physical and financial constraints, so only a limited proportion of children have this option. As mentioned earlier, this can also vary across districts. The second option is to enroll in a public middle school in Beijing, but, as will be discussed later, this often requires an entrance exam and a range of fees and documentation, making enrollment difficult. The third option is to return to their hometowns. In the past, most migrant children would go home for middle school because of expensive public school fees. Based on conversations with parents and researchers, however, a larger proportion of parents now hope to keep their children in Beijing for at least part of middle school before sending them home.[18] The obstacles migrant schools in different districts face in offering middle school education can therefore affect migrant children's educational opportunities.

## *A low quality of teaching*

According to an officer of the migrant school teachers' association in Beijing, there were about 7,000 migrant school teachers in the city by 2010. Most of these teachers are young, female rural migrants. These individuals choose to become migrant school teachers for various reasons. Some are recent graduates unable to find other work. Others come across the occupation by chance or are introduced to it by friends or relatives. Still others choose it because they enjoy teaching.

Two key factors have contributed to the low quality of teaching in migrant schools: high teacher mobility, which can affect licensed and unlicensed schools, and the continued hiring of uncertified teachers by the schools, particularly unlicensed ones. First, high rates of teacher turnover are primarily driven by three factors: low salaries (discussed earlier), job instability because of the high mobility of migrant schools (which will be discussed later), and the difficult nature of their jobs. In terms of the third, these teachers generally have heavier workloads than their public school counterparts. While public school classes are limited to 40 students in Beijing,[19] the average class size in Beijing's migrant schools frequently exceeds 40, with sometimes over 50–60 students per class (Zhang 2010). Within the sample, five schools had average class sizes of at least 50 students.[20] Moreover, while public school teachers traditionally teach a more stable, settled part of the population, migrant school teachers face high levels of student mobility. As one long-time principal explained, the high student mobility is a result of factors including the frequent relocations of migrant schools, the reality that migrant communities and migrant schools are often in danger of being demolished, and the mobile lifestyles of migrant workers. Of the 12 schools that kept rough records on student mobility, about half said that at least 30 percent of their students were considered to be mobile. At one licensed primary school with over 1,100 students, for example, the principal expressed that, each semester, over 300 students leave the school and another 300 or so enroll (FL2P1). At one unlicensed primary school, the principal stated that only three or four of the 34 students in the sixth grade class had been attending the school since the first grade (SU2P1). At another unlicensed school, a third grader in one family interviewed had already changed schools four times because of the demolition of migrant villages and school closures (SU1F4).

Besides high student mobility, migrant school teachers face a range of other issues. Unlike local urban parents, migrant workers, especially those who are more poorly educated, may not know how to teach their children at home, and some may even be violent or abusive. This affects the everyday responsibilities of migrant school teachers. During an interview at a licensed migrant school, for instance, the teacher had to leave the room several times because of a missing student, who had been beaten by his father and had not returned home for two days. The teacher had to then track down and meet with the student's father (XL1T1). According to other principals and teachers and student volunteers interviewed, such occurrences are not uncommon.

As a result, principals and parents repeatedly expressed that the teachers, especially younger ones, often treat their time at migrant schools as temporary and leave when they find better jobs or because they cannot support their families on such low salaries.[21] At one school, the principal was only able to recall one semester since 1999 when no teachers had left the school (SU1P1). At another school, the principal stated that about half of the 14 teachers were mobile, with teachers leaving each semester (PU1P1). In discussing the high level of teacher turnover at their child's school, one parent pointed out that one of the teachers had recently quit and chosen to sell vegetables instead (HL1F4). As a consequence, principals may frequently find themselves scrambling to find teachers throughout the year. For example, the principal of one unlicensed school – where as many as half of the 46 teachers were considered to be mobile – contacted me at the start of the school year saying: "Our school is currently in urgent need of teachers. Could we please trouble you to help recommend some?" (FU2P1). Even students are frequently aware of the reasons underlying the high turnover rate. One fifth grader at a licensed migrant school, for instance, stated that her teachers change all the time, explaining that their salaries are too low and the teachers are fed up. She supported this conclusion with an example, saying that she recently saw two of her teachers talking at school, one of whom was holding about 1,700 RMB (roughly 250 USD). After commenting on how much money it was, she was shocked when one of the teachers stated that it was actually both of their salaries for the month (SL2F6).

Second, the quality of teachers migrant schools are able to attract remains low, and – not unlike the situation during the late 1990s (see Han 2001: 12; Lü 2007: 228–9) – the educational background of migrant school teachers and the proportion of teachers with teaching certificates still lag behind public schools (Song *et al.* 2009). Within the sample of schools, teachers were often graduates of vocational secondary schools (*zhongzhuan*) or junior colleges (*dazhuan*). Unlike public school teachers, many migrant school teachers lack teaching experience and certification. While licensed migrant schools are required to fulfill government standards for teaching certification, unlicensed schools frequently have a high proportion of uncertified teachers. At over one-third of the 17 schools visited in the three selected districts, all of which were unlicensed, principals expressed that at least half of their teachers were uncertified (see Table 6.5). Interestingly, unlike Haidian and Fengtai, there was only one school in Shijingshan where the majority of teachers were uncertified, likely a reflection of the district's close attention to teacher certification in regulating migrant schools (see Chapter 5).

Since they can only afford to offer low salaries, some principals, mainly those at unlicensed schools, do not require their teachers to have certificates at all. At one such school in the sample, the principal admitted that only two of their 17

*Table 6.5* Proportion of teachers with certification at migrant schools in the sample

| District | Legal status | Estimated percentage of teachers with teaching certificates |
|---|---|---|
| Haidian | Licensed (unlicensed branch) | 67% |
| | Licensed | Almost 100% |
| | Unlicensed | 40% |
| | Unlicensed | 50% |
| | Unlicensed | Almost 100% |
| | Unlicensed | 12% |
| Shijingshan | Licensed | 100% |
| | Licensed | Almost 100% |
| | Licensed | 100% |
| | Unlicensed | >90% |
| | Unlicensed | Minority |
| | Unlicensed | Majority |
| | Unlicensed | 80% |
| Fengtai | Licensed | Majority |
| | Licensed | 100% |
| | Unlicensed | 30% |
| | Unlicensed | <50% |

Source: Author's fieldwork (2009–10).

teachers were certified (HU2P1). Further exacerbating the problem is the fact that, unlike public schools, where teachers are given regular training, migrant school principals generally lack the resources to provide training (Zhang 2010). Along with the high levels of teacher turnover, this has had negative consequences for the quality of teaching in migrant schools (see Figure 6.1).

As a result, migrant schools in Beijing continue to offer low quality teaching. This was acknowledged by principals in the sample, evident in the following quotes:

> [Since] the tuition we charge is low, the salaries we pay our teachers are low. … So the school lacks the appeal [to attract better quality teachers]. … There is turnover every year.
>
> (HL1P1)

> In the earlier years, my goal in running the school was to make sure that the children had a school to go to. Now, my goal in running the school is to make sure that the children are getting a good education.
>
> (YL1P1)

> If you were to randomly choose a public school, its conditions would be better than our school. So the result is that, if on a civilization exam public school students were able to get an average of 80–90 points, our students might only get 50–60 points. Because the opportunities are not equal, the outcomes are not equal.
>
> (YL2P1)

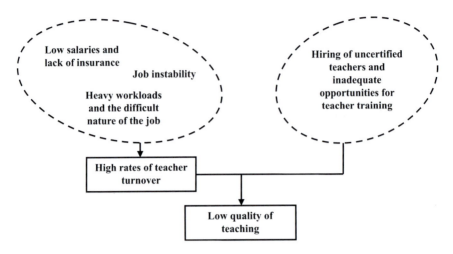

*Figure 6.1* Factors contributing to the low quality of teaching at migrant schools
Source: Author's fieldwork (2009–10).

While their lack of financial resources has prohibited them from hiring better quality teachers, low teacher salaries and the unstable and difficult nature of the job have resulted in high teacher turnover, with major consequences for the quality of teaching at licensed and unlicensed schools. Indeed, the quality of teaching and facilities at migrant schools in Beijing still lags behind urban public schools and, according to Lai *et al.* (2012: 15–16), even rural schools.

As a result, the quality of teaching at migrant schools remains a widespread concern, even for families in the sample that did not mention tuition as a substantial problem. The following remarks are examples of this concern:

> This [migrant] school faces restrictions [in providing quality education]. The gap between this school and public schools is large.
>
> (HL1F7)

> The difference between [the quality of teaching in] this school and public schools is too great. I don't know where some of these teachers came from.
>
> (SL2F2)

> The quality of teaching is too poor. … Some teachers have even said [to our child]: "Your grades are so good. You shouldn't be going to school here."
>
> (FU2F2)

> The teachers are always changing [because] the school doesn't give them enough money.
>
> (SL2F6)

Though many are aware that this gap between public and migrant schools is a result of the physical and financial limitations of migrant schools, most parents in the sample expressed worries about the quality of education offered by migrant schools, particularly when it came to the qualifications of teachers and high levels of teacher turnover.

### Instability

One of the issues that most defines the situations of migrant schools in Beijing is their instability. Unlike public schools, migrant schools have often been in danger of being shut down or demolished and have frequently had to change locations (Han 2001: 5; Kwong 2004: 1085–6). Among the 17 schools visited in Haidian, Shijingshan, and Fengtai, only two had never moved (see Table 6.6). One school in particular had moved five times across three districts (SU1P1). Relocating has become a way of life for most of these schools, particularly those that are unlicensed. When I asked an interviewee at one school that had moved 11 times within a decade about the numerous moves, she simply replied: "We're used to it" (HL1P3). The fear of being closed or demolished, however, has made some principals hesitant to invest in improving their schools (Han 2001: 5). Instability has, therefore, also contributed to the poor physical conditions of the schools.

In most cases, this instability is either because of the risk of being closed for failing to meet government standards or because of demolition. The former, though common to unlicensed migrant schools across the city, can be higher in some districts than others. The best example is the case of Fengtai, where the

*Table 6.6* Number of relocations among migrant schools in the sample

| District | Legal status | Year founded | Number of relocations |
|----------|--------------|--------------|------------------------|
| Haidian | Licensed (unlicensed branch) | 1994 | 11 |
| | Licensed | 1999 | 4 |
| | Unlicensed | 1994 | 4 |
| | Unlicensed | 1994 | 2 |
| | Unlicensed | 1995 | 1 |
| | Unlicensed | 1996 | 2 |
| Shijingshan | Licensed | 1997 | 4 |
| | Licensed | 1998 | 2 |
| | Licensed | 1998 | 2 |
| | Unlicensed | 1999 | 5 |
| | Unlicensed | 2000 | 1 |
| | Unlicensed | 2000 | 1 |
| | Unlicensed | 2000 | 0 |
| Fengtai | Licensed | 2000 | 1 |
| | Licensed | 2005 | 0 |
| | Unlicensed | 1999 | 2 |
| | Unlicensed | 2005 | 3 |

Source: Author's fieldwork (2009–10).

district's more assertive approach in closing down migrant schools in the early to mid-2000s made the situations of the schools and their students particularly unstable. As discussed in Chapter 5, most students affected by the closures had to attend migrant schools in other districts or return to their hometowns. Interestingly, among the migrant schools in Fengtai during this period, there was little movement *within* the district, and schools that did relocate usually moved to other districts instead.

The latter, demolition, is certainly not a new occurrence and has been a core element of Beijing's pursuit of urbanization, even in the 1990s. According to principals, the city may have had as many as 500 migrant schools at its height, but the number has been declining. Over time, migrant communities have been pushed farther and farther away from the city's center, and, as of 2010, there were essentially no migrant enclaves left within the city's Fourth Ring Road.[22] Razing prior to the 2008 Beijing Olympics received a lot of media coverage, which put pressure on the municipal government to temporarily slow down its quest for urbanization. Recent rounds of demolition, however, have been threatening the survival of migrant enclaves and migrant schools – licensed and unlicensed – to a greater extent than before, such that even some of the relatively well-established, well-supported schools may no longer exist in a few more years. Within the sample, 13 of the 22 schools were in danger of being demolished as of mid-2010. While some principals stated that they would try to relocate, or at least wait and see what happens, nearly half indicated that the impending demolitions might signify the end of their schools. Many communicated that they were simply too exhausted after years of struggling to keep their schools running. One principal, whose school was established in 1994, said that, after their community – with a migrant population of about 60,000 – is demolished, there is a chance that they will not continue as they are very tired and "cannot manage it" (*banbuqi*) (HU3P1). For one of the city's earliest migrant schools, one of its branches was about to be demolished at the time of fieldwork, while the other two branches would likely be demolished within a few years. The principal revealed that they would most likely not move the school to another location because there is nowhere to go and they are "truly exhausted" (*shizai pibei*). He stated: "This is the extent of our efforts" (HL1P1). Another principal – who had recently invested his own money into building a new school after his previous one had been demolished – summarized the situation: "Moving [a school] all the time, who could take it?" (YL1P1). The difficulty of finding another place to rent was another major factor. As one principal expressed:

> [With our type of school], even if you move to a new location, no one is willing to rent buildings to you. … Even if someone is willing to rent to you, … it would cost at least 400,000 RMB [around 59,000 USD] per year. … Without external [financial] support, this school absolutely cannot relocate. If it's demolished, it's demolished.
>
> (SU2P1)

Indeed, though there were over 300 migrant schools in Beijing at the time of fieldwork, follow-up conversations with a few principals and researchers revealed that the estimated number had dropped to somewhere between 200 and 300 by late 2011 and somewhere between 100 and 200 by mid-2013. This lack of stability significantly affects how these schools are run. As one principal stated: "We've already told our teachers that, for every day this school is still in existence, we must continue to be responsible for these children" (HU2P1).

These closures and demolitions are often decided by the districts, and differences have emerged in terms of the extent to which district governments demolish or shut down schools and how they handle the distribution of the students to other schools. Though knowledge of student allocation following demolitions and closures and the politics behind it remains extremely limited, it is possible to shed light on some of the variations by examining recent cases.

For example, even though it has tended to focus its management of migrant schools on safety regulation, Shijingshan has reportedly done better than other districts in distributing migrant children to public schools after demolitions. In 2011, the district demolished a migrant community in which there were around 30,000 migrants and three unlicensed migrant schools, involving a total of about 1,300 students and over 50 teachers. A follow-up conversation with the principal of one of these schools revealed that the district education commission allocated almost all of the students involved to a few public schools nearby for free, and a proportion of the migrant school teachers were also transferred to the public schools with their students. Moreover, based on information from principals and researchers, migrant children affected by demolitions and closures in districts like Chaoyang and Haidian, where the gap between the best and worst public schools is relatively large, may frequently be allocated to poorer quality public schools (*jichu boruo xuexiao*). In contrast, the gap between the best and worst public schools in Shijingshan is smaller and, as a result, migrant children affected by closures or demolitions may be distributed to schools that are not considerably worse than those primarily attended by local students.

Despite Chaoyang's more positive reputation in the policy area (see Chapter 5), migrant schools in the district have not been unaffected by plans for urban expansion, and the district government has reportedly not done as well in allocating migrant children after recent closures and demolitions. For example, Chaoyang was one of the several districts that demolished over 30 migrant schools in 2010 (see Ni and Zhao 2010). Based on information provided by an NGO in the sample, while some children were able to follow their schools to new locations or find new schools to attend, many had to return to their hometowns or were unable to find new schools at all. In the case of the Chaoyang branch of a school in the sample that was demolished that year, most students had to find other migrant schools to attend in Chaoyang and Daxing. According to the principal, the small proportion of children who were able to enroll in public schools did so without government assistance, and, in most cases, these public schools were of poorer quality and charged tuition and miscellaneous fees of around 3,000–4,000 RMB per year (HL1P1).[23]

The demolition and closure of migrant schools in Haidian, Chaoyang, and Daxing in 2011 are further cases in point. Much of the media reported on the closing of 24 migrant schools by the three districts,[24] but follow-up conversations with principals suggested a more complicated picture involving different objectives and approaches. In Haidian, four migrant schools were demolished or closed, primarily because they were built on government land or considered unsafe. Although the education commission distributed about half of the students to public schools, the rest had to either go to other migrant schools or return to their hometowns. In Chaoyang, nine unlicensed schools were closed during this round. Instead of allocating the students involved to public schools, the education commission distributed at least half of them to about four private (*minban*) schools (which it had converted from public schools for this purpose). While retired public school teachers were appointed as the principals of these new schools, the teachers were transferred from the migrant schools themselves. So even though the principals and locations changed, the quality of teaching basically remained the same, as did the fees charged. Of the remaining children affected, most went to other migrant schools or back to their hometowns. In Daxing, the district government made plans to close over ten migrant schools on the grounds that they did not possess real estate licenses (*fangchanzheng*), technically an issue to be taken up with the landlords rather than the schools. Resulting pressure from the media, however, played a role in delaying action to close these schools. In other words, 13 schools were closed or demolished during this particular round, and each district had different motives and strategies, with different consequences for the students. Though knowledge of the politics behind such demolitions and closures remains very limited, the above discussion indicates that different district approaches can have direct implications for the survival of migrant schools and the continued schooling of their students, illustrating the importance of understanding district-level dynamics within the context of municipal-level standards.

Following from the three stages proposed by Han (2003) (discussed in Chapter 3), we are now witnessing a fourth stage in the development of migrant schools in Beijing, one in which these schools are, once again, struggling to survive. This has major consequences for the students. As one principal asked: "What will happen to these migrant children if they do not get an education?" (HL1P1). Indeed, parents interviewed expressed a great deal of concern about the uncertain future of their children's education in light of pending demolitions or closures, especially since no one had given them advice or discussed their options with them.[25]

The instability of migrant schools has serious, longer-term implications for the development and growth of these children. Given their already mobile lifestyle, as well as the fact that they attend schools that may be unlicensed, it is vital that these children have a strong support system from their schools and families. But this is not always the case. They may often not get adequate time and attention from their parents, and it is difficult for them to get a sense of stability from their schools and teachers given the reasons explored above. According to China

Labour Bulletin (2008), "migrant children in cities consequently develop psychological [and behavioral] problems disturbingly similar to those left behind." The outcomes are made even more complex because of differing district-level approaches towards shutting down or demolishing the schools.

## Difficulties acquiring licenses

Though it has been over a decade since district governments in Beijing started to license migrant schools, it continues to be difficult for these schools to get licensed, and they remain vulnerable to government closures. In order to get government approval, migrant schools in Beijing must fulfill a range of conditions, and all facilities and equipment must reach a certain standard. Evidence shows, however, that there is a general lack of transparency in the licensing process, and many principals and researchers were unclear or inconsistent about the actual standards being used. As a result, principals of unlicensed schools put great emphasis on the difficulties of getting licensed; many had applied several times unsuccessfully, while others did not even bother. One principal stated: "We don't have anything. We know we cannot apply because we don't meet the standards. Applying would be pointless" (HU2P1). Another principal shared that he had applied twice before the local education commission told him to stop as his school did not meet the standards (FU1P1). According to a principal in Shijingshan, in mid-2006, officials from numerous district government departments visited the district's 18 migrant schools and told them that they needed to improve (*zhenggai*). After a series of meetings, the education commission closed eight of them but did not disclose why those particular schools were shut down and the others were not. The principal stated that the requirements for a license are similarly unclear, so "there is no use in applying" (SU2P1). More than one source (mainly a few well-connected principals) also stated that the municipal government had already announced internally the decision to suspend the licensing of migrant schools in the city. This is in stark contrast to Shanghai, which reportedly licensed over 60 migrant schools per year in recent years, and Wuhan, where one district alone licensed over 30 migrant schools (Beijing Migrant School Principals' Association 2009).

Whether or not a migrant school is licensed is often left for the district governments to decide. As previously discussed, Haidian's approach of limited management has made it hesitant to license these schools; the district only has two licensed migrant schools, while Shijingshan and Fengtai – both of which have less than half the number of migrant schools than Haidian – each have three. Still, all three districts have a much lower number of licensed migrant schools when compared to Chaoyang, which, at the time of fieldwork, had 14 (out of a total of over 80 migrant schools), and Changping, which had 16 (out of roughly 50–60 migrant schools). This is despite the fact that Chaoyang's outside population of 963,000 is only slightly larger than Haidian's (which is 848,000), and Changping's outside population of 305,000 is even smaller than Fengtai's (which is 447,000) (see Chapter 5). Thus, assuming that there is no significant variation in terms of the physical conditions of migrant schools by district, district governments play a direct role in determining the difficulties faced by migrant schools in acquiring licenses (see Figure 6.2).

An additional issue is that government approval does not necessarily mean that migrant schools are immune to the problems discussed above. As mentioned in Chapter 4, licensed migrant schools do receive some governmental support; the municipal government provides assistance in the form of supplies and equipment, and students receive a small subsidy each term. Yet, based on the sample, even these schools face difficulties, and government support remains limited. According to one principal, for example, the equipment and supplies they have received from the district education commission since being licensed are frequently just old items passed down from public schools (SL1P1). In a report on his school's situation, another principal wrote:

> As a migrant school, the primary difficulty we face is the shortage of funds. Our school fees are: on average, 350 RMB per student per term. In cases where students' families face difficulties, the fees are reduced. Fees collected are used to pay rent, utilities, transportation expenses for students, teachers' salaries, the purchase of basic teaching instruments and equipment, [fees for] necessary school construction, etc., all in order to maintain the normal operation of the school. Under such circumstances, even if the school wants to further improve the conditions and the treatment of teachers, we often run into difficulties because of insufficient funds.
>
> (HL2P1)

Thus, as stated by a teacher who had taught at both licensed and unlicensed migrant schools:

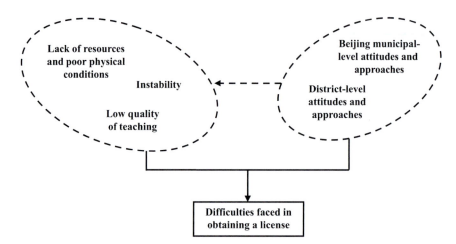

*Figure 6.2* Factors influencing the difficulties faced by migrant schools in acquiring licenses.
Source: Author's fieldwork (2009–10).

Currently, I'll put it this way, in terms of "licensed" and "unlicensed" [migrant schools], there isn't a clear concept. It's only formal language. Usually, schools that have relatively better relations with government actors or schools that are in slightly better condition can get licensed. ... But it's just formal language. There is not much difference.

(XL1T1)

Ultimately, even though licensed schools may still face a range of problems, licensing remains an important step in at least formalizing the existence of migrant schools and guaranteeing them a level of governmental support. Whether or not a migrant school is licensed also has direct implications for its stability; while licensed schools are not immune to demolition, they will at least not be shut down for failing to meet official standards.

The fact that serious barriers to licensing remain has not only made it more difficult for principals to improve their schools, but it has also had consequences for the teachers and students. For students, the lack of a license affects the stability of their schooling. Children attending unlicensed migrant schools that are shut down usually have to go to their local street office to present a range of documents and apply for a temporary student certificate before contacting nearby public schools; in other words, enrollment is not guaranteed. For teachers, whether or not the school is licensed affects their job stability, as teachers at unlicensed schools are more likely to lose their jobs because of government closures. This then has additional consequences for teacher turnover rates and subsequently the quality of teaching.

## The continued importance of migrant schools in Beijing

Since the early 1990s, the problem of migrant children's education in Beijing has been shifting from one of *access* to one of *quality*, but recent rounds of demolition and efforts to shut down unlicensed migrant schools indicate that access still remains a serious problem. As one principal pointed out, the Law on Promoting Private Education (2002) stipulates that private (*minban*) schools (including their teachers and students) should enjoy equal treatment as public schools, but this is still far from the reality in Beijing. One can argue, as some interviewees did, that the situation of migrant schools has already seen great improvement since the early 1990s; not only are they no longer seen as "underground" schools, but they are also more standardized and better supported. While this may be true to an extent, the above discussion illustrates that, licensed or not, migrant schools in Beijing (and their students) continue to be "outside of the system" (*zai tixi wai*) (GR2). What is more, demolition and increased government efforts to close unlicensed migrant schools are making the issue much more urgent.

It is commonly argued that public schools are the better option for migrant children. For one, according to the Compulsory Education Law, public school education at the primary and middle school levels is technically free of tuition.

Attending public schools would also presumably allow for migrant children to become more socially integrated. In addition, based on the above discussion and the findings of studies including Song *et al.* (2009) and Lai *et al.* (2012), the overall quality of education and teaching offered by migrant schools in Beijing remains considerably poorer than that offered by public schools. Yet, while placing migrant children into public schools is a necessary long-term goal, such a focus in the immediate future would only lead the Beijing municipal and district governments to neglect the continued role of migrant schools.

This section highlights several reasons why the municipal and district governments should not assume that focusing on migrant schools is of secondary importance. It shows that, despite the poor quality of migrant schools and the policy focus on public schools, migrant schools still serve a critical function for migrant communities in Beijing and provide a service for many migrant children for which there is currently no adequate alternative.

### Problems with existing estimates

The actual proportion of migrant children in public schools remains unclear and highly debatable, making it unwise to assume that the role of migrant schools is declining, at least in the near future. First of all, there is considerable variation among existing estimates. Recent government figures suggest that most migrant children in Beijing are in public schools. According to the "Notice of the General Office of the Beijing Municipal People's Government on the Work of Strengthening the Safety of Non-Approved Self-Run Migrant Schools" (2006), for instance, over 62 percent of the city's compulsory school-aged children of the floating population were already in public schools by the mid-2000s. Other estimates, however, suggest a different picture. Li (2009: 65) maintains that in large cities like Beijing, Shanghai, and Guangzhou, less than two-thirds and sometimes less than half of the migrant children are able to attend local public schools. According to Beijing Migrant School Principals' Association (2009), half of the over 400,000 migrant children in Beijing still attend migrant schools. Wang (2008: 693) writes that an estimated 47 percent of Beijing's migrant children attend public schools, and Lai *et al.* (2012: 3) cite that 70 percent are in migrant schools.

Second, as discussed in Chapters 2 and 3, measuring the number of migrant children in public schools is fundamentally difficult. As one researcher in the field explained, it is likely that over 60 percent of the children in Beijing's *floating population* are attending public schools, but the children of rural–urban migrant workers are, in principle, only a subset of this population. While these terms are frequently used interchangeably by officials and academics alike, there are no accurate estimates of the percentage of *migrant workers' children* attending public schools in Beijing.

Third, existing estimates may not include all migrant children. Official statistics, as well as many estimates made by researchers, may be based on figures that exclude a number of migrant schools, though how many is unclear. Indeed, it is not uncommon for migrant schools that were previously shut down to secretly reopen their doors. For example, as one principal disclosed, a number of the unlicensed schools that were closed down in Haidian reopened as "preschools," when in reality they were still primary schools. In Shijingshan, one school I stumbled across had over 2,000 students at its peak. Soon after it was shut down in 2006, it reopened its doors without publicizing its identity as a school for migrant children. The size of its student body had decreased to about 200–300 students, but the fact that it had resumed operation is significant. It is likely that such schools are not included in official reports and figures.

## The continued demand for migrant schools in Beijing

Evidence also shows that there remains a demand for migrant schools in Beijing. Among the principals and teachers interviewed, there were mixed views on the advantages of migrant schools versus public schools for migrant children. On the one hand, public schools generally offer a higher quality of education and teaching, have better physical conditions and facilities, and provide more standardized management. On the other hand, migrant schools typically have flexible enrollment procedures, charge low fees, are conveniently located, lack discrimination, and may use similar teaching materials to those used in the sending areas. Interviews with migrant parents, however, showed that, even though most hope for their children to attend public schools, there is still a need for migrant schools. While seemingly contradictory, this demand is primarily because of three reasons: barriers to public school education, the lack of discrimination in migrant schools, and the services offered by migrant schools.[26]

### Barriers to public school education

Despite concerns about the quality of migrant schools, public schools continue to be an elusive option for many migrant families.[27] Entrance into public schools remains difficult, as migrant families are regularly required to pay a range of fees and present various documents. In the late 1990s, public schools charged children of the outside population temporary schooling fees and sponsorship fees, ranging from a few thousand to tens of thousands of RMB (Lü 2007: 218). With policies calling for the equal treatment of migrant children in the acceptance of fees, these schools are no longer permitted to charge migrant children temporary schooling fees. Yet public schools in Beijing regularly charge migrant children various other fees, and how much they charge can be up to their discretion.

According to parents in the sample, sponsorship fees, for example, can often cost at least 10,000–20,000 RMB (about 1,500–3,000 USD). For migrant children wishing to enter a public primary school after the first grade or a public middle school after the seventh grade, public schools may charge a special fee known as the *chabanfei*, literally a fee to be inserted into a class or grade level. Though the amount varies across schools, this fee can cost migrant parents several thousand RMB. Upon enrollment, there are usually additional fees (e.g.

for food, books, and school events) that can sometimes add up to over 2,000 RMB per term. Entrance into top public schools can cost considerably more. Based on conversations with a few migrant parents with children in such schools, the entrance fee for migrant children can be as high as 60,000 RMB for top primary schools and 180,000 RMB for top middle schools, which most migrant families cannot afford. Fees charged by public schools therefore continue to constitute a major obstacle for migrant children.

Public schools also require that migrant children present a range of documents before enrollment. The number of certificates required in Beijing is most frequently cited as five, typically referring to the temporary residence permit, household registration booklet, work permit, proof of residency, and certificate verifying a lack of guardianship in the place of origin (Rural Education Action Project 2009). According to a government-based researcher, though, some schools require as many as seven or eight. Migrant workers often do not have all of these certificates, making enrollment difficult.

While the municipal and district governments may make the regulations, public schools themselves usually make the final decisions when it comes to entrance requirements. Overall, there was agreement among parents and other interviewees that the entrance policies of most public schools in Beijing are not particularly welcoming to migrant children. Parents expressed that it was too difficult to get into public schools, especially those of better quality, as they did not have all the documents required and/or the fees were too expensive. Of the parents in the sample who went to local public schools to enquire about entrance requirements, the fee that was most frequently asked for was the sponsorship fee, ranging from 6,000 to 100,000 RMB, though the most common amount cited was usually 10,000–20,000 RMB. Even poorer quality public schools may require a sponsorship fee of 15,000 RMB. As one parent concluded: "Instead of charging temporary schooling fees, they charge sponsorship fees. All they did was change the name" (HL1F6). Ultimately, different schools adopt different policies towards migrant students. One parent, for instance, stated that a local public primary school required them to pay all six years of school-related fees upfront in order for their child to enroll, with the fees amounting to about 12,000 RMB (HL1F5). Another parent recalled going to a public school near the Fifth Ring Road only to be turned away before being able to get any information about entrance requirements (SL2F4).

There are some migrant families that have children in both migrant and public schools, as was the case with three families in the sample. This is a phenomenon that has likely only surfaced in more recent years. Interestingly, the reasons that prohibited these families from enrolling all of their children in public schools have to do precisely with the requirements just discussed. In the first case, the older child was a seventh grader at a migrant school, while the younger child was a third grader at a public school. The reason for this was that the children had come to Beijing two years earlier, and the public school would not allow the older child to enroll as a fifth grader (HL2F3). In the second case, a *chabanfei* of 4,000–5,000 RMB was too expensive for the family, so the oldest child had to enroll in a migrant school (SU2F2). And in the third case, the parents were only able to get the elder of their two children into a public school after using some connections to get all of the required documents (SU2F3).

Thus, while most migrant parents hope that their children can get a higher-quality education in public schools, entrance requirements continue to constitute a major barrier. Moreover, as argued by one researcher, the lack of transparency in terms of the fees public schools charge migrant children has made the schools a less attractive option. In addition, officials and public schools themselves regularly claim that most public schools in Beijing are already full and that placing all migrant children into these schools is therefore an unrealistic short-term goal (see Chapter 5). As one migrant school principal summarized: "Children only come to our school because public schools cannot accept all of them" (FL2P1).

Furthermore, as the number of migrant schools declines because of demolitions and government closures, it is unlikely that all of the children involved will be placed into public schools given the barriers discussed. If unable to find another migrant school to attend, a significant number of these children may be left without schools to attend in Beijing and may have to return to their hometowns for schooling. While many may return to their hometowns for the latter part of middle school or for high school anyway, demolitions and closures may be forcing them to do so at an earlier age, with serious implications for their childhood development. Indeed, in many such cases, even if they return to their hometown, at least one of their parents may decide to continue working in Beijing to support the family. In other words, the surviving migrant schools play an additional role by providing these children with the opportunity to stay with their parents in the city for a longer period of time in a context in which barriers to public school education persist.

### The lack of discrimination in migrant schools

The phrase *yishi tongren* (equal treatment) has made frequent appearances in recent central and Beijing municipal policies discussing the treatment of migrant children (see Chapter 4). Still, discrimination by teachers and students in public schools can be a problem, and local parents may often be opposed to their children attending school with migrant children (Wang 2008: 693). Depending on the proportion of students that are migrants, migrant children may also sometimes be placed into separate classrooms (Wang 2009: 300–1).[28] As a result, it is common for migrant children attending public schools to lack self-confidence. For example, one retired public school teacher from Beijing, who was teaching at a migrant school at the time of fieldwork, recalled observing a noticeable sense of inferiority (*zibei*) among the one or two migrant children in each of his classes at the public school (SU4T1). The lack of discrimination is therefore an attractive trait of migrant schools. As one principal asserted:

> At this kind of school, the teachers are migrant workers, and the students are the children of migrant workers. There is absolutely no sense of

discrimination among the students, teachers, and administrators, and no one looks down on anyone else. We are all equal. So in this kind of environment, our students can study and live very happily.

(YL1P1)

### Services offered by migrant schools

Migrant schools offer services catering to the needs of migrant families. Similar to the situation in the 1990s (see Han 2001: 6), one of the primary reasons families in the sample chose their child's school was that it was close to their home and more convenient (as opposed to public schools, which tend to be farther away). In addition, migrant schools have flexible enrollment procedures and accept students throughout the school year. They are also open for longer hours; many allow parents to drop off their children as early as 5 a.m. and pick them up as late as 6 p.m. in order to accommodate migrant workers' long work days. Many give discounts to families with more than one child enrolled. At some schools, families facing particularly difficult financial situations may also be given discounts or may not be charged tuition at all. At one unlicensed school in Fengtai, for instance, about 40 percent of the students were regularly given discounts (FU2P1). Moreover, the similar curricula often used by migrant schools and schools in their home provinces may help facilitate the transition of these children when they return home (for middle school or high school).[29] Thus migrant schools not only "address both psychological and economic barriers to education in the state system" (Chen and Liang 2007: 125), but they also provide services that are not offered anywhere else in Beijing's schooling system. As one parent put it: "These schools only exist because there is a need for them" (HL1F4).

Each of these three factors has contributed to a continued demand for migrant schools in Beijing. When asked what aspects of their children's education were most important to them, parents in the sample placed great emphasis on the quality of education and teaching. At the same time, most were aware of the gap between migrant and public schools in this area. The fact that these parents enroll their children in migrant schools anyway is a reflection of both the barriers faced in attending public schools and the convenience, flexibility, and sense of community that migrant schools provide. The reemergence of migrant schools in Fengtai in the mid- to late 2000s and the reopening of several migrant schools as "preschools" after being closed in Haidian are useful examples of this continued demand. Thus, putting aside any perceptions of migrant school principals as profit-seeking individuals (see Chapter 3),[30] it is crucial not to downplay the role and contribution of migrant schools over time. As one principal expressed it:

We are silently doing a service for the country, for the nation. ... I made all of the investments [into this school] myself, but by training these children I am doing something for the country, for society, and for the families. Isn't that all good? ... At least I am not training these children to become thieves and robbers – that is not possible. At least I am teaching them.

(YL1P1)

Even at the government level there is an awareness of the continued market and need for migrant schools in Beijing. The district officials interviewed emphasized that their public schools are basically full and also expressed that migrant schools are often more convenient for migrant families because of, for example, their locations and flexible enrollment procedures. The Haidian official, for instance, provided several reasons why the schools still exist: first, many migrant children do not have the documentation required to attend public schools; second, a strong sense of community and native-place ties bind migrants together; third, many migrant school principals may misinform their students, saying that enrolling in public schools is complex and requires the payment of high fees; fourth, migrant schools provide services that cater to the needs of the migrant population; and, finally, public schools are generally full and located too far away from migrant communities.

## The important effects of decentralization on migrant schools and their students

The discussion in this and previous chapters illustrates that the decentralization of responsibility to receiving governments and public schools through the policy of "two priorities" has had major consequences for migrant schools in Beijing, with implications for the quality and stability of the education migrant children are receiving and subsequently trends in social stratification. The lack of support for migrant schools in Beijing municipal policies has directly affected the stability and legal status of the schools, as well as their poor conditions and low quality of teaching. Evidence shows that licensed *and* unlicensed schools in the city continue to face many of the same basic problems, illustrating that this lack of policy support has had serious consequences for migrant schools as a whole. At the same time, district-level approaches have also affected the situations of these schools, resulting in differences between the stability of the schools and the difficulties they face in getting licensed. Understanding the impacts of both the municipal and district approaches is therefore a critical step towards identifying more targeted measures to improve the situations of migrant schools and their students, an especially important task given that these schools remain a crucial source of education for migrant children in Beijing.

As discussed in Chapter 2, studies often point to the key role of the *hukou* system in accounting for the educational problems of migrant children in China. However, central-level policy changes, as well as some recent developments in Beijing like the decision to include migrant children in the lottery system for enrolling in public middle schools, indicate that it is possible to weaken or at least challenge the impact of institutional barriers on the exclusion of migrant children and the situations of migrant schools, even in cities with large migrant populations.

The recent experience of Shanghai is a useful example (see Chapter 4). The municipal and district-level situations explored in the previous two chapters and the consequences for migrant schools discussed above provide further evidence of the basic significance of examining the local politics surrounding policy implementation. The findings show that the situations of migrant schools and their students are shaped by social and political concerns at the municipal level and a range of district-level factors. In other words, the impact of the *hukou* system on the educational exclusion of these children is not straightforward. Ultimately, in order to more fully understand the intricacies of educational provision for migrant children and their implications for trends in social stratification, the *hukou* system, while fundamentally important, must be considered in conjunction with local factors and dynamics.

Thus the above discussion provides a valuable case that illustrates the need to analyze the implementation process to better understand the local consequences and sheds light on the effects of decentralized decision making on migrant schools and their students in Beijing. The findings confirm that, despite the potential benefits, the outcomes of decentralization can be highly complex. As King and Cordeiro Guerra (2005: 179) argue in discussing decentralization and reform in the realm of education: "[T]he reform process is never smooth. It is likely to be punctuated by bursts of progress and frequent setbacks, which may lead to rising frustration and growing mistrust among stakeholders who see themselves as losers under the reform process."

In view of the limited policy support given to migrant schools at the municipal level and the variation among district approaches, as well as the continued existence of the problems discussed above, critical questions arise regarding whether or not actors *outside* the government are able to have an impact. What role do civil society actors play in this picture? What can a stronger understanding of their involvement contribute to knowledge of Beijing's policy environment in this area? Turning to the final remaining piece of the framework set out in Figure 2.1 in Chapter 2, the next chapter demonstrates that an exploration of the municipal and district-level approaches and their impact on the situations of migrant schools is not complete without also considering the role of civil society. Examining the nature of civil society involvement will shed further light on how policy implementation in the area operates in Beijing, including which actors are involved and why, and the ultimate consequences for migrant schools and their students.

## Notes

1  This quote was translated from a 2009 issue of the migrant school teachers' association's magazine.
2  Based on schools in the sample and findings from previous research (e.g. Duan and Liang 2005; Wang 2008), there is no clear indication that the physical conditions of migrant schools in Beijing vary among districts. Any variation – in terms of, for example, facilities, size, and infrastructure – is often between individual schools rather than schools across districts. Ultimately, however, it is difficult to measure given their high mobility.

3 Given the mobile and unstable nature of the schools, the exact proportion of migrant schools in Beijing that offer both primary and middle school education is unclear. Within the sample, nine schools offered primary and middle school education (up through the ninth grade), one offered classes up through the eighth grade, and one offered classes up through the seventh grade. Based on fieldwork, there is one migrant school in Beijing that offers only middle school education.

4 Migrant schools in the sample at which both levels were licensed could support more students at the middle school level than schools at which only the primary school level was licensed. The four licensed schools visited in Shijingshan and Fengtai that offered middle school each had at least 200 middle school students, whereas the licensed school in Haidian only had about 150.

5 Almost all migrant schools in Beijing are rented or built on rented land (Beijing Migrant School Principals' Association 2009). Within the sample, the costs of rent ranged from 30,000 to 600,000 RMB.

6 In addition, unlike public school teachers, migrant school teachers are not subsidized during winter and summer holidays, a total of about three months every year. To support themselves and their families, many take up additional, low-paying jobs during these holidays (e.g. working as nannies, tutors, cleaners, construction workers, and street vendors) (Zhang 2010).

7 There is, however, often a range of salaries *within* schools, depending, for example, on level of experience.

8 Public school teachers are usually provided pension, medical, unemployment, work-related injury, and maternity insurance.

9 As will be discussed in Chapter 7, this also reflects the tendency of civil society actors to work in particular districts.

10 At schools that are short on teachers, principals (and sometimes their spouses) may also teach classes and take on additional responsibilities like driving the school bus.

11 Because of factors like increasing costs of rent, many migrant school principals have also been increasing their tuition fees.

12 In comparison, based on China Household Income Project (CHIP) survey data, the average household per capita disposable income in 1995 was 4,429 RMB in urban areas and 1,564 RMB in rural areas (calculated without including subsidies for housing and imputed rent) (Sicular *et al.* 2010: 91, table 4.1).

13 Based on CHIP survey data, the average household per capita disposable income in urban areas had already reached 8,038 RMB by 2002 (Sicular *et al.* 2010: 91, table 4.1).

14 Almost all the families visited lived in small, single-room homes that were just large enough to fit one or two beds. While most could afford a small television, the majority did not have appliances like refrigerators or adequate space for their children to do homework.

15 To date, no studies have compared characteristics of migrant workers like income and educational background across districts, largely because of their high mobility. Knowledge of the extent to which such differences exist remains extremely limited.

16 This is also an indication of the diverse nature of migrant communities (see Ma and Xiang 1998: 548).

17 Migrant children who stay in Beijing for middle school usually have two main options if they wish to continue their education after graduation. One is to attend vocational school in Beijing before entering the workforce. Of the schools in the sample, this was a common path chosen. At one school, for instance, the principal stated that over two-thirds of their middle school graduates attend vocational schools in Beijing (HL2P1). At another school, the principal stated that about 80 percent of the students pursue this route (SL3P1). The second option is to go back to their hometowns for high school. According to principals and teachers, in cases where children are not getting good grades, parents often choose not to send them home, particularly if there is

nobody there to take care of them. It is generally the better performing students who go back for high school. Yet an increasing number of migrant children are born and/ or raised in Beijing and are unaccustomed to life in rural areas. The issue of post-primary and post-middle school education (commonly referred to as *shengxue wenti*) is therefore a top concern among migrant parents.

18 For most migrant children, by the time they complete primary school, there are only three years left before they must return to their hometowns if they wish to attend high school. As a result, many parents with children in migrant schools – especially those who are unable to enroll their children in public middle schools – choose to send their children home for at least the last year or two of middle school so they can get used to the living and school environment. Going back, however, raises additional problems. Difficulties adjusting and differences in curricula may result in children having to repeat a grade upon their return. Certain subjects may also be taught at different stages. As one parent pointed out, her daughter, who was born in Beijing but would be "returning" to the family's hometown for the sixth grade, had been studying English at her migrant school since the first grade, when schools in her hometown only start teaching English in the fifth grade (SL2F6).

19 In 2009, for instance, the average class size was 31 among public primary schools and 33 among public middle schools in Beijing (Wang 2011).

20 In addition, the average number of class hours per week among Beijing's migrant school teachers is about 24, which is 1.5 times greater than that among public primary school teachers (Wang 2011).

21 There are, of course, exceptions. One teacher from Hebei, a woman in her early thirties, had started teaching at a licensed migrant school in the sample six years earlier. Though she subsequently got a Beijing *hukou* and a teaching certificate, which qualified her to be a public school teacher, she chose instead to stay at the school, saying that she felt a sense of loyalty to the school, the children, and the cause (HL2T3). Another teacher, a middle-aged woman from Inner Mongolia, had been teaching at migrant schools in Beijing since 1998. At her first migrant school, she received a total of 800 RMB for her first four months of teaching. With her current monthly salary of a little over 1,000 RMB, she pointed out that she could earn more working as a cleaner (*baojie*). Still, she continues to teach because the children need to have good teachers (SU1T1).

22 As Heikkila (2007: 74) maintains: "[For reasons] including a perception of social disorder and crime, these urban villages are viewed as problematic by local government authorities and by many urban residents [in cities like Beijing]. Recent government reforms seek to convert these places to designated urban areas."

23 According to the principal, such schools accept migrant children because of their own shortages of students.

24 See, for example, Chin (2011) and Zhang (2011).

25 While landlords are often given subsidies when migrant enclaves are demolished, migrant families are generally not given any assistance. In addition, based on a notice one principal in the sample received from the Haidian education commission in mid-2006, students attending migrant schools that are shut down must go to their local street office to present various documents and apply for a temporary student certificate before contacting the public school assigned to them. In many cases, however, the situation may not be clear-cut, and parents are often unaware of their options and must find new schools for their children to attend on their own.

26 See Kwong (2006: 172) and Chen and Liang (2007: 125–6) for additional discussion of this demand.

27 As discussed in Chapter 5, there are a small number of public schools in Beijing at which the majority of students are migrant children. Based on fieldwork, these schools may sometimes only charge a few hundred RMB per term, but they are usually of poorer quality and have limited space.

28 According to a researcher in the sample, this is usually done for reasons of convenience (e.g. if the school has a separate branch closer to a migrant community or if different teaching materials need to be used).
29 The Ministry of Education stipulates that students in China must take their high school entrance examination in the county in which they are officially registered. These exams are based on the curriculum used by the school system in the particular locality. Given that school systems in rural counties often use the standard "national curriculum," migrant schools in cities tend to also follow the national curriculum so that their students can be better prepared for the entrance examination in their home county (Rural Education Action Project 2009).
30 Zhang (2010), for example, makes the case that a school with 500 students and 15 teachers can make one million RMB per year from students' fees (2,000 RMB per student per year). Subtracting expenses for teacher salaries (100,000 RMB per year) and rent (200,000 RMB per year), the school would still be left with 700,000 RMB.

# Bibliography

Beijing Migrant School Principals' Association. "Huiyi yiti" [Topics for Discussion]. Discussion notes prepared for a migrant school principals' forum, China Youth University for Political Sciences, Beijing, China, December 2009.

Chen, Yiu Por and Zai Liang. "Educational Attainment of Migrant Children: The Forgotten Story of China's Urbanization." In *Education and Reform in China*, ed. Emily Hannum and Albert Park. Oxford: Routledge, 2007, pp. 117–32.

Chin, Josh. "Will School Closures Prompt Migrants to Flee?" *The Wall Street Journal*, August 19, 2011. http://blogs.wsj.com/chinarealtime/2011/08/19/will-school-closures-prompt-migrants-to-flee/ (accessed August 28, 2011).

China Labour Bulletin. "The Children of Migrant Workers in China." 2008. www.clb.org.hk/en/node/100316 (accessed December 3, 2008).

Davies, Lynn, Clive Harber, and Chris Dzimadzi. "Educational Decentralisation in Malawi: A Study of Process." *Compare* 33, no. 2 (2003): 139–54.

Duan, Chengrong and Hong Liang. "Guanyu liudong ertong yiwu jiaoyu wenti de diaocha yanjiu" ["A Study on the Compulsory Education for Temporary Migrant Children"]. *Renkou yu jingji* [*Population & Economics*] 1 (2005): 11–17.

Han, Jialing. "Beijingshi liudong ertong yiwu jiaoyu zhuangkuang diaocha baogao" [Report on the Investigation of the Compulsory Education Situation of Children of the Floating Population in Beijing]. *Qingnian yanjiu* [*Youth Studies*] 8 and 9 (2001): 1–7, 10–18.

Han, Jialing. "Beijingshi 'dagong zidi xuexiao' de xingcheng, fazhan yu weilai" [The Formation, Development, and Future of Migrant Schools in Beijing]. In *Zhongguo minban jiaoyu zuzhi yu zhidu yanjiu* [Research on the Organization and System of Private Education in China], ed. Xiaobing Sun. Beijing: Zhongguo qingnian chubanshe [China Youth Press], 2003, pp. 402–16.

Heikkila, Eric J. "Three Questions Regarding Urbanization in China." *Journal of Planning Education and Research* 27, no. 1 (Fall 2007): 65–81.

King, Elizabeth M. and Susana Cordeiro Guerra. "Education Reforms in East Asia: Policy, Process, and Impact." In *East Asia Decentralizes: Making Local Government Work*, ed. World Bank. Washington, DC: World Bank, 2005, pp. 179–207. http://siteresources.worldbank.org/INTEAPDECEN/Resources/dc-full-report.pdf (accessed November 4, 2008).

Kwong, Julia. "Educating Migrant Children: Negotiations between the State and Civil Society." *The China Quarterly* 180 (December 2004): 1073–88.

Kwong, Julia. "The Integration of Migrant Children in Beijing Schools." In *Education and Social Change in China: Inequality in a Market Economy*, ed. Gerard A. Postiglione. Armonk, NY: M. E. Sharpe, 2006, pp. 163–78.

Lai, Fang, Chengfang Liu, Renfu Luo, Linxiu Zhang, Xiaochen Ma, Yujie Bai, Brian Sharbono, and Scott Rozelle. "Private Migrant Schools or Rural/Urban Public Schools: Where Should China Educate Its Migrant Children?" REAP Working Paper No. 224, Stanford University, Rural Education Action Project, Stanford, CA, 2012. http://iis-db.stanford.edu/pubs/23180/migrant_paper_final_sdr_fang_acm_sdr_march26_sdr.pdf (accessed August 3, 2012).

Li, Xinling. "Zhubu tupo 'zhidu pingjing,' cujin yiwu jiaoyu junheng fazhan" ["Break the 'System Bottleneck' Gradually, Promote the Balanced Development of Compulsory Education"]. In *Zhongguo jiaoyu fazhan baogao (2009) (Jiaoyu lanpishu)* [*Annual Report on China's Education (2009) (Blue Book of Education)*], ed. Dongping Yang. Beijing: Shehui kexue wenxian chubanshe [Social Sciences Academic Press], 2009, pp. 64–75.

Litvack, Jennie, Junaid Ahmad, and Richard Bird. *Rethinking Decentralization in Developing Countries*. Washington, DC: World Bank, 1998. www1.worldbank.org/publicsector/decentralization/Rethinking%20Decentralization.pdf (accessed May 6, 2011).

Lü, Shaoqing. *Liushou haishi liudong? "Mingong chao" zhong de ertong yanjiu* [*Left Behind or Migration? An Empirical Study on Children of Rural Migrants*]. Beijing: Zhongguo nongye chubanshe [China Agriculture Press], 2007.

Ma, Laurence J. C. and Biao Xiang. "Native Place, Migration and the Emergence of Peasant Enclaves in Beijing." *The China Quarterly* 155 (September 1998): 546–81.

Ni, Guanghui and Yuanyuan Zhao. "Jing: 30 duo suo dagong zidi xuexiao chaiqian, shu qianming haizi ruxue nan" [Beijing: The Demolition of Over 30 Migrant Schools, Thousands of Children Face Difficulties Enrolling in School]. *Renmin ribao* [*People's Daily*], March 1, 2010. http://news.xinhuanet.com/employment/2010-03/01/content_13072448.htm (accessed April 22, 2010).

Rural Education Action Project. "Education for Migrant Children." 2009. http://reap.stanford.edu/docs/education_for_migrant_children/ (accessed April 19, 2011).

Sicular, Terry, Ximing Yue, Björn A. Gustafsson, and Shi Li. "How Large Is China's Rural–Urban Income Gap?" In *One Country, Two Societies: Rural–Urban Inequality in Contemporary China*, ed. Martin King Whyte. Cambridge, MA: Harvard University Press, 2010, pp. 85–104.

Song, Yingquan, Prashant Loyalka, and Jianguo Wei. "Does Going to Public Schools Matter for Migrant Children's Academic Achievement in China?" Manuscript, Peking University, China Institute for Educational Finance Research, Beijing, China, 2009.

Wang, Chunhua. "Beijing dagong zidi jiaoshi shouru buji nongmingong, quefan shehui baozhang" [Migrant School Teachers' Salaries Lower than That of Migrant Workers, Lack Social Security]. *Gongren ribao* [*Workers' Daily*], April 27, 2011. www.bj.xinhuanet.com/bjpd_sdzx/2011-04/27/content_22635749.htm (accessed May 2, 2011).

Wang, Lu. "The Marginality of Migrant Children in the Urban Chinese Educational System." *British Journal of Sociology of Education* 29, no. 6 (November 2008): 691–703.

Wang, Zhichao. "Systematic Barriers to Schooling of Migrant Workers' Children and Policy Recommendations." *Frontiers of Education in China* 4, no. 2 (June 2009): 298–311.

Zhang, Dong. "Beijing dagong zidi xin xuenian: 'Wo xihuan zheli de laoshi'" [A New Academic Year for Migrant Children: "I Like the Teachers Here"]. *Zhongguo jiaoyubao* [*China Education Daily*], September 2, 2011. www.jyb.cn/basc/xw/201109/t20110902_451824.html (accessed November 11, 2011).

Zhang, Shujun. "Nongmingong zidi xuexiao jiaoshi xianzhuang nan" [The Difficult Situation Faced by Migrant School Teachers]. Speech delivered at the Department of Sociology at Tsinghua University, Beijing, China, January 3, 2010. www.jinchengwugong.com/jiaoyupindao1.asp?id=101 (accessed August 13, 2010).

# 7 The survival and development of migrant schools in Beijing
## The role of civil society

[Civil society] is becoming more and more involved ... [but] its impact is not great. The arm is no match for the thigh [*gebo ningbuguo datui*].

(HL1P1)

Not only does decentralization increase the involvement of different levels of government, but it can also create space for civil society in the delivery of services like education.[1] In China, civil society has become increasingly involved in welfare service provision for marginalized groups including laborers and children since the early 1990s (Howell 2007: 18–20). The case of migrant children's education in Beijing is, at first glance, no exception. As mentioned in Chapter 3, local researcher Zhao Shukai is usually credited for being the first to discover the existence of migrant schools in Beijing in 1996, and the local media subsequently played a key role in bringing migrant children's education to the attention of the government and society. Since then, an increasing number of civil society actors have become active in mobilizing on behalf of migrant children and their education in the capital city.

In light of the overall lack of support for migrant schools from the Beijing municipal government and the emergence of different district policy approaches, important questions arise concerning civil society involvement in this policy area. What role do civil society actors play, and are they able to influence the situations of migrant schools and their students? If so, what are the main channels through which they are able to have an impact, or, if not, what factors are inhibiting them? What are the implications for the understanding of migrant children's education in Beijing? Examining these questions will shed further light on the dynamics shaping the situations of migrant schools and their students at the municipal and district levels.

This chapter focuses on the main sets of actors outside the government that have become involved in migrant children's education in Beijing and operate with the goal of improving the educational situations of migrant children in some way: academics and researchers, the media, university student organizations, NGOs, migrant school principals' and teachers' associations, and migrant parent activists. It explores the involvement of these actors, including their interaction with both the government and migrant schools (see Figure 7.1). Evidence shows that their overall capacity to impact migrant children's education in

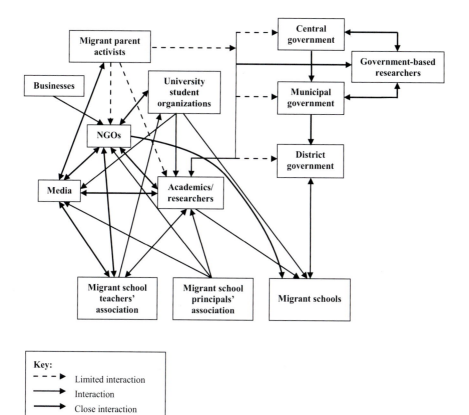

*Figure 7.1* General areas of interaction between government, civil society, and migrant schools in Beijing.

Source: Author's fieldwork (2009–10).

Beijing has been limited, mainly in terms of their influence on government and policy, the situations of migrant schools and their students, and the sharing of knowledge and information. Their limited impact has been shaped by a general lack of support for civil society from the municipal government in an area that is, in its view, closely linked to population growth and social instability, as well as low levels of collaboration among key actors involved. District-level situations and policy approaches have had an additional impact on where in the city these actors tend to work, with consequences for the amount of external attention and support migrant schools in different districts receive.

## Civil society and social welfare provision in China

Since the 1980s, decentralization has created room for civil society involvement in the delivery of services in China (Davis 1989; Teets 2008: 7–8). Starting in the 1980s, the CPC began to promote the role of new kinds of societal organizations, including professional associations, trade associations, and cultural clubs. As a part of its efforts to move China towards a system of "small government, large society" (*xiao zhengfu, da shehui*), it also started to encourage these organizations to carry out tasks formerly done by the government, including social welfare provision. In particular, the 1990s saw the emergence and rise of civil society associations focused on the provision of services for marginalized groups including workers, women, children, the poor, and people with disabilities (Howell 2007: 17–19).

The increase in the number of such organizations was rooted in political and economic developments. For example, with the deepening of market reforms during the 1990s, the negative outcomes of reform became more serious, evident in trends in urban poverty, unemployment, and income gaps. At the same time, with limited political reform, ensuring social stability became a top goal of the Chinese leadership. These new civil society organizations would therefore help play a much-needed role in reducing both poverty and social tensions and discontent. Their involvement would also create more job opportunities, which could help tackle unemployment (Howell 2007: 20). The lack of adequate state investment in social welfare services and social relief and the resulting limited capacity of the government to provide welfare provided an additional stimulus for the emergence of these actors (Shang 2002: 206).

The nature of the relationship between government and civil society in social welfare provision in China varies. In some areas, government control over these actors has loosened. Shang (2002: 204), for instance, points to a shift from "welfare statism" to "welfare pluralism" in the case of care for orphaned or abandoned children, indicating that civil society has become more influential in the policy process. In most cases, however, the relationship is complex, and government actors adopt differing strategies towards civil society depending on the context. As Cheng *et al.* (2010: 1104) contend:

> In general, they have to respond to increasing demand for various types of social services. But their considerations of social stability and definitions of their respective baselines are complicated and may even be contradictory, with mixed elements coexisting: detachment, neglect, tolerance, support, and sanction.

Indeed, a range of government approaches have emerged. Officials may tolerate those actors that restrict their size and act in line with policy goals. In other cases, they may adopt strategies to retain control, either formally (e.g. by increasing management through policy) or informally (e.g. by trying to limit the development of such actors). They may also adopt a strategy of "absorption" as a regulatory mechanism, which could involve presenting awards or titles of a political nature, building relationships between the actors and local government departments, and appointing actors to political positions (cited by Cheng *et al.* 2010: 1095–6, 1098–102).

Ultimately, the role of civil society in welfare provision in China is complicated and varies across both contexts and policy areas (Chamberlain 1993: 212; Cheng *et al.* 2010: 1104). Issues involving gender, for example, are generally considered to be less sensitive than those involving labor; as a result, "just as attempts to organize around labour point to the boundaries of Party-state tolerance for civil society, organizing around gender can indicate how wide the space for organizing can be pushed" (Howell 2003: 207). Indeed, while it might seem beneficial to provide some political support to labor NGOs as a way of promoting social harmony, many labor NGOs in China continue to lack legal authorization. Local governments therefore usually choose to not pay attention to them and adopt an impartial position towards them while letting them continue their work (Cheng *et al.* 2010: 1089–90).

The extent to which civil society actors are able to build relationships with government actors has become a major factor shaping their role in social welfare provision. Those that do not interact with the government may struggle to survive or flourish, while those that have closer relationships with government actors may be less likely to face such difficulties, though they may eventually be absorbed into the government's sphere of control (Cheng *et al.* 2010: 1095). All of this has consequences for the services and amount of support available to the groups these actors serve, making closer examinations of their involvement in different policy areas and contexts crucial.

Despite growing interest in the role of civil society in areas like gender and labor, few studies have explored such dynamics for migrant children's education. Perhaps the only exception is Kwong (2004), which focuses on state–civil society relations in migrant children's education; however, it does not analyze district-level variations in detail and was also written prior to the emergence of actors including many of the NGOs now involved. Important questions then arise concerning the impact of civil society in this policy area. As Howell (2007: 21) puts it: "Have societal actors begun to carve out a public sphere that allows critical debate around issues that were otherwise regarded as only a matter for the Party/state? Is governance becoming more plural, more democratic, more negotiated than before?"

The rest of this chapter examines the civil society actors involved in migrant children's education in Beijing, including their structure (who the key actors are and what activities they are engaged in), their motives for being involved and their relationship to the policy environment in which they operate (the extent to which they are able to interact with and attain recognition and support from the government), and their capacity to impact the situations of migrant schools and their students.[2] Evidence shows that, largely because of the perception of migrant children's education as a policy area with potential implications for population growth and social instability, government actors in Beijing have, for the most part, chosen to either ignore or tolerate the civil society actors involved. The result has been a low level of state–civil society interaction in the policy area, and the role of these actors has been heavily defined by the views and concerns of the municipal and district governments, ultimately limiting their capacity to have a large-scale impact on migrant children's education in the city.

# The role of civil society in migrant children's education in Beijing

Not only is there a continued demand for migrant schools in Beijing (as established in Chapter 6), but the *visibility* of these schools has also increased, in large part because of the work of civil society. As previously discussed, during the mid- to late 1990s, the Chinese government saw migrant schools as illegal entities and had little knowledge about them. Though still vulnerable to being shut down, most migrant schools in Beijing no longer operate as "underground" schools. This section illustrates that migrant children's education – and migrant schools in particular – has attracted attention from an increasing number of civil society actors in Beijing since the mid- to late 1990s. They include academics and researchers, the media, university student organizations, and NGOs, as well as actors within the migrant community that often lack government recognition (including migrant school principals' and teachers' associations and parent activists).[3] The involvement of these various actors is driven by a combination of three key motives: to provide support directly to migrant schools and their students and teachers, to raise awareness about the problems of migrant schools and their students, and to influence government and policy.

In light of the general lack of support for migrant schools from the municipal government and the differing district policy approaches, evidence is used to evaluate the extent to which these actors have been able to – through their work and relationships – achieve these objectives and ultimately improve the situations of migrant schools and their students and why. In conducting this evaluation, emphasis is placed on the reality that civil society actors typically seek out the migrant communities and schools they work with, rather than the other way around. As one principal explained, each migrant school's relationships "have a lot to do with the reputations of the school and the principal" (SU1P1), and actors like researchers and NGOs often recommend schools to others based on these reputations. These actors can therefore significantly affect the amount of external attention and support migrant schools in different districts receive, making a closer examination of their role critical.

## *The key actors involved*

### *Academics and researchers*

Although government and society were first made aware of migrant schools in Beijing through the efforts of a local researcher in 1996, few studies were conducted on the subject in Beijing during the late 1990s, key exceptions being Lü (2007) and Han (2001). Very few have researched the subject continuously since the 1990s; based on fieldwork, those who conduct research on the topic tend to do so for a short period of time before moving on to other subjects. This overall lack of sustained interest – at least in part a result of the basic difficulties of conducting research on the subject and the resulting perception that there is little room for ongoing exploration – has contributed to a lack of extensive research on migrant children's education.

The role of academics and researchers in the area revolves primarily around research, usually with the goal of raising awareness about the problems of migrant schools and their students. Some local researchers collaborate with researchers from outside of China, helping to increase awareness about the subject abroad. Their work can also include organizing discussion forums with other scholars, government-based researchers, migrant school principals, and NGOs, as well as creating programs or organizations to support migrant schools and their students (e.g. by teaching migrant children about self-esteem or, in one case, by subsidizing teachers' salaries). In addition, research may serve as a channel through which to influence policy. Not only do many of the academics and researchers involved exchange information and ideas with government-based researchers at the central and municipal levels, but some also submit their research findings to the government. The latter, however, does not occur frequently and also depends to a large extent on the nature of the relationship between their universities or research institutions and the government. Within the sample, for instance, only one institute submitted policy briefs based on their research on various topics to the central government several times a year. According to an established researcher in the field, the government consulted academics and researchers about migrant children's education more frequently in the early to mid-2000s, given its lack of knowledge about the subject at the time, but the level of interaction has since declined, and their impact in the policy area is unclear.

Moreover, there was a tendency among academics and researchers in the sample to focus their research on schools in Chaoyang and Haidian districts (both of which have high concentrations of academic and research institutes) and to a lesser extent schools in Shijingshan, Changping, and Daxing districts. The focus on schools in less controversial districts has contributed to a general trend among many of them to disregard or downplay the importance of district-level variations in the policy area. This has greatly shaped the existing body of research, as studies on the subject often provide evidence based on particular schools in these districts and then discuss the findings at the municipal level, rather than comparing district-level situations (e.g. Kwong 2004; Goodburn 2009).

Migrant schools in different districts therefore receive differing amounts of attention and support from academics and researchers. For example, the principals at four of the six schools visited in Haidian expressed having regular contact with academics and researchers, compared to three of the seven schools visited in Shijingshan. All four schools visited in Fengtai, however, had little to no previous contact with academics and researchers; at one of the district's unlicensed schools, the principal noted that I was the first to visit the school since its creation in 2005 (FU1P1). Interestingly, one of the existing contact lists of migrant schools in the city, compiled by a team of researchers, did not include any of the licensed or unlicensed schools in Fengtai that were visited during fieldwork or that were mentioned by the officials and principals in the sample, further evidence that the district's schools are isolated from the academic sphere. As a result, there has been a general lack of knowledge about Fengtai's situation. One prominent researcher I spoke with, for instance, was unaware that the district had three licensed migrant schools.[4] All of this is especially significant in light of the potential capacity of academics and researchers to influence policy through research.

## The media

As mentioned in Chapter 3, the media played a key role in bringing migrant children's education to the attention of the government and society in the mid-1990s. Based on fieldwork, the earliest newspapers to report on the obstacles faced by migrant children in attaining education included *Zhongguo jiaoyubao* (*China Education Daily*), under the Ministry of Education; *Guangming ribao* (*Guangming Daily*), under the Propaganda Department of the CPC; and *Nongmin ribao* (*Peasants' Daily*), under the Ministry of Agriculture.[5] Though much of the media attention since then has also been from state-run media, independent media have played a role in reporting about the subject as well. In recent years, much of the coverage, local and international, has been focused on the demolition and shutting down of migrant schools and the impact on the students (e.g. when the "Notice of the General Office of the Beijing Municipal People's Government on the Work of Strengthening the Safety of Non-Approved Self-Run Migrant Schools" was issued in 2006, when several districts demolished over 30 migrant schools in 2010, and when Haidian, Chaoyang, and Daxing made plans to close or demolish 24 migrant schools in 2011) (see, for instance, Ren and Mao 2006; Ni and Zhao 2010; Zhuang and Lin 2010; BBC News Asia-Pacific 2011; Jacobs 2011; Shi *et al.* 2011; Zhang 2011). In addition, local independent media play a role by helping to publicize NGO events and programs and are frequently present at relevant symposiums held by actors like researchers and NGOs.

By bringing issues like demolition and school closures to the public's attention, the media have occasionally been able to put pressure on the municipal and district governments in this area. As shown in Chapter 5, the Shijingshan and especially Haidian officials interviewed discussed feeling such pressure at various times. However, the media's impact has varied. Media coverage put some pressure on the municipal and Haidian district governments in 2006 and the Daxing district government in 2011 but was unable to stimulate much change when several districts, including Chaoyang, shut down over 30 schools in 2010 (see Chapter 6). Though it is difficult to assess the precise factors influencing decision making because of the lack of transparency, principals and researchers in the sample expressed that the media's capacity to generate change in the policy area remains low.

## University student organizations

University student groups were also among the earliest actors outside of the government to become involved. During the late 1990s, local researcher Zhao

Shukai recruited students from a local university to assist with research on rural development and migrant workers. This led to the creation of a students' association at the university with a similar focus, which began volunteering at migrant schools around 2000. The number of student groups doing volunteer work at migrant schools has increased over time, and these groups usually go to the schools on their own or through NGOs. Their main objective is to provide support for migrant school students and improve the quality of education they receive, primarily by tutoring, teaching classes, organizing events, and donating school supplies.

The overall involvement of such groups is still limited, and, while they may have a direct impact on the individual children they work with (e.g. by helping with schoolwork and serving as role models), their capacity to have a large-scale, long-term impact is small. Of the 22 migrant schools in the sample, seven had little to no interaction with student volunteers. This included three licensed schools, illustrating that a license does not necessarily lead to stronger connections with such actors. Principals expressed that university students tend to visit their schools irregularly and infrequently or may simply organize one-off events. Only about half of the principals expressed that university students came to their schools on a regular, usually weekly, basis. The number of students that visit migrant schools to tutor students also tends to be small (e.g. fewer than ten students per visit), and student groups may only send volunteers to one or two schools each year. The limited involvement of these organizations is largely a result of financial and time constraints, the high turnover rate among members, and the fact that migrant children's education may not be the primary focus of their voluntary work. Conversations with student volunteers revealed that some principals may consequently prefer that university students not come to their schools at all because of reasons such as concerns about the negative effects of short-term, unstable programs on the children and safety considerations when, for example, volunteers organize programs during weekends when schools are unstaffed.

In other cases, migrant schools did not have student volunteers because such groups had never contacted them. Out of the four inner suburban districts, student groups tend to choose schools in Chaoyang, Haidian, and Shijingshan. Here, distance is a key factor; many of the city's major universities are in Haidian and Chaoyang, and it is easier for students to travel to migrant schools in nearby areas. As a result, whereas all six schools visited in Haidian and about six of the seven schools visited in Shijingshan had relationships with university student volunteers, only one of the four schools visited in Fengtai (a licensed school) had university students coming on a weekly basis. At one of the unlicensed schools in Fengtai, the principal recalled that university students in Haidian had once contacted the school to arrange tutoring but pulled out after learning the school's location (FU1P1). What is more, some student groups choose not to select migrant schools on their own and have instead become volunteers through NGOs, in which case the schools are selected by the NGOs themselves. As will be discussed below, this can also lead to the exclusion of schools in particular districts.

*Non-governmental organizations*

There is an increasing number of NGOs working on migrant children's education in Beijing. The majority became involved in the mid-2000s when the issue had begun to attract more societal attention.[6] These organizations mainly arrange programs and events for migrant schools and their students, sometimes through their own community centers, and are often present at relevant forums held by researchers and other organizations. Their primary objectives can include providing support for and improving the situations of migrant school students (e.g. through tutoring and teacher training); fostering the healthy growth and development of migrant children and encouraging their creativity through art, music, and sport; increasing societal awareness about the problems migrant children face; and engaging in policy advocacy.[7] The majority of the local NGOs in the sample relied, at least in part, on financial support from sources outside of mainland China (including Hong Kong), illustrating the important role of external funding in their survival.

Within the sample, organizations varied in type, the nature of their work, and the extent to which their work was focused on migrant children's education. Though the local NGOs in the sample were all registered with the government, most focused on providing services directly to particular migrant communities or migrant schools and were often relatively small in scale. There were, of course, exceptions; for example, starting in 2007, one foundation sponsored the establishment of three non-governmental migrant schools in the city as a part of its work in the area (YOF2S1).

Most NGOs in the sample served a number of communities and schools in various locations and districts, though a few were primarily engaged in serving single communities. NGOs that are physically based in migrant communities are, like migrant schools, also vulnerable to being demolished. At one such organization, for instance, an interviewee described that it was already at its third location since its creation in the mid-2000s and was in the process of looking for a fourth:

> We only came here because of demolition in Haidian and Chaoyang. It's unstable ... this is our biggest problem. ... Right now we have nowhere to move because so many other migrant villages are also being demolished. ... There are many obstacles. It will be good if we can survive.
>
> (SOC1S1)

The number of organizations that choose this model therefore remains limited.

NGOs that are not based within a particular community frequently choose the migrant schools they work with based on location, need, and the willingness of the principals to work with them. Because of limited resources, NGOs that work closely with individual schools often work with no more than ten schools, usually unlicensed ones.[8] They also tend to concentrate their work in certain districts; based on the NGOs in the sample, Chaoyang received the most attention, followed by Haidian, Shijingshan, Changping, and Daxing (see Table 7.1). Again, schools in Fengtai received considerably less attention.

Table 7.1 NGOs in the sample and the districts where they work

| Location of NGO (district) | Main district(s) where they work | | | | | | | | | |
|---|---|---|---|---|---|---|---|---|---|---|
| | Fengtai | Shijingshan | Haidian | Chaoyang | Changping | Daxing | Tongzhou | Dongcheng | All | Varies |
| Changping | | * | | | * | * | | | | |
| Changping | | | | | | | | | * | |
| Chaoyang | | * | * | * | * | | | | | |
| Chaoyang | | * | * | * | | | | | | |
| Chaoyang | | * | * | * | * | * | * | | | |
| Chaoyang | | | * | * | * | * | * | | | |
| Chaoyang | | | * | * | * | * | | | | |
| Chaoyang | | | | * | | | | | | |
| Chaoyang | | | | | | | | | | * |
| Dongcheng | * | | * | * | | | | * | | |
| Dongcheng | | | | | | | | * | | |
| Shijingshan | | * | | | | | | | | |

Source: Author's fieldwork (2009–10).

In addition to providing services for migrant communities and schools, NGOs also help increase awareness about migrant children's education. One example is their role in bringing businesses into the picture. As mentioned by staff at several NGOs, a small number of businesses have started to take interest in the area and, through NGOs, donate items to migrant schools and sponsor NGO events and programs; that is, NGOs provide them with information about and access to the schools. However, their involvement is still limited. Moreover, since NGOs tend to work with schools in particular districts, more isolated schools do not benefit from such interaction.

Overall, the capacity of these NGOs to substantially improve the situations of migrant schools remains low. First, their general inability to interact with the government has affected their capacity to have a significant, long-term impact on migrant schools and their students. Their attempts to impact policy have included efforts with other actors like the media, researchers, and principals to put pressure on the government. For instance, at least two organizations in the sample interacted with Haidian officials in opposing the decision to shut down unlicensed migrant schools in 2006. Yet such interaction has been infrequent, and most NGOs involved have not been able to build close working relationships with government actors. As a staff member at one NGO admitted:

> In terms of interaction with the government, I think this is an area where we haven't done too well. ... We are currently working hard on this. ... We are hoping that [our projects] can acquire recognition from the education commission (for example, Chaoyang's district education commission). ... This kind of recognition is what migrant schools need the most. Actually, I think that there are many things that we cannot change ourselves. ... The most important thing is for the government to pay more attention to and suggest ways in which we can resolve the problems. The main force needs to come from the government. ... We haven't been able to establish the channels. We don't have the capacity to build the relationships. We don't know how to access them. ... Ideally we would build relationships with a few municipal government officials, but, if that's not possible, building relationships with the district government and education commission would also be very good.
>
> (YOL3S1)

Only two NGOs in the sample, both in Chaoyang, expressed having had some limited contact with municipal officials (e.g. in the labor bureau), while two others, in Changping and Chaoyang, expressed having had limited contact with their district education commission. The majority did not have close relationships with the municipal and district education commissions. As one NGO staff member maintained: "The government doesn't have any interest [in interacting with us]" (POC1S1). This has had direct consequences for the extent to which these organizations are able to impact the situation, reflected in the following remark made by one interviewee:

The main point is that government support is needed. ... [The work we do (like training and events)] cannot resolve many of the problems. ... Many [migrant school] principals are good people, and many teachers are good people. But the efforts of [such] individuals cannot resolve the issues. So, in this area, it's very difficult for us without having support from the government.

(SOC1S1)

Second, based on interviews, NGOs may sometimes encounter difficulties working at migrant schools, with further consequences for their capacity to improve the situations of the schools and their students. Some principals, for example, have safety concerns when an organization wishes to run its programs during weekends when the school is unstaffed. In addition, some teachers and parents feel that participating in NGO programs would take valuable time away from the students' schoolwork and subsequently affect their grades.

*Migrant school principals' association*

In 1999, a group of principals created an association for migrant school principals, a notable development given the previously low level of interaction among them.[9] A Hong Kong-based organization provided financial assistance, while a local university provided meeting space. The association was created to serve as a forum for principals to meet and share information about policy-related developments and key problems faced by their schools. In the early stages of its existence, the main issues discussed centered on seeking legal status and stability. By the late 2000s, its focus had extended to issues concerning the low salaries and lack of insurance among their teachers, demolition, and the need to eliminate tuition fees at migrant schools. At the time of fieldwork, it included principals from most of the districts (including Haidian, Chaoyang, Shijingshan, Daxing, Tongzhou, Changping, Shunyi, Fangshan, Yanqing, Huairou, and Xuanwu). According to a representative, the association lacks members from Fengtai because of the district's history and the small number of remaining schools.

Though the association is primarily a forum for principals, actors like academics and researchers, NGOs, lawyers, and the media have sometimes been invited to its meetings. It has, however, had very little interaction with the municipal government, which sees it as a potential threat. Indeed, past attempts to express its views to the government and make policy recommendations have been unsuccessful; according to the representative interviewed, it has occasionally submitted reports to the municipal government and education commission, but such efforts have not resulted in much action. Moreover, the number and frequency of its meetings have declined because, as an association without government authorization, it cannot hold meetings legally. Principals have also become increasingly busy dealing with matters such as impending demolitions and government closures, making it more difficult to organize meetings or hold events. So, despite its relatively long history, its impact has been low. As the representative interviewed asserted: "We haven't made too many accomplishments.

... The government manages governmental affairs. We can only express our wishes" (HL1P1). During a follow-up conversation in mid-2013, this principal revealed that the association was basically no longer active.

There are also, at the district level, private (*minban*) education associations (which typically operate under the district education commission and include licensed migrant schools) and a small number of migrant schools' associations. Based on fieldwork, Chaoyang, Changping, Tongzhou, and Shijingshan each have a migrant schools' association, though these associations are generally disorganized and meet infrequently. Chaoyang's migrant schools' association and private (*minban*) education association have somewhat better reputations. According to a long-time principal in the district, the district's *minban* education association has served as a forum for the principals of licensed *and* unlicensed migrant schools to express their views to the district education commission and has, on occasion, been able to influence local decisions. In 2008, for example, principals in the association met to discuss the use of school buses by migrant schools, which had been contributing to competition among the schools and had also raised safety concerns. The principals decided to eliminate the use of the buses and submitted a resolution to the district education commission, which then approved the decision, allowing migrant children to attend migrant schools closest to their homes.

Such occurrences, however, remain infrequent, and the overall capacity of the district-level associations to impact policy is low. Most districts do not have one specifically for migrant schools, and the few associations that do exist usually do not meet regularly and receive little attention or support from the district governments. Out of the three districts of focus in this study, only Shijingshan had a migrant schools' association. According to principals in the sample, the association, which was created around 2005, was the first such district-level association in Beijing and includes licensed and unlicensed migrant schools. However, even though it has occasionally brought issues to the district education commission, meetings are not held on a regular basis, and its influence remains very limited. In the case of Haidian, the lack of an association was explained by one long-time principal as follows:

> Haidian was the leading district in shutting down migrant schools in 2006, so it doesn't have any interest in [supporting a migrant schools' association]. ... Some [of the district's migrant schools] have also become "preschools" and don't call themselves primary schools anymore [making the existence of an association less likely].
>
> (HL1P1)

Fengtai also lacks such an association. Principals in the district stated that migrant schools in Fengtai are relatively isolated from each other, and interaction among them – particularly between licensed and unlicensed schools and among unlicensed schools themselves – is very limited.

Ultimately, a model closer to the one found in Chaoyang has, thus far, not been adopted by other districts, and, at least among the other inner suburban districts, it is unlikely that they will be based on two factors: the attitudes of the Shijingshan, Haidian, and Fengtai district education commissions towards migrant schools, and the increasingly aggressive demolition of migrant schools. In terms of the latter, the number of migrant schools in each district has been declining, making it less likely that district education commissions would want to devote time and resources into supporting such associations.

### Migrant school teachers' association

In 2009, a migrant school teachers' association was also created. Made up of and run by migrant school teachers, it receives support from a local NGO and a research center jointly run by a local university and a university in Hong Kong. The association's primary goals include improving the lives of migrant school teachers, strengthening their teaching ability, and protecting their rights and ensuring that they enjoy the same treatment as public school teachers. At the time of fieldwork, it had over 100 members, representing over 100 licensed and unlicensed schools across almost all of the districts. Similar to the migrant school principals' association, however, it also lacks members from Fengtai.

Though the organization has events or meetings about once a month, most of its focus is on publishing a monthly newspaper and magazine for migrant school teachers. Both publications serve as a channel through which teachers can write about their views, problems, concerns, and goals, and discuss policies and developments. According to an officer of the association:

> Most teachers aren't able to watch television and cannot go on the Internet. Many don't know how to use the Internet or don't have the resources to do so. They may not be able to go to Internet cafés, and their schools may not have computers. Schools may also not have newspapers. This school's copy of the newspaper is bought by me every morning. Many teachers don't have televisions, and their schools don't have televisions. ... Information about the schools, teachers, and students is put into the magazine so that teachers can all read it.
>
> (XL1T1)

It is difficult to assess the association's impact given its short history. By mid-2010, it had begun to build relationships with several NGOs, the local media, and academics, helping to increase awareness about the problems of migrant school teachers in the process. Yet it had not been able to interact with the government and lacked direct channels to impact policy. Though its influence may grow as it builds more relationships, there remain obstacles to its success as a potential forum for larger change. At the time of fieldwork, not only did it lack government approval and an office of its own, but, according to the officer interviewed, membership was still limited; even within the sample, many teachers interviewed had not heard of it, while others were too busy to participate or were simply not interested.

*Migrant parent activists*

Based on interviews with principals, teachers, and parents, most migrant workers with children in migrant schools have not adopted strategies to try to change their children's educational situation. Most are too busy to spend a substantial amount of time with their children, and most do not regularly interact with their children's principals and teachers, let alone actors like NGOs, academics, and the government. In addition, most lack knowledge about their children's rights, as well as the time and opportunities to try to understand the relevant policies. The majority of parents interviewed emphasized that they are too poorly educated to understand the policies, frequently referring to themselves as "uncultured" (*mei wenhua*).[10] When asked whom they turn to for help when it comes to their children's education, parents said that they primarily rely on themselves (*kao ziji*) but may sometimes seek help or information from relatives, other community members, or migrant school teachers. None discussed taking any type of action beyond this. For example, when asked whether or not they have taken any action in response to problems concerning their children's education, the parents in one family replied by stating that they are "uncultured," so they can only seek their children's teachers for help (FU2F1). When asked about their familiarity with the policy situation and their children's educational rights, one parent responded by stating that it is very important to understand the policies, but they have had no opportunities to learn about them. The parent added that, even if their children's teachers gave them such information, they would not be able to understand it, as they only have "primary school culture" (*xiaoxue wenhua*) (SL2F3). As one parent put it: "We had very simple schooling. We don't understand much" (HU2F1).[11]

In contrast, a small proportion of the more well-off migrant parents – mainly those whose children attend local public schools – have taken to activism in the area since the mid- to late 2000s. These parents have begun to adopt action in the hopes of improving their children's educational opportunities and ensuring that they are given the same treatment as local children.

By the time of fieldwork, there had been two major cases of such action. The first was an effort to have migrant children included in the computerized lottery system for entry into Beijing's public middle schools. According to a leading parent involved, in early 2010, a group of migrant workers with children in public schools in Haidian organized a petition, as well as several rallies outside the Beijing and Haidian education commissions. Initially the effort of a few parents, the group eventually grew to over 30, and more than 2,000 people signed the petition. Though it cannot be said for certain, it is speculated that this effort – and the local media attention it attracted – played at least a small role in the decision that year to include migrant children in the lottery system for entry into public middle schools in Beijing (Yang 2010). Second, parents organized a petition to cancel the requirement for migrant children to return to their place of *hukou* registration for their university entrance exam, a barrier that has prevented migrant children from attending high school in the cities. According to a parent involved, over 7,000 signatures had been collected by mid-2010. In late 2010,

*Gongren ribao* (*Workers' Daily*) reported that the petition – signed by 13,000 people, about 90 percent of which were migrant parents in Beijing – had been submitted to the government's education departments but had yet to result in any response (Yang 2010). In August 2012, the State Council did issue a set of basic principles regarding the gradual lifting of *hukou* restrictions on the exam. However, not only must migrant parents and students meet certain eligibility criteria, but the Ministry of Education also stated that local provincial and city governments would be allowed to determine their own policies based on population trends and available resources (Cheng 2012). A follow-up conversation with a prominent migrant school principal in mid-2013 indicated that migrant students in Beijing are still only able to attend vocational schools and junior colleges.

Both of these efforts were primarily organized by migrant parents with children in public schools, with some support from a local NGO. According to a long-time researcher in the area, the parents involved have been relatively wealthier and more cultured. As a result, the issues they address are not necessarily those most urgent to children in migrant schools. For example, a leading parent activist involved in the two cases discussed above expressed that, if the university entrance exam issue is resolved (and migrant children are allowed to remain in the cities for high school), then other key educational problems faced by migrant children, including those related to middle school education and the high school entrance exam, will no longer be issues. One parent involved also maintained that research on *compulsory* education for migrant children is becoming outdated, and another asserted that researchers should focus more on issues concerning higher education. Such assertions indicate that the views and problems of migrants with children in migrant schools may be largely overlooked by these parent activists. Ultimately, however, the impact of these activists remains low; only a small proportion of migrant parents have become involved, and local government actors have generally avoided interacting with them.

## The limited impact of civil society

As mentioned earlier, there are three key motives among the civil society actors involved: to provide support to migrant schools and their students and teachers, to raise awareness and spread information about the situations of migrant schools and their students, and to influence government and policy. The above discussion illustrates that those actors aiming to influence government and policy have encountered many obstacles, and state–civil society interaction in the area remains limited. In regard to providing support to and substantially improving the situations of migrant schools, evidence indicates that the overall impact of these actors has been low as well. Examples can be found in the following statements made by principals in the sample:

> These actors don't have much of an impact [on our school]. Researchers may come and conduct studies, but some are objective, and [their research] won't immediately have an impact. ... They might have a larger impact

on migrant children as a group [but they won't have much impact on our school's situation].

(PL1P1)

[Actors like] NGOs come and do a little tutoring and provide some help to the students, but they cannot resolve the basic problems. The government is still the key.

(HU1P1)

[Our sources of support] aren't fixed. In terms of regular support, [the main source of support] is the government. ... If you rely on [other actors] to try to resolve the problems, the impact will be limited. ... The government has the real strength, so we have to rely on the government.

(HL2P1)

Based on the sample of schools, direct support from organizations or universities outside of mainland China has also been small in scale and is often limited to donations to a few select migrant schools. In addition, the extent to which migrant schools benefit from the work of civil society can vary among licensed schools, between licensed and unlicensed schools, and to a certain extent among unlicensed schools, illustrating the complex impact these actors have on the schools.

What is more, civil society actors have had a limited impact on the sharing of information, with major consequences for their existing knowledge about the local policy environment (and how it affects migrant schools and their students) and subsequently their ability to provide more targeted services and support. While efforts by actors like NGOs and the media have helped increase public awareness about the general problems of migrant schools over time, there remain serious gaps in knowledge, particularly concerning policies at the central and especially municipal and district levels. For example, among the individuals interviewed at the 12 local NGOs in the sample, half expressed that they were either unfamiliar with the municipal and district policies or had some knowledge of the municipal policies but no knowledge of district-level situations. Most academics and researchers in the sample also did not have in-depth knowledge about the district-level situations. Such gaps in knowledge have had consequences for migrant families. The majority of parents interviewed were unfamiliar with the policies and situations at the municipal and district levels, and only six families expressed having a little knowledge from watching the news or talking to friends and relatives. None had received such information from other actors like NGOs. Yet nearly 90 percent of them stressed the importance of learning about the policies and the educational opportunities available to their children.

### Factors limiting the impact of civil society

Four key factors have shaped the involvement of these actors and limited their capacity to have a large-scale impact. First, the lack of transparency in decision making and the low level of state–civil society interaction in the policy area limit their influence, and, based on fieldwork, the municipal and district governments generally either disregard or tolerate their existence. The obstacles civil society actors face – both in building relationships with key actors in the municipal and district governments and in improving the situations of migrant schools – illustrate the continued dominance of the government in determining the fate of migrant schools and their students.

A second factor involves the levels of interaction between the various actors. Not only is state–civil society interaction low, but there is also limited collaboration among many civil society actors themselves, as well as between civil society actors and many migrant schools. There is, for instance, little collaboration between the principals' and teachers' associations. Moreover, interaction between academics and researchers and many migrant schools remains limited, and families with children in these schools often lack the channels to interact with actors like researchers, NGOs, and the media. There are of course exceptions; for example, many of the researchers and NGOs involved regularly exchange information and ideas with each other. Overall, however, there is still a lack of interaction in key areas in which closer collaboration could more greatly benefit migrant schools and their students.

This limited interaction is at least in part a result of the existence of tensions between certain actors. For example, the lack of collaboration between the principals' and teachers' associations stems largely from concerns among many principals that their teachers will acquire too much power and make demands that they are unable to meet. Such principals have therefore adopted a position in which they "do not oppose [the teachers' association] but also do not support [it]" (XL1T1). In addition, a common view, especially among academics and researchers and some NGOs, is that migrant school principals run their schools like businesses (see Chapter 3). As Wang (2008: 693) asserts: "It is a matter of growing concern that many [migrant schools] are run essentially for profit rather than to provide basic education services." This view – based primarily on the unconfirmed observation of many academics and researchers that these principals pocket a substantial amount of the money earned through tuition after paying teachers' salaries and other expenses like rent – can then affect the views of government officials, who may consult these academics and researchers. Indeed, the perception of migrant school principals as profit-seeking individuals was mentioned by the Haidian official interviewed but not by the Shijingshan and Fengtai officials, particularly interesting in light of the higher level of interaction between researchers and the Haidian district government (see Chapter 5). While many principals continue to see building relationships with academics and researchers as an opportunity to help their schools, this perception has inhibited the establishment of close relationships between certain key academics and researchers and government actors on the one hand and migrant schools on the other. All of this sheds additional light on the complex factors shaping civil society involvement in the area, with implications for the capacity of these actors to collaborate and generate larger change.

Third, district policy approaches and reputations have an important impact on the work of civil society actors in the policy area. This is most apparent when looking at Fengtai, where licensed and unlicensed migrant schools are relatively isolated, not only from each other, but also from migrant schools in other districts and actors like NGOs, researchers, and university student groups. When asked whether or not they organize events or programs in Fengtai or about their knowledge of the district's situation, several NGOs, researchers, and even migrant school principals and teachers from other districts simply responded by saying that Fengtai no longer has many migrant schools, often emphasizing that there were none in the district at one point in time. In other words, Fengtai has been brushed aside by many, even though it had roughly the same number of migrant schools as Shijingshan at the time of fieldwork. Interestingly, among the unlicensed schools visited in Haidian, Shijingshan, and Fengtai, the school with the most connections (e.g. with researchers, universities, and NGOs) was located in Shijingshan, the least controversial of the three districts. Thus district-level situations and policy approaches can significantly affect where civil society actors focus their work, with consequences for the amount of external support migrant schools in the different districts receive.

Further complicating the situation is that the amount of interaction between the district education commissions and civil society actors also varies. Based on interviews, Shijingshan's education commission has occasionally consulted academics and researchers, whose expertise can help guide and inform policy decisions, but it has seldom interacted with other actors like NGOs. Despite some tensions with the local media, Haidian's education commission has developed close relationships with academics and researchers and has sometimes interacted with NGOs; in collaboration with one organization, for example, the district created an association that provides teacher training for a number of licensed and unlicensed migrant schools. In contrast, Fengtai's education commission has had very little contact with civil society actors like researchers and NGOs.

These differences affect the extent to which pressure from such actors is able to influence district-level decision making. Indeed, unlike those in Fengtai, the officials interviewed in Shijingshan and especially Haidian expressed sometimes feeling pressure from the media, migrant school principals, and migrant parents. As mentioned in Chapter 5, pressure from the media played a role in driving the Shijingshan education commission's prompt response when the sudden closure of a migrant school by its principal left about 170 students without a school to attend. In Haidian, pressure from actors like the media and NGOs affected the education commission's decision in 2006 to allow some schools it had tried to shut down to continue operation. Though such occurrences have been relatively isolated and infrequent, they provide further evidence of the complex relationship between civil society involvement and district-level dynamics.

A fourth factor affecting the work of many of these actors is related to location and distance. As previously shown, the reality is that most NGOs in this area are located in Chaoyang and Changping, while many universities and research institutions are concentrated in Haidian and Chaoyang. Distance then has become an additional factor limiting the number of civil society actors working with schools in particular districts.

## The limited impact of civil society and continued feelings of exclusion among principals, teachers, and families

The above findings illustrate the complexity of civil society involvement in migrant children's education in Beijing and have important implications for migrant schools and their students at both the municipal and district levels. At the municipal level, there remain strong feelings of social exclusion among migrant school principals and teachers and families with children attending migrant schools, demonstrating not only that they do not receive much government support but that their situations have also not been significantly improved by civil society. Interviewees expressed feeling an overall lack of support and subsequently power to generate larger change (see Table 7.2).

At the same time, while difficult to measure given the problems concerning data discussed in Chapters 2 and 3, the level of exclusion experienced by principals, teachers, and families also differs across districts. For migrant schools themselves, the amount of interaction with and support from actors like researchers and NGOs can vary across districts. Migrant schools in Fengtai, for example, generally receive much less societal attention than schools in Haidian. At one of the district's licensed migrant schools, for instance, the principal pointed out that their school has had extremely little interaction with actors like NGOs, academics, and the media and has had to instead rely on the district education commission for any support or assistance (FL1P1). The lack of training opportunities and insurance for migrant school teachers, as well as the lack of opportunities to engage with and learn from public school teachers, can vary across districts as well. And although the lack of interaction between migrant school students and their public school counterparts is largely a general trend – and feelings of discrimination and unequal treatment were reflected by most families in the sample – migrant schools that are better connected are more likely to have opportunities for such interaction, which usually means schools in districts like Chaoyang and Haidian. Furthermore, the lack of channels through which migrant parents receive support and information about their children's educational options is also a general trend, but the tendency for actors like NGOs to work in particular areas does exclude migrant communities in certain districts, the best example being those in Fengtai. Such trends have implications for the extent to which migrant parents lack a voice. For example, even though those involved in recent petitions and rallies were mainly parents of migrant children attending public schools, the fact that they were predominantly based in Haidian indicates that there are differences among the districts.

Ultimately, there was a general feeling among migrant school principals and teachers in the sample that the municipal and district governments are focused

*Table 7.2* Continued evidence of exclusion: views of principals, teachers, and families in the sample

| | |
|---|---|
| Migrant school principals | *A lack of government support and assistance:*<br>• As one principal stated: "We principals are all tired. … Beijing is doing subtraction. That is, the number of migrant schools can only decrease and must not increase." (HL1P1)<br><br>• According to one principal: "We have brought [many issues like teachers' insurance] to the attention of the municipal education commission, as well as district education commission leaders. … You could say we have talked about the issues with officials at large meetings and small meetings. … They don't respond. They say the problem[s] cannot be resolved. We want to improve our teachers' well-being and at least protect their livelihood. But we cannot do it. We are powerless. We aren't able to do it. Looking at the response of the government departments, what can we do?" (YL1P1)<br><br>• One principal stated that he was familiar with the central and Beijing municipal policies but added: "Whether or not I'm familiar with them, what difference does it make?" (SU1P1)<br><br>*Feelings of exclusion among unlicensed schools:*<br>• As one principal asserted: "We are a school that is not recognized by the education commission, that doesn't have a license. So we cannot get any financial assistance from society." (HU2P1)<br><br>• When asked about the school's lack of relationships with civil society actors, one principal simply said: "Schools without licenses are like children without *hukou* [*hei hukou haizi*]." (XU1P1) |
| Migrant school teachers | *A lack of government and societal support:*<br>• When asked about her interaction with actors like the district education commission or NGOs, one teacher said that she had never had any contact with government actors and had only occasionally interacted with a few NGOs, comparing migrant workers like herself to "people living in a crevice" (*shenghuo zai jiafeng de ren*). (SU2T3)<br><br>• The following was translated from a quote made by a teacher in a 2009 issue of the migrant school teachers' association's newspaper: "When [one migrant school was recently] demolished, the teachers did not get any compensation or assistance in finding another job. This reminds me of my own previous experience. When the school [where I was teaching] was demolished, the principal was overwrought, and no one asked about where the teachers would go. We could only look for a way out by ourselves. Demolition was inevitable, the school was powerless, and we migrant school teachers were even more of a disadvantaged group. Who is to blame? Who will resolve this? It's all empty talk. Real implementation requires more time. Our basic needs of clothing, food, housing, and transport for one day are inevitably linked to money. Don't wait, don't ask, don't delay. We can only rely on ourselves." |
| Migrant families | *A lack of interaction with and support from the government:*<br>• When asked if they interacted with or received support from local government actors like the education commission, street office, or neighborhood committee, one parent quickly said: "No." The daughter immediately chimed in saying: "We're outsiders [*waidiren*]." (FU2F1) |

*A lack of channels to acquire information:*

- As one parent expressed, learning about the policies is very important because they want to "help their children find a way out [*zhao chulu*]." The problem is that they do not have any opportunities to learn about the policy situation, and their school has not given them any relevant information about their children's options. (SU2F3)

*A lack of voice:*

- One parent expressed that understanding the policies is not that important because they are migrant workers and any views they might raise would just be treated as "empty talk" (*konghua*). (SU2F1)

*Feelings of social exclusion:*

- As one parent summarized, the situation is "unfair," as their children cannot get into "the good schools." As migrants, they "lack the conditions to compete with Beijing children." (SU2F3)

- As one interviewee stated: "I have lived in Beijing for 30 years, and I haven't even been integrated into society. When I live in the city areas I am uncomfortable, but when I come [to this village] I feel comfortable. I have been here for 30 years, my home is here. ... But it's still difficult for me to become integrated. To hope that migrant workers become integrated into society as soon as they come is a joke. How can we be integrated? We don't have the conditions. Even if we were integrated, we would still be living in places like basements [*dixiashi*]. There is a lot of discrimination." (SOC1S1)

Source: Author's fieldwork (2009–10).

more on issues of safety and public security than on improving the schools and that civil society actors therefore lack the power to generate broader change. As a result, a growing sense of disillusionment and hopelessness has emerged among a proportion of these principals and teachers. Some, for instance, expressed that research and media coverage on the subject are essentially useless and will not lead to positive change for their schools or the larger problems of migrant children. These feelings of hopelessness can be seen in the following remarks made by principals and teachers in the sample:

> The difficulties we face cannot be resolved. ... The issue should be resolved by society but they haven't done anything.
>
> (HU4P1)

> Many [researchers] and reporters come. But what can you all accomplish? What can you do for [migrant children and migrant schools]?
>
> (SU3P1)

> Talking [about the problems migrant school teachers face] is of no use. ... There is no point. ... [Understanding the policies] is useless. ... The problems cannot be resolved. Who would be willing to give money to a migrant school?
>
> (HL2T1)

Doing research and asking us questions cannot resolve any of our problems.
(SU4T2)

Despite the above, it is vital not to discount the work of civil society, including the important impact it can have on specific migrant schools or communities, and there are reasons to remain hopeful about its future role. Civil society actors have, thus far, played a critical part in bringing more attention to migrant children's education in Beijing. Their impact on the heightened visibility of migrant schools since the mid-1990s – evidenced, for instance, by increased international media coverage – is especially noteworthy. Some of these actors have also begun developing more innovative ways to assist migrant children that have gradually expanded the scope of civil society involvement in the policy area (the sponsoring of the creation of a few non-governmental migrant schools by a local foundation being an example).

## Towards a more comprehensive understanding of the policy environment surrounding migrant children's education in Beijing

There is "enormous diversity in how [civil society] is understood and manifested in different contexts around the world" (Malena and Heinrich 2007: 339). The role and impact of civil society actors can therefore vary considerably across different settings and policy areas (Edwards *et al.* 1999: 130; Malena and Heinrich 2007: 341). In the realm of migrant children's education in Beijing, the increased involvement of civil society is notable given the overall lack of government and policy support for migrant schools and their students. These actors do work that is of symbolic and political importance; that is, by working in an area such as migrant children's education, they highlight the potential limitations of government authority and the possibilities for broader socio-political reform (see Howell 2003: 208).

This chapter shows, however, that, despite their initial role in bringing migrant children's education to the attention of the government and society, civil society actors in Beijing have been unable to have a large-scale impact in the policy area. This is largely a result of the low level of government support for their work and limited state–civil society interaction, which, as established earlier in the chapter, is an integral factor shaping the impact of civil society on welfare provision in China. Based on fieldwork, the Beijing municipal and district governments have not taken discernible steps to control or absorb the civil society actors discussed above or given them extensive support or recognition. Instead, they have primarily *tolerated* those actors that have refrained from openly opposing government objectives (including university student groups and most of the NGOs involved) and *ignored* those that lack government authorization and are seen as a potential threat to policy goals (mainly the principals' and teachers' associations and parent activists). While coverage of key developments and problems by independent and state-run media has put pressure on local government actors on certain occasions, the media's capacity to stimulate broader policy change is still low. Academics and researchers are in the best position to bring about larger change in the area, but their overall level of interaction with the government has declined since the early to mid-2000s, and their impact is unclear. In other words, in spite of their increased involvement since the mid- to late 1990s, civil society actors in Beijing have not been able to play a substantial role in the policy process in this area, providing a counterexample to the findings of Teets (2008: 3), who argues:

> Through the ability of these [civil society] organizations to transmit credible information to local government about societal interests and to transmit information to society and higher levels of government about local officials' reputation and behavior, they facilitate more pluralism and accountability in the policy process at the local level.

Moreover, a deeper exploration indicates that the role and impact of these actors have also been influenced by district-level dynamics, with consequences for the amount of attention and support migrant schools in different districts receive.

The above exploration illustrates the complex, political nature of the policy environment surrounding migrant children's education in Beijing. Given that the policy area has been closely linked to issues concerning migration and labor – an area of welfare provision in China in which civil society actors like NGOs have often had little policy impact (Cheng *et al.* 2010) – it is perhaps not surprising that the actors discussed above have been unable to acquire much influence in the local policy process. This analysis provides an example of a case in which the role and impact of civil society actors involved in welfare provision are significantly shaped by the extent to which they are seen by the local government as representing issues that might provoke social instability, consistent with the arguments raised by Howell (2007: 19) and Cheng *et al.* (2010: 1089–90, 1104). These findings therefore strengthen the understanding of policy implementation in the area, including which actors are included or excluded and why, and shed further light on the range of factors affecting the situations of migrant schools and their students at the municipal and district levels, with subsequent implications for patterns of exclusion.

Ultimately, while the lack of substantial government support for the work of the civil society actors discussed has had serious consequences for the role they are able to play, the increased involvement of civil society in what continues to be seen as a delicate policy area is, in itself, a significant indicator of the potential for larger change. Based on the findings discussed above and in previous chapters, the next and final chapter proposes ways in which both the government and civil society can work towards improving the situation of migrant schools and their students and highlights the importance of adopting a more collaborative approach.

## Notes

1  According to Malena and Heinrich (2007: 338): "Despite its varied interpretations, civil society can be broadly understood as the space in society where collective citizen action takes place. This notion, however, of a *societal space* animated by a complex set of actors, activities, interests, and values has in fact proved extremely difficult to operationalise." According to Kaldor (2003: 11–20), there are four major categories of civil society actors: (1) *social movements*, "organizations, groups of people, and individuals, who act together to bring about transformation in society"; (2) *non-governmental organizations*, which are "voluntary, in contrast to compulsory organizations like the state or some traditional, religious organizations, and they do not make profits, like corporations"; (3) *social organizations*, "organizations representing particular sectors of society defined in social terms" that include "professional organizations (societies of lawyers, doctors, employers, trade unions or farmers) [and] community groups of women or youth"; and (4) *national or religious movements*, "organizations based on particular sections of society, defined in terms of culture, kin or religion."
2  These characteristics are primarily adapted from a framework discussed by Malena and Heinrich (2007: 341).
3  While the principals' and teachers' associations might be considered as being a part of migrant schools, they have become largely independent actors in their own right. They can be seen as what Kaldor (2003) refers to as "social organizations" and are therefore included in this discussion.
4  One of the only major studies to include Fengtai as a core case was Lü (2007), the research for which was primarily conducted in 1999–2000. The other districts focused on were Chaoyang and Haidian.
5  See Jiao (1996) and Yuan (1997) for two early examples.
6  Based on fieldwork, the earliest NGO involved was created in the late 1990s by a researcher and provided community-based services for migrants. Most, however, were either created in the mid-2000s or only started to pay attention to migrant children's education in the mid-2000s.
7  See Appendix C for additional information about the work of these organizations.
8  There were exceptions. One organization in the sample, for instance, worked with six licensed schools and only one unlicensed school based on the recognition that unlicensed schools are more likely to be shut down at any given time and are therefore less stable (YOL4S2).
9  According to Lü (2007: 233–4), there was little interaction among migrant schools in the mid- to late 1990s.
10  Most parents in the sample were either primary or middle school graduates, and a couple of the parents interviewed had had no previous schooling (see Appendix B).
11  There are, of course, exceptions. See, for example, Shi *et al.* (2011).

## Bibliography

BBC News Asia-Pacific. "Migrant Schools Closed in Chinese Capital." August 17, 2011. www.bbc.co.uk/news/world-asia-pacific-14556906 (accessed August 27, 2011).

Chamberlain, Heath B. "On the Search for Civil Society in China." *Modern China* 19, no. 2 (April 1993): 199–215.

Cheng, Joseph Y. S., Kinglun Ngok, and Wenjia Zhuang. "The Survival and Development Space for China's Labor NGOs: Informal Politics and Its Uncertainty." *Asian Survey* 50, no. 6 (November/December 2010): 1082–106.

Cheng, Yingqi. "Migrant Children to Sit *Gaokao* in Cities." *China Daily*, September 7, 2012. www.chinadaily.com.cn/china/2012-09/07/content_15740993.htm (accessed January 21, 2013).

Davis, Deborah. "Chinese Social Welfare: Policies and Outcomes." *The China Quarterly* 119 (September 1989): 577–97.

Edwards, Michael, David Hulme, and Tina Wallace. "NGOs in a Global Future: Marrying Local Delivery to Worldwide Leverage." *Public Administration and Development* 19, no. 2 (May 1999): 117–36.

Goodburn, Charlotte. "Learning from Migrant Education: A Case Study of the Schooling of Rural Migrant Children in Beijing." *International Journal of Educational Development* 29, no. 5 (September 2009): 495–504.

Han, Jialing. "Beijingshi liudong ertong yiwu jiaoyu zhuangkuang diaocha baogao" [Report on the Investigation of the Compulsory Education Situation of Children of the Floating Population in Beijing]. *Qingnian yanjiu* [*Youth Studies*] 8 and 9 (2001): 1–7, 10–18.

Howell, Jude. "Women's Organizations and Civil Society in China: Making a Difference." *International Feminist Journal of Politics* 5, no. 2 (July 2003): 191–215.

Howell, Jude. "Civil Society in China: Chipping Away at the Edges." *Development* 50, no. 3 (September 2007): 17–23.

Jacobs, Andrew. "China Takes Aim at Rural Influx." *The New York Times*, August 29, 2011. www.nytimes.com/2011/08/30/world/asia/30china.html?_r=1&ref=china (accessed August 31, 2011).

Jiao, Xin. "Liudong renkou zinü jiuxue youwang" [There is Hope for Children of the Floating Population to Go to School]. *Zhongguo jiaoyubao* [*China Education Daily*], June 7, 1996, p. 1.

Kaldor, Mary. "Civil Society and Accountability." *Journal of Human Development* 4, no. 1 (2003): 5–27.

Kwong, Julia. "Educating Migrant Children: Negotiations between the State and Civil Society." *The China Quarterly* 180 (December 2004): 1073–88.

Lü, Shaoqing. *Liushou haishi liudong? "Mingong chao" zhong de ertong yanjiu* [*Left Behind or Migration? An Empirical Study on Children of Rural Migrants*]. Beijing: Zhongguo nongye chubanshe [China Agriculture Press], 2007.

Malena, Carmen and Volkhart Finn Heinrich. "Can We Measure Civil Society? A Proposed Methodology for International Comparative Research." *Development in Practice* 17, no. 3 (June 2007): 338–52.

Ni, Guanghui and Yuanyuan Zhao. "Jing: 30 duo suo dagong zidi xuexiao chaiqian, shu qianming haizi ruxue nan" [Beijing: The Demolition of Over 30 Migrant Schools, Thousands of Children Face Difficulties Enrolling in School]. *Renmin ribao* [*People's Daily*], March 1, 2010. http://news.xinhuanet.com/employment/2010-03/01/content_13072448.htm (accessed April 22, 2010).

Ren, Bo and Zhipeng Mao. "Closure of Migrant Children Schools Exposes Education Deficiency." *Caijing Magazine*, September 4, 2006. http://english.caijing.com.cn/2006-09-04/100043075.html (accessed June 6, 2009).

Shang, Xiaoyuan. "Looking for a Better Way to Care for Children: Cooperation between the State and Civil Society in China." *Social Service Review* 76, no. 2 (June 2002): 203–28.

Shi, Minglei, Jialin Wang, and Ding Du. "Beijing 30 suo dagong zidi xiao shou guanting tongzhi yingxiang 3 wanming xuesheng" [30 Migrant Schools in Beijing Receive Closure Notices, 30,000 Students Impacted]. *Xinjingbao* [*The Beijing News*], August 16, 2011. http://news.sina.com.cn/c/2011-08-16/040122996001.shtml (accessed October 10, 2011).

Teets, Jessica C. "Improving Governance in China: The Role of Civil Society in Local Public Policy." Paper presented at the annual meeting of the Midwest Political Science

Association National Conference, Chicago, IL, April 3, 2008. www.allacademic.com/ meta/p_mla_apa_research_citation/2/6/7/4/9/p267492_index.html (accessed November 4, 2008).

Wang, Lu. "The Marginality of Migrant Children in the Urban Chinese Educational System." *British Journal of Sociology of Education* 29, no. 6 (November 2008): 691–703.

Yang, Shijian. "Gaokao nantuo hukou jiban, feijingji jiazhang huyu quxiao huji xianzhi" [Difficulties Escaping *Hukou* Restraints for the University Entrance Exam, Migrant Parents Appeal to Cancel Household Registration Restrictions]. *Gongren ribao* [*Workers' Daily*], December 9, 2010. www.chinanews.com/edu/2010/12-09/2710122.shtml (accessed March 14, 2012).

Yuan, Xinwen. "Bierang 'liudong de haizi' chengwei xin wenmang" [Don't Let "Floating Children" Become the New Illiterates]. *Guangming ribao* [*Guangming Daily*], March 24, 1997, p. 1.

Zhang, Dong. "Beijing dagong zidi xin xuenian: 'Wo xihuan zheli de laoshi'" [A New Academic Year for Migrant Children: "I Like the Teachers Here"]. *Zhongguo jiaoyubao* [*China Education Daily*], September 2, 2011. www.jyb.cn/basc/xw/201109/ t20110902_451824.html (accessed November 11, 2011).

Zhuang, Qinghong and Xiaoge Lin. "Beijing 30 suo dagong zidi xuexiao jiang chaiqian xiaoshi, boji shangwan haizi" [30 Migrant Schools in Beijing Will Be Demolished and Disappear, Affecting Thousands of Children]. *Zhongguo qingnianbao* [*China Youth Daily*], February 23, 2010. http://news.xinhuanet.com/edu/2010-02/23/content_ 13028254.htm (accessed August 2, 2012).

# 8  Implications for the future

As emphasized throughout this book, migrant schools remain a crucial source of education for migrant children in the capital city. In light of the Beijing municipal and district policy approaches discussed, including recent rounds of demolition and efforts to shut down unlicensed migrant schools, the level of government and societal support these schools receive is, now more than ever, a subject of critical importance. As the number of migrant families grows, the extent to which migrant children still face barriers in attaining basic education will have enormous consequences for the continued social exclusion of this segment of society. This final chapter summarizes the key findings of the study and their implications, both for migrant children themselves and for the understanding of the complex linkages between migration, education, and policy in urban China. It then discusses why it is both necessary and beneficial for the government to take immediate action and provides a list of policy and program recommendations and suggestions for future research.

## The complexities of policy implementation and implications for social stratification

As previously discussed, studies on rural–urban migration in China often emphasize the predominant role of the *hukou* system when accounting for the problems migrants encounter in the cities, including the educational problems of migrant children. However, central-level policy changes, as well as developments in cities like Shanghai, indicate that it is possible to challenge the impact of institutional barriers on the social exclusion of migrant children and the situation of migrant schools, even in cities with large migrant populations. In other words, the *hukou* system, while of fundamental importance, must be considered alongside the complex effects of decentralization and local context when trying to understand the problems migrant workers and their families face in Chinese cities. This study illustrates the critical role of policy implementation and local factors in the policy process, consistent with the growing discussion of decentralization in China by Wong (2007) and others. It sheds particular light on the significance of these local dynamics in a context in which the Chinese government at different levels is trying to cope with an increasingly large rural migrant population in the cities.

The empirical findings of this study can be summarized as follows. Chapter 4 shows that, whereas central policies on migrant children's education have called for the increased management of and support for migrant schools, the Beijing municipal government has largely omitted the latter from its policies, primarily because of concerns about population growth and social instability. Even though central policies since the early 2000s have highlighted the importance of educational provision for migrant children, Beijing – home to the central government – has actually been one of the more reluctant cities to comply. Using Shijingshan, Fengtai, and Haidian districts as cases, Chapter 5 illustrates that policy implementation has been made more complicated because of district-level variations. Based on the three trajectories identified, there are significant differences between what district governments, and district education commissions in particular, view as the main issue at hand (including its level of importance or urgency) and the approaches adopted in response. Though the district officials interviewed each conveyed a desire to ensure that migrant children receive compulsory education, the complex, political nature of educational provision for this group has meant that some districts are better able or equipped – or sometimes more willing – to address the issue than others. The approaches adopted have been influenced by social, demographic, economic, and political factors, including the size of the district and its migrant population, the number of migrant schools, the district's financial situation, other policy interests and priorities, and external pressures from actors like the media. The factors that have been most instrumental in driving each district's approach also vary, signifying that implementation does not operate in a systematic manner.

Not only do these findings demonstrate the degree of flexibility given to district governments in the implementation process, but they also have implications for the situations of migrant schools and their students. Chapter 6 shows that decentralization has led to a gap between central-level policy ideals and the local reality in Beijing and that the situations of migrant schools in the city continue to be shaped by four key problem areas: a general lack of resources and poor physical conditions, a low quality of teaching, instability, and difficulties acquiring licenses. Evidence indicates that the municipal *and* district-level approaches have had a critical impact on the survival and development of migrant schools in these four areas. Only when both levels are considered can one begin to more fully understand the situations of these schools and their students.

In addition, these policy approaches affect migrant schools indirectly, through civil society. Given the policy environment in Beijing, the increased involvement of civil society actors is a significant development. However, Chapter 7 illustrates that the capacity of these actors to generate larger policy change remains, on the whole, low. Most NGOs and university student organizations focus on providing services to migrant schools and migrant children directly, often on a small scale because of limited resources, and have lacked strong channels to interact with the government. The principals' and teachers' associations and parent activists are seen as potential threats to policy goals and have generally been ignored by the government. Though independent and state-run media frequently report on major policy decisions and developments, their capacity to stimulate change has been inconsistent, shedding light on the sometimes unpredictable nature of the decision-making process. Academics and researchers are best positioned to influence policy, but their overall level of interaction with government actors in the area has somewhat declined since the early to mid-2000s, and their impact on the policy process remains unclear. Limited collaboration among these various sets of actors has further inhibited the ability of civil society to generate policy change. What is more, district-level situations and policy approaches have influenced where in the city these actors tend to work, and the extent to which district governments interact with and support them has affected their capacity to assist migrant schools and their students. Ultimately, the municipal and district governments retain control of the policy process, with minimal external interference, and there has emerged a fundamental divide between the actors officially responsible for migrant children's education (local governments and public schools) on the one hand, and the intended beneficiaries (migrant children and migrant schools) and civil society on the other.

The outcomes of decentralized decision making – and the reasons behind them – can be far from straightforward, and these findings demonstrate that the case of migrant children's education in Beijing is no exception. Drawing on the broader literature on policy processes and decentralization, as well as literature on policy processes, migration, urbanization, and educational inequality in China, this analysis contributes a more nuanced understanding of the process by which policies in the area are implemented and the micro-politics of educational provision for these children in the capital city. It shows that failing to analyze this process, including the roles of policy history and local context, would lead to an incomplete understanding of the diversity of factors affecting migrant schools and their students and subsequently patterns of social exclusion. Though knowledge of the precise motives driving policy implementation is limited by the lack of transparent decision making, these findings illustrate that implementation in this area is far from administrative in nature and is influenced by social, economic, and political considerations at the municipal and district levels, with direct consequences for migrant children's education. Thus this study not only makes a valuable contribution to the conceptualization of policy processes in an urban Chinese context, but it also sheds light on the potential long-term effects of decentralization and differential policy implementation on trends in social stratification and the complex relationship between migration, education, and policy in China's cities.

## Towards increased social stratification and social instability: the costs of inaction to the government and society

In light of the continued demand for migrant schools in Beijing and the absence of accessible alternatives, the lack of support and assistance to these schools will have serious implications for the educational opportunities available to migrant children and, consequently, their growth and development. As previously established, however, many municipal and district officials in Beijing still view migrant children's education as a delicate policy area with implications for population growth and social stability. This constitutes a serious obstacle to reform, and adopting change will be challenging to say the least. Yet educational provision for migrant children in Beijing has become an increasingly pressing issue, especially in light of recent demolitions and closures of migrant schools. This section highlights three reasons why it is in the best interests of the central, Beijing municipal, and district governments not to allow the current situation in Beijing to persist.

First, if the demolition and shutting down of migrant schools in Beijing continue at the current rate, more and more migrant children will be left without schools to attend in the city. Recent events indicate that it is unlikely that all, or even a majority, of the migrant children involved are being placed into public schools. Instead, many have to return to their hometowns for further schooling. Though the exact proportion is unknown, estimates made by researchers and migrant school principals in the sample suggest that the situation is increasingly severe. For example, as was discussed in Chapter 6, following the demolition and closure of 13 migrant schools in Haidian and Chaoyang districts in 2011, it was estimated that a substantial number of children may have been unable to find new schools to attend and returned to their hometowns. While this technically increases the percentage of migrant children attending public schools in Beijing, it is only because a proportion of the city's migrant children have had to leave.

It may frequently be the case that, when migrant children return to their hometowns for further schooling, at least one parent stays in the city to support the family. Any rise in the number of migrant children going back to their hometowns without their parents should be concerning for the Chinese government given the problems "left-behind" children typically face (see Chapter 2).[1] As previously discussed, a growing percentage of migrant children are born and/or raised in cities and have not spent substantial periods of time living in rural areas. Upon their return, many are left under the care of grandparents or other relatives and lack emotional and psychological support. As a result, they may develop feelings of depression, anxiety, anger, and low self-confidence, all of which can affect their academic performance and growth and development. Moreover, the curricula used by migrant schools and schools in their hometowns can sometimes differ, which can lead to a decline in student performance and subsequently self-esteem (see Lü 2007; China Labour Bulletin 2008). If the current situation in Beijing persists, migrant children who are unable to enroll in a migrant or public school upon reaching school age may have to return to their hometowns at an even earlier age and could be denied a chance for a better education and a childhood with their parents by their sides. The potential consequences are severe; for example, as emphasized by China Labour Bulletin (2008), left-behind children are more vulnerable to commit or become victims of crimes.

Second, if the current situation persists, migrant children who stay in Beijing are likely to face a range of difficulties that will ultimately create more problems for the municipal and district governments. Children who are unable to enroll in public schools may keep bouncing from one migrant school to another as the government continues demolishing and shutting them down, with major consequences for the quality and stability of the education received. These children may end up entering the workforce after middle school or even earlier, contributing to a growing proportion of poorly educated, low-skilled migrant workers in the city.[2] This will have implications for societal development that the government will not be able to ignore. Not only would it negatively affect the migrant population itself, but it could also perpetuate or intensify trends in social stratification and exclusion, widen existing rural–urban disparities, and affect crime rates and social stability, the third of which has been a top concern driving the attitudes and approaches of the Beijing municipal and district governments towards migrant children's education in the first place. For the central government, continuing down the current path in Beijing would, by jeopardizing the growth and development of current and future generations of migrants, be detrimental to central-level efforts to reduce rural–urban inequalities, not to mention the building of a "harmonious society" advocated by former President Hu Jintao.

Third, migrant workers, who make up a significant proportion of Beijing's population, take on a range of necessary jobs that local residents do not want – jobs typically referred to as "dirty, tiring, arduous, and dangerous" (*zang lei ku xian*) – and make a critical contribution to the capital's economy. And, as many interviewees pointed out during fieldwork, the city's pursuit of urbanization, including the rapid construction of new office and apartment buildings after the demolition of migrant enclaves, would not be possible without the use of migrant labor. But the current policy environment concerning migrant children's education in Beijing could, if left unchanged, influence the decisions of these migrants to stay in the city, particularly when other cities, including Shanghai, have been more supportive, or it could lower the incentives for migrant workers with school-aged children to migrate to Beijing in the future. It could also lead to a higher proportion of migrant workers in Beijing who leave their children behind. Thus, in the long run, it is in the best interests of the central, Beijing municipal, and district governments to ensure that the capital city does not continue down a path that threatens the existence of migrant schools and the education and growth and development of migrant children.

## Policy and program recommendations

This study demonstrates that the Beijing municipal and district governments have fallen short of meeting the basic objectives stated in central policies and the basic needs of migrant children in migrant schools. There is an urgent need for formal policy change, with a focus on how the municipal and district governments and civil society can work towards meeting these needs and objectives. Before moving on, a few points should be emphasized. First, given the complexity surrounding the problems discussed, change will not happen overnight. As

Hannum (1999: 193) reminds us, trying to balance economic and societal objectives is a particularly difficult policy problem for developing countries, China being no exception. Second, there is no single solution to the problems discussed. A range of local factors and constraints can influence how the municipal and district governments view and approach migrant children's education. It is necessary to target any general proposals towards the particular context in which they are to be implemented; this requires innovative approaches including, for example, involvement from important local stakeholders and the mobilization of resources, and these approaches can be tested through pilot programs. As one researcher asserted, any solution should involve the use of "multiple levels, multiple channels, and multiple models" (GR1). The following is a list of recommendations based on the study's findings, with the ultimate goal of improving educational opportunities for migrant children in Beijing.

## 1. Clearer standards for policy implementation

Since the municipal and district governments continue to determine the fates of migrant schools in Beijing, it is useful to start with recommendations concerning policy implementation. This book illustrates that the policy of "two priorities," while a significant step forward, has given the Beijing municipal government the freedom to interpret central policies based on its views and concerns about population growth and social instability, and district governments the flexibility to implement central and municipal policies based on local circumstances. With decentralization in the delivery of services in China extending back to the 1980s (Davis 1989), it is uncertain whether or not the central government will create more specific guidelines for local governments in this area, especially in light of the differences between the pace and scale of reforms across localities. It is therefore necessary in the immediate future to identify steps that can be adopted at the municipal and district levels.

- *More specific guidelines for implementation.* Ultimately, there needs to be a clearer baseline for districts to follow. Beijing municipal policies are – not unlike their central-level counterparts – too vague in terms of the standards set and the language used, allowing districts to further diverge from central-level aspirations. Municipal policies should more strictly adhere to the principles and standards in central policies, particularly those regarding migrant schools. Once clearer guidelines are in place, the municipal government should enforce the standards and collaborate with the districts in their work. District governments should then set clearer guidelines for actors at the sub-district level (e.g. street offices and neighborhood committees).

### Necessary conditions

To achieve better, more standardized implementation at the district level, the first step needs to be taken by the municipal government. This would greatly enhance the capacity to hold district governments accountable. However, in light of the current policy environment in Beijing, it would be naive to expect major change immediately. There will need to be a greater recognition of the incentives discussed above and a change in attitude towards migrant children's education among influential municipal officials. Pressure from central-level leaders could be a potential stimulus for such change, though the likelihood of sustained pressure from the central government is unclear.

## 2. Increased support for migrant schools and monitoring of public schools

While the dual focus on the role of local governments and public schools is both pragmatic and necessary, a range of obstacles still prevent many migrant children from attending Beijing's public schools, and migrant schools remain a critical source of education for these children. It is therefore necessary to focus on both eliminating the barriers to public school education and improving the quality of migrant schools (see also Lü and Zhang 2004: 80–2; Wang 2008: 145–6). Given the lack of an official, comprehensive list of migrant schools in Beijing and the high mobility of the schools, ensuring the inclusion of all migrant schools will be challenging. The effort should be made to bring together existing lists and information compiled by the district education commissions, researchers, NGOs, and principals, and this information should be regularly updated based on demolitions and closures.

- *Management, guidance, and support for migrant schools.* Since it is unlikely that all migrant children will be absorbed into Beijing's public school system in the near future, the remaining migrant schools are valuable entities. More concerted efforts to improve the quality of these schools and their capacity to serve migrant children should be made in the immediate term, with the longer-term goal of ensuring that migrant children are more fully integrated into the public school system or a system of public schools and government-subsidized migrant schools similar to that in Shanghai.

  - *Management and guidance.* The municipal and district governments' "management" of migrant schools is currently focused more on safety concerns than on improving the quality of the schools. While the focus on safety is certainly important and necessary, there is also an urgent need for more standardized management and guidance in areas like teaching so that the way these schools are run is not determined solely by individual principals, some of whom may lack adequate training and experience.
  - *Support.* The municipal and district governments should increase their support for licensed *and* unlicensed migrant schools, particularly in terms of financial assistance and efforts to improve the quality of teaching (as in Shanghai). After demolitions and closures, the allocation of students

should be more systematic and transparent, and teachers should be given more concrete support. Schools that are demolished should be given assistance in finding new locaions.

- *Closer monitoring of public schools.* Public schools in Beijing have had a substantial amount of freedom in determining the entrance requirements for migrant children, and the few standards that exist (e.g. the elimination of various fees) have often not been adequately enforced. The municipal and district governments should create a system of checks and balances to ensure that eliminated fees are not charged and that the number of documents required is both consistent and reasonable.

## Necessary conditions

The process by which migrant schools are improved and barriers to enrollment in public schools are eliminated will be gradual. In order for these recommendations to be achieved, the guidelines should be explicitly defined in municipal policies so that districts have a clear set of standards to follow. The municipal government should also increase its share of the responsibility to eliminate disparities among districts in terms of the levels of assistance given to migrant schools.

### 3. Increased support for migrant school teachers

At the Fifth High-Level Group Meeting on Education for All in November 2005, then Premier Wen Jiabao stated:

> In China, respecting teachers is a traditional virtue. The nearly 10 million primary school teachers in this country are held in high esteem for their contributions to education. We have all along given major importance to setting up a sound teacher's training system, and we have never stopped improving teachers' working and living conditions. In our rural areas and least developed regions, most teachers are on a government payroll.
>
> (Wen 2005)

Migrant school teachers in Beijing, however, continue to receive low salaries, and most do not have insurance. In addition, though some migrant schools receive teacher training from their district education commission or NGOs, many still lack regular opportunities for training. The result has been a high proportion of poorly qualified teachers and high levels of teacher turnover, with consequences for the quality of education provided (see Lü and Zhang 2004: 75; Kwong 2006: 172).

- *Training.* Lü and Zhang (2004: 82) suggest the establishment of "[s]pecific qualification requirements and assessment standards ... for the school operators and a system of regular performance assessments for the teachers." To increase the likelihood that such requirements would be met, standardized training should be provided to all migrant school principals and teachers on a regular basis. This training should be the responsibility of the municipal and district education commissions and should involve teaching methods, curriculum, information about policies, and opportunities to exchange information and knowledge with public school principals and teachers. Licensed and unlicensed migrant schools across the districts should be included, so as not to widen the gap among migrant schools.

- *Subsidized salaries and insurance.* The Beijing municipal government should subsidize migrant school teachers' salaries, as has been done in Shanghai. Higher salaries and better treatment for these teachers would help the schools attract better quality teachers and lower teacher turnover.

*Necessary conditions*

Migrant school teachers have not been given adequate attention in the Beijing municipal and district policies. If the quality of education at migrant schools is to be improved, municipal policies should introduce targeted measures to improve the teaching ability and treatment of these teachers.

## 4. Increased state–civil society collaboration

While migrant children's education is primarily the responsibility of the government, the potential contribution of civil society should not be overlooked. The situation in Beijing calls for a more collaborative approach, in which the government should take advantage of the local knowledge, networks, and skills different sets of actors have to offer.

- *Greater collaboration.* Improving the situation of migrant schools requires cooperation between the municipal and district governments and civil society. This would enhance the capacity of actors like NGOs to assist migrant schools and would bring about a much needed change in the implementation process. In building these relationships, the government and civil society should ensure that licensed and unlicensed migrant schools across the districts, including the more peripheral and poorer ones, receive appropriate levels of attention and support.

*Necessary conditions*

In light of the current policy environment, these relationships will require time to build. The effort can start with academics and researchers, who are best positioned to influence policy and can serve as a key link between the various actors. Here, the continued perception of migrant school principals as profit-seeking individuals remains an obstacle, but the hope is that, with regular principal training and more systematic management of migrant schools by district governments, this will become less and less of a barrier. Ultimately, the municipal and district governments should see building these relationships as beneficial, as a way to increase their outreach and reputation and as a channel through which they can lessen their own burden, since civil society can be a source of additional resources (e.g. knowledge, manpower, and funding). For civil society actors, these relationships would boost their legitimacy, as well as enhance their understanding of the policy process and subsequently their capacity to generate larger change.

### 5. More systematic dissemination of information

The channels through which migrant workers with children in migrant schools can get information about their children's educational rights and options are limited. This has resulted in a general lack of knowledge and clarity about relevant policies and public school entrance requirements.

- *Disseminating information to teachers and parents.* To ensure that parents receive the necessary information and support, increased interaction between civil society, migrant school teachers, and parents is required. NGOs could, for example, create a simple publication for parents with summaries of relevant policies, information about NGO services and events, and a directory of nearby schools. In cases where a publication may not be appropriate (e.g. for parents who are illiterate), NGO staff and volunteers could regularly visit migrant schools and communities to talk to teachers and parents about these topics. Again, efforts should be made to include licensed and unlicensed schools across the districts.

### Necessary conditions

The successful dissemination of information requires the civil society actors involved to first familiarize themselves with the policies. As discussed in Chapter 7, many of these individuals lack a strong understanding of the local policies and situations, particularly at the district level. Appropriate channels should therefore be created. Academics and researchers generally have the greatest knowledge of the policies among these actors, though many are still unfamiliar with district-level dynamics. The first step would be for them to enhance their knowledge of the municipal *and* district-level situations and share the information with actors like NGOs.

### 6. Clearer allocation and use of funding

When it comes to government spending on migrant children's education, two key problems have emerged. First, financial disparities across districts have contributed to differences among policy approaches. Second, a lack of transparency has greatly limited the knowledge of government expenditure in the area.

- *Increased financial support from the municipal government.* Beijing municipal policies should more clearly spell out the distribution of financial responsibilities. The municipal government should also increase its level of financial support so that any constraints at the district level do not play such a large role in discouraging or restricting district governments in their work.[3]
- *Increased spending on migrant schools.* The municipal government's promise of new desks, chairs, podiums, and lights (*sanxin yiliang*) only applies to licensed migrant schools, and the supplies that migrant schools receive from public schools are often inadequate (see Chapters 4 and 6). For the quality of these schools to be improved, increased government spending is needed. In addition, the current subsidy for students attending licensed migrant schools in Beijing is negligible, especially since most of the city's migrant schools are unlicensed. The municipal government should, in line with the Compulsory Education Law, ensure that all migrant school students are not required to pay tuition. Eliminating tuition for these children would ultimately also increase the financial capacity of their parents to support their post-middle school education.

## Necessary conditions

Given the lack of access to data concerning financial expenditure on migrant children's education, these recommendations will be difficult to achieve. Those best positioned to acquire the information to begin identifying areas for reform are researchers in universities or institutes that have close working relationships with the relevant government departments. Areas in which further research would be especially beneficial include: trends in the use of educational funds on migrant schools relative to public schools; how the allocation of resources is determined and the impact on migrant schools in different districts; and the division of responsibilities and how, if at all, it is enforced.

## Future research

This study sheds important light on the growing urgency surrounding educational provision for migrant children in the capital city. Yet, despite the increased attention towards migrant children's education from those within China and abroad, it remains an understudied topic, and there is much room for further examination. Future research can include a larger-scale comparison of the demolition and shutting down of migrant schools across districts in Beijing, including the extent to which schools are being demolished or closed down and the approaches adopted towards the students and teachers. More research can also be done on migrant children's post-primary school education in different districts (e.g. the extent to which children receiving their primary school education in migrant schools are able to enroll in public middle schools, as well as the experiences of migrant children after middle school). A stronger knowledge of both would help in identifying more targeted measures to improve educational opportunities for migrant children in Beijing.

Since policy processes are context-specific, this study's findings cannot necessarily be applied to other cities. A natural next step would be to conduct similar studies in other cities with large migrant populations. For example, similar research in Shanghai would shed light on the extent to which recent steps taken by the municipal government there have been translated at the district level. Such research could also be conducted in cities like Wuhan and Xiamen to determine whether or not differential policy implementation affects cities with smaller migrant populations at a comparable level.

Additionally, the questions raised by this study can be extended to other policy areas like housing and health care. As discussed in Chapter 2, central-level leaders encouraged a shift towards the more positive treatment of migrant workers in the early 2000s. And there was, to an extent, a greater acceptance of migrant workers and a willingness to recognize their contributions to society and economic growth throughout much of the decade. There is reason to suspect, however, that this trend may be approaching its limits, at least in some localities. The findings of this study and recent developments in Beijing suggest the reemergence (or perhaps intensification) of concerns about the potential threat of the increasing inflow of migrant workers to local living standards and the local provision of services. As migrant workers and their families continue to increase as a percentage of local populations in cities like Beijing, the general sense of growing economic difficulties and increasing competition for services and the benefits of economic growth may become more and more of an issue. Further research is required.

## Notes

1 The problems of left-behind children have been attracting increasing government attention. In 2007, for instance, the All-China Women's Federation, the Ministry of Education, and several other organs in the central government initiated the "Same Sky" campaign, a major part of which involved creating a network of support for these children (Wang 2007).
2 As mentioned in Chapter 6, it is often the better performing students who return to their hometowns for high school.
3 Wang (2008: 145), for example, suggests creating local systems of shared financial responsibility for migrant children's education.

## Bibliography

China Labour Bulletin. "The Children of Migrant Workers in China." 2008. www.clb.org.hk/en/node/100316 (accessed December 3, 2008).

Davis, Deborah. "Chinese Social Welfare: Policies and Outcomes." *The China Quarterly* 119 (September 1989): 577–97.

Hannum, Emily. "Political Change and the Urban–Rural Gap in Basic Education in China, 1949–1990." *Comparative Education Review* 43, no. 2 (May 1999): 193–211.

Kwong, Julia. "The Integration of Migrant Children in Beijing Schools." In *Education and Social Change in China: Inequality in a Market Economy*, ed. Gerard A. Postiglione. Armonk, NY: M. E. Sharpe, 2006, pp. 163–78.

Lü, Shaoqing. *Liushou haishi liudong? "Mingong chao" zhong de ertong yanjiu* [*Left Behind or Migration? An Empirical Study on Children of Rural Migrants*]. Beijing: Zhongguo nongye chubanshe [China Agriculture Press], 2007.

Lü, Shaoqing and Shouli Zhang. "Urban/Rural Disparity and Migrant Children's Education: An Investigation into Schools for Children of Transient Workers in Beijing." *Chinese Education and Society* 37, no. 5 (September/October 2004): 56–83.

Wang, Xiaoyan. "Nongmingong zinü jiaoyu: wenti yu jianyi" ["Education for Children of Rural Migrant Workers: Problems and Suggestions"]. In *Shenru tuijin jiaoyu gongping (2008) (Jiaoyu lanpishu)* [*Promote Further Justice in Education (2008) (Blue Book of Education)*], ed. Dongping Yang. Beijing: Shehui kexue wenxian chubanshe [Social Sciences Academic Press], 2008, pp. 136–46.

Wang, Ying. "Special Effort Launched to Help 'Left-Behind' Children." *China Daily*, May 29, 2007. www.chinadaily.com.cn/china/2007-05/29/content_882123.htm (accessed March 23, 2012).

Wen, Jiabao. "Opening Speech." Speech delivered at the Fifth High-Level Group Meeting on Education for All, Beijing, China, November 28–30, 2005. www.unesco.org/education/efa/global_co/policy_group/HLG5_presentations/Opening/china.doc (accessed December 9, 2010).

Wong, Christine. "Fiscal Management for a Harmonious Society: Assessing the Central Government's Capacity to Implement National Policies." BICC Working Paper No. 4, British Inter-University China Centre, Oxford, 2007. http://bicc.blogs.ilrt.org/files/2012/06/04-Wong.pdf (accessed October 21, 2013).

# Appendix A Interviewees

Migrant school principals in the sample

| Code* | District | Legal status |
|---|---|---|
| HL1P1 | Haidian | Licensed (unlicensed branch) |
| HL1P2 | Haidian | Licensed (unlicensed branch) |
| HL1P3 | Haidian | Licensed (unlicensed branch) |
| HL2P1 | Haidian | Licensed |
| HU1P1 | Haidian | Unlicensed |
| HU2P1 | Haidian | Unlicensed |
| HU3P1 | Haidian | Unlicensed |
| HU4P1 | Haidian | Unlicensed |
| SL1P1 | Shijingshan | Licensed |
| SL2P1 | Shijingshan | Licensed |
| SL3P1 | Shijingshan | Licensed |
| SU1P1 | Shijingshan | Unlicensed |
| SU2P1 | Shijingshan | Unlicensed |
| SU3P1 | Shijingshan | Unlicensed |
| SU4P1 | Shijingshan | Unlicensed |
| FL1P1 | Fengtai | Licensed |
| FL2P1 | Fengtai | Licensed |
| FU1P1 | Fengtai | Unlicensed |
| FU2P1 | Fengtai | Unlicensed |
| YL1P1 | Chaoyang | Licensed |
| YL2P1 | Chaoyang | Licensed |
| PL1P1 | Changping | Licensed |
| PU1P1 | Changping | Unlicensed |
| XU1P1 | Daxing | Unlicensed |

*In the codes used for interviews with principals, teachers, and families, the first letter corresponds to the district, and the second letter corresponds to the type of school (licensed migrant school, unlicensed migrant school, or public school).

Migrant school teachers in the sample

| Code | District | Gender |
|------|----------|--------|
| HL1T1 | Haidian | Female |
| HL1T2 | Haidian | Female |
| HL1T3 | Haidian | Female |
| HL2T1 | Haidian | Male |
| HL2T2 | Haidian | Female |
| HL2T3* | Haidian | Female |
| HU2T1 | Haidian | Female |
| HU2T2 | Haidian | Female |
| HU3T1 | Haidian | Female |
| SU1T1 | Shijingshan | Female |
| SU2T1 | Shijingshan | Female |
| SU2T2 | Shijingshan | Male |
| SU2T3 | Shijingshan | Female |
| SU4T1 | Shijingshan | Male |
| SU4T2 | Shijingshan | Male |
| FL2T1 | Fengtai | Female |
| FL2T2 | Fengtai | Female |
| FL2T3 | Fengtai | Female |
| FL2T4 | Fengtai | Female |
| FL2T5 | Fengtai | Female |
| FL2T6 | Fengtai | Female |
| FL2T7 | Fengtai | Female |
| FU1T1 | Fengtai | Female |
| FU2T1 | Fengtai | Male |
| YL2T1 | Chaoyang | Female |
| YL2T2 | Chaoyang | Female |
| PU1T1 | Changping | Female |
| XL1T1* | Daxing | Male |

*These teachers are not considered to be part of the core sample of teachers interviewed.

Migrant families in the sample

| Code | District | Student | | | Total number of children in the family |
|------|----------|---------|------|-------|------|
| | | *Gender* | *Age* | *Grade* | |
| HL1F1 | Haidian | Female | 10 | 5 | 2 |
| HL1F2 | Haidian | Female | 8 | 2 | 2 |
| HL1F3 | Haidian | Female | 12 | 6 | 2 |
| HL1F4 | Haidian | Male | 10 | 3 | 1 |
| HL1F5 | Haidian | Female | 9 | 4 | 3 |
| HL1F6 | Haidian | Female | 12 | 5 | 1 |
| HL1F7 | Haidian | Female | 12 | 5 | 1 |
| HL2F1 | Haidian | Female | 14 | 7 | 2 |
| HL2F2 | Haidian | Female | 12 | 7 | 1 |
| HL2F3 | Haidian | Male | 13 | 7 | 2 |
| HL2F4 | Haidian | Male | 14 | 7 | 3 |
| HU2F1 | Haidian | Female | 16 | 6 | 3 |
| HU2F2 | Haidian | Female | 11 | 4 | 3 |
| HU2F3 | Haidian | Female | 10 | 3 | 3 |
| SL2F1 | Shijingshan | Female | 10 | 5 | 2 |
| SL2F2 | Shijingshan | Male | 8 | 3 | 1 |
| SL2F3 | Shijingshan | Male | 11 | 3 | 3 |
| SL2F4 | Shijingshan | Male | 11 | 4 | 2 |
| SL2F5 | Shijingshan | Female | 9 | 2 | 2 |
| SL2F6 | Shijingshan | Female | 12 | 5 | 2 |
| SL2F7 | Shijingshan | Female | 7 | 1 | 2 |
| SL2F8 | Shijingshan | Female | 8 | 1 | 1 |
| SU1F1 | Shijingshan | Male | 9 | 4 | 2 |
| SU1F2 | Shijingshan | Female | 9 | 3 | 3 |
| SU1F3 | Shijingshan | Male | 11 | 5 | 4 |
| SU1F4 | Shijingshan | Male | 9 | 3 | 2 |
| SU2F1 | Shijingshan | Male | 13 | 6 | 4 |
| SU2F2 | Shijingshan | Female | 11 | 4 | 3 |
| SU2F3 | Shijingshan | Female | 12 | 6 | 2 |
| SP1F1 | Shijingshan | Male | 12 | 6 | 2 |
| FL2F1 | Fengtai | Male | 10 | 4 | 2 |
| FL2F2 | Fengtai | Female | 9 | 4 | 1 |
| FL2F3 | Fengtai | Male | 5 | Preschool | 1 |
| FU1F1 | Fengtai | Female | 11 | 4 | 5 |
| FU1F2 | Fengtai | Male | 10 | 4 | 1 |
| FU1F3 | Fengtai | Female | 11 | 5 | 1 |
| FU2F1 | Fengtai | Male | 10 | 2 | 3 |
| FU2F2 | Fengtai | Female | 15 | 8 | 4 |
| FP1F1 | Fengtai | Male | 8 | 1 | 1 |
| FP2F1 | Fengtai | Female | 8 | 2 | 1 |

Government-based researchers in the sample

| Code | Level of government |
|------|---------------------|
| GR1 | Central |
| GR2 | Central |

Academics and researchers in the sample

| Code | District |
|------|----------|
| A1 | Chaoyang |
| A2 | Chaoyang |
| A3 | Haidian |
| A4 | Haidian |
| A5 | Haidian |
| A6 | Haidian |
| A7 | Haidian |
| A8 | Haidian |
| A9 | Haidian |

University students in the sample

| Code | District |
|------|----------|
| U1S1 | Haidian |
| U2S1 | Haidian |
| U2S2 | Haidian |
| U3S1 | Chaoyang |
| U4S1 | Chaoyang |

Organization leaders and staff in the sample

| Category | Code | District |
|----------|------|----------|
| Local NGO | POL1S1 | Changping |
|  | YOL1S1 | Chaoyang |
|  | YOL1S2 |  |
|  | YOL2S1 | Chaoyang |
|  | YOL3S1 | Chaoyang |
|  | YOL4S1 | Chaoyang |
|  | YOL4S2 |  |
|  | YOL4S3 |  |
|  | YOL5S1 | Chaoyang |
|  | COL1S1 | Dongcheng |
| Local NGO (community-based) | POC1S1 | Changping |
|  | YOC1S1 | Chaoyang |
|  | COC1S1 | Dongcheng |
|  | SOC1S1 | Shijingshan |
|  | SOC1S2 |  |
| Foundation | YOF1S1 | Chaoyang |
|  | YOF2S1 | Chaoyang |
| International organization | YOI1S1 | Chaoyang |

# Appendix B Migrant families in the sample

Main composition of migrant families in the sample

| District | Total number of children | Number of children in Beijing | Number of children in primary or middle school | Number of children in primary or middle school in Beijing | Number of children in migrant school in Beijing | Number of children in public school in Beijing |
|---|---|---|---|---|---|---|
| Haidian | 2 | 1 | 1 | 1 | 1 | 0 |
| | 2 | 1 | 2 | 1 | 1 | 0 |
| | 2 | 2 | 1 | 1 | 1 | 0 |
| | 1 | 1 | 1 | 1 | 1 | 0 |
| | 3 | 3 | 3 | 3 | 3 | 0 |
| | 1 | 1 | 1 | 1 | 1 | 0 |
| | 1 | 1 | 1 | 1 | 1 | 0 |
| | 2 | 2 | 2 | 2 | 2 | 0 |
| | 1 | 1 | 1 | 1 | 1 | 0 |
| | 2 | 2 | 2 | 2 | 1 | 1 |
| | 3 | 2 | 1 | 1 | 1 | 0 |
| | 3 | 1 | 2 | 1 | 1 | 0 |
| | 3 | 2 | 3 | 2 | 2 | 0 |
| | 3 | 2 | 1 | 1 | 2* | 0 |
| Shijingshan | 2 | 2 | 1 | 1 | 2* | 0 |
| | 1 | 1 | 1 | 1 | 1 | 0 |
| | 3 | 3 | 2 | 2 | 2 | 0 |
| | 2 | 2 | 1 | 1 | 1 | 0 |
| | 2 | 1 | 2 | 1 | 1 | 0 |
| | 2 | 2 | 2 | 2 | 2 | 0 |
| | 2 | 1 | 1 | 1 | 1 | 0 |
| | 1 | 1 | 1 | 1 | 1 | 0 |
| | 2 | 2 | 1 | 1 | 1 | 0 |
| | 3 | 3 | 2 | 2 | 2 | 0 |
| | 4 | 4 | 4 | 4 | 4 | 0 |
| | 2 | 2 | 1 | 1 | 2* | 0 |
| | 4 | 4 | 2 | 2 | 2 | 0 |
| | 3 | 3 | 2 | 2 | 2* | 1 |
| | 2 | 2 | 2 | 2 | 1 | 1 |
| | 2 | 2 | 1 | 1 | 0 | 1 |

| District | Total number of children | Number of children in Beijing | Number of children in primary or middle school | Number of children in primary or middle school in Beijing | Number of children in migrant school in Beijing | Number of children in public school in Beijing |
|---|---|---|---|---|---|---|
| Fengtai | 2 | 1 | 1 | 1 | 1 | 0 |
| | 1 | 1 | 1 | 1 | 1 | 0 |
| | 1 | 1 | 0 | 0 | 1* | 0 |
| | 5 | 1 | 1 | 1 | 1 | 0 |
| | 1 | 1 | 1 | 1 | 1 | 0 |
| | 1 | 1 | 1 | 1 | 1 | 0 |
| | 3 | 3 | 2 | 2 | 2 | 0 |
| | 4 | 4 | 4 | 4 | 4 | 0 |
| | 1 | 1 | 1 | 1 | 0 | 1 |
| | 1 | 1 | 1 | 1 | 0 | 1 |

* These figures include one child who was in a preschool class at a migrant school.

Educational attainment and monthly salaries of migrant parents in the sample

| Type of school attended by student* | Educational attainment | | Salary (RMB/month)** | | |
|---|---|---|---|---|---|
| | Father | Mother | Father | Mother | Total |
| Haidian | | | | | |
| L (UL) | University | High school | 3,000 | 1,500 | 4,500 |
| L (UL) | Middle school | Did not finish middle | NA | NA | 5–6,000 |
| L (UL) | High school | Junior college/vocational | <2,000 | 1,100 | <3,100 |
| L (UL) | Middle school | High school | 2,000 | >1,000 | >3,000 |
| L (UL) | Primary school | Middle school | >1,000 | >1,000 | >2,000 |
| L (UL) | Middle school | High school | 3–4,000 | 3–4,000 | 6–8,000 |
| L (UL) | Middle school | High school | 12,000 | 3,000 | 15,000 |
| L | Primary school | Did not finish primary | NA | NA | 2–3,000 |
| L | High school | High school | 3,000 | 1,000 | 4,000 |
| L | Middle school | Did not finish primary | NA | NA | 5–6,000 |
| L | Middle school | Did not finish primary | NA | NA | 3–4,000 |
| UL | Middle school | Primary school | NA | NA | 2,000 |
| UL | Primary school | Middle school | >1,500 | 1,200 | >2,700 |
| UL | Unknown (divorced) | No schooling | – | 900 | 900 |
| Shijingshan | | | | | |
| L | High school | High school | >2,000 | 0 | >2,000 |
| L | Did not finish primary | High school | 3,000 | 0 | 3,000 |
| L | Did not finish primary | Did not finish primary | – | – | – |
| L | Middle school | Middle school | NA | NA | 2,000 |
| L | High school | Middle school | NA | NA | >1,000 |
| L | High school | Primary school | 3,000 | 1,200 | 3,200 |
| L | Primary school | Middle school | 1,300 | 1,000 | 2,300 |
| L | High school | Middle school | NA | NA | 2,000 |
| UL | Did not finish middle | Primary school | >3,000 | >1,000 | >4,000 |
| UL | Primary school | Did not finish primary | 1,000 | 1,500 | 2,500 |
| UL | Did not finish middle | Did not finish primary | 2,000 | 2,000 | 4,000 |
| UL | Middle school | Primary school | NA | NA | >10,000 |
| UL | Middle school | Middle school | >3,000 | 0 | >3,000 |
| UL | Middle school | Middle school | >4,000 | 0 | >4,000 |

| | Type | Education | | | |
|---|---|---|---|---|---|
| Fengtai | UL | Primary school | 1–2,000 | 1,300 | 2–3,000 |
| | P | Middle school | >2,000 | 0 | >2,000 |
| | L | Middle school | – | 1,000 | – |
| | L | Junior college/vocational | 1,000 | 900 | 1,900 |
| | L | Junior college/vocational | 2,000 | >900 | >2,900 |
| | UL | Middle school | NA | NA | – |
| | UL | Middle school | >1,000 | 1–2,000 | 2–3,000 |
| | UL | Middle school | – | – | >3,000 |
| | UL | No schooling | 3,000 | 0 | 3,000 |
| | UL | Primary school | NA | NA | 2–3,000 |
| | P | High school | >2,000 | 800 | >2,800 |
| | P | Junior college/vocational | >4,000 | >1,000 | >5,000 |

* "L" refers to licensed migrant schools; "UL" refers to unlicensed migrant schools; "L (UL)" refers to the unlicensed branch of a licensed migrant school; "p" refers to public schools.

** Areas marked "–" in the salary column signify parents who were uncomfortable revealing their salaries. Areas marked with "NA" signify families where parents worked together and did not make separate incomes.

# Appendix C Non-governmental organizations in the sample

Profile of the local NGOs in the sample

| Year founded | Mission | Main scope of work in the area |
|---|---|---|
| 1996 | To provide support and assistance to the poor, with the goal of ensuring that their basic needs are met | • Runs a migrant workers' event center<br>• Assists 11 migrant schools in areas concerning funding, books, and equipment |
| 1996 | To provide services for female migrant workers, protect their legal rights and interests, and promote their personal development | • Does work concerning migrant women's survival and development, the protection of migrant women's rights, and migrant children's education<br>• Provides guidance for students and parents and training for teachers at seven migrant schools |
| 1999 | To facilitate the social integration of migrant workers and promote their equal treatment in society | • Conducts research on issues concerning migrant workers and their families and sometimes submits the findings to the government<br>• Runs a community center that houses a library for migrant families and a collection of news and relevant information<br>• Organizes educational activities and counseling for migrant children on topics related to education, city life, and health and safety<br>• Organizes seminars for migrant parents on topics like parenting, legal issues, and their children's education |
| 2002 | To provide cultural education services for migrant workers; to promote migrant children's healthy growth and cultural development, increase social awareness, and encourage policy advocacy | • Runs a museum dedicated to the culture and art of migrant workers and coordinates an arts festival for migrant children<br>• Provides services and events for 11 migrant schools<br>• Distributes a monthly publication on issues concerning migrants to over 30 migrant schools |

| Year founded | Mission | Main scope of work in the area |
|---|---|---|
| 2003 | To empower migrant workers and promote the harmonious development of urban and rural areas, with a focus on policy advocacy and the education of citizens | • Runs programs concerning migrant children's growth and development, provides training for migrant school teachers and migrant parents, and offers health services in migrant communities<br>• Produces a publication series documenting the needs and experiences of migrant workers |
| 2004 | To promote educational equality; to promote the healthy growth and development of migrant children and provide services related to their education | • Organizes events and symposiums related to migrant children's education for parents, teachers, volunteers, and others to discuss relevant issues<br>• Runs a children's center at a migrant school |
| 2005 | To provide services to migrant workers, including those related to migrant children's education | • Runs an activity center for the women and children of a migrant community<br>• Organizes participatory trainings and seminars<br>• Provides services for preschool children<br>• Sells clothes to residents of the community at low prices |
| 2006 | To provide services to migrant children and migrant parents and improve the situations of migrant school teachers | • Offers services and programs for migrant children and their parents, including a library for migrant children and computer training for parents<br>• Organizes programs for migrant school teachers |
| 2006 | To provide services and support to migrant children and youth through a range of programs in schools and migrant communities | • Runs migrant community centers and offers tutoring and after-school programs for students, organizes seminars and workshops for families, and provides various types of training (including vocational training and migrant school teacher training)<br>• Works to enhance the capacity of NGOs to serve migrant communities through the sharing of resources and information |
| 2007 | To provide funds and resources for public welfare projects and organizations, with a focus on improving educational opportunities for migrant children | • Provides grants for non-profit organizations working on migrant children's education<br>• Sponsors the creation of non-governmental schools for migrant children |

*(Continued)*

Continued

| *Year founded* | *Mission* | *Main scope of work in the area* |
|---|---|---|
| 2007 | To serve and support migrant workers and their families | • Organizes events and provides services for the residents of a migrant community<br>• Advocates for the rights of migrant workers and the educational rights of migrant children (especially those attending public schools)<br>• Does not work with migrant schools or their students |
| 2008 | To provide services and events for migrant children | • Works primarily in conjunction with other NGOs (by supporting or contributing to their programs) |

# Appendix D Policy documents and legislation cited

Central policies and legislation

| Month/Year | Issuing body | Document title |
|---|---|---|
| Adopted in December 1982 | Adopted at the Fifth Session of the Fifth National People's Congress | Constitution of the People's Republic of China *Zhonghua renmin gongheguo xianfa* |
| Adopted in April 1986, effective as of July 1986 | Adopted at the Fourth Session of the Sixth National People's Congress | Compulsory Education Law of the People's Republic of China *Zhonghua renmin gongheguo yiwu jiaoyufa* |
| Adopted in March 1995, effective as of September 1995 | Adopted at the Third Session of the Eighth National People's Congress | Education Law of the People's Republic of China *Zhonghua renmin gongheguo jiaoyufa* |
| April 1996 | State Education Commission | "Trial Measures for the Schooling of Children and Youth among the Floating Population in Cities and Towns" *Chengzhen liudong renkou zhong shiling ertong shaonian jiuxue banfa (shixing)* |
| March 1998 | State Education Commission, Ministry of Public Security | "Provisional Measures for the Schooling of Children and Youth in the Floating Population" *Liudong ertong shaonian jiuxue zanxing banfa* |
| May 2001 | State Council | "Decision of the State Council on the Reform and Development of Basic Education" *Guowuyuan guanyu jichu jiaoyu gaige yu fazhan de jueding* |

*(Continued)*

Continued

| Month/Year | Issuing body | Document title |
| --- | --- | --- |
| Adopted in December 2002, effective as of September 2003 | Adopted at the Thirty-First Session of the Standing Committee of the Ninth National People's Congress | Law on Promoting Private Education<br>*Zhonghua renmin gongheguo minban jiaoyu cujinfa* |
| January 2003 | General Office of the State Council | "Circular of the General Office of the State Council on Strengthening Employment Management and Service Work for Rural Migrant Workers"<br>*Guowuyuan bangongting guanyu zuohao nongmin jincheng wugong jiuye guanli he fuwu gongzuo de tongzhi* |
| September 2003 | Ministry of Education, State Commission Office for Public Sector Reform, Ministry of Public Security, National Development and Reform Commission, Ministry of Finance, Ministry of Labor and Social Security | "Suggestions to Provide Better Compulsory Education to the Children of Migrant Workers in Cities"<br>*Guanyu jinyibu zuohao jincheng wugong jiuye nongmin zinü yiwu jiaoyu gongzuo de yijian* |
| December 2003 | Ministry of Finance, Ministry of Labor and Social Security, Ministry of Public Security, Ministry of Education, National Population and Family Planning Commission | "Notification on Issues Concerning the Incorporation of Management Funds for Migrant Workers and Other Related Funds into the Scope of the Financial Budget and Expenditure"<br>*Guanyu jiang nongmingong guanli deng youguan jingfei naru caizheng yusuan zhichu fanwei youguan wenti de tongzhi* |
| March 2004 | Ministry of Finance | "Notification on Regulating the Management of Fees and Promoting Higher Incomes for Peasants"<br>*Guanyu guifan shoufei guanli cujin nongmin zengjia shouru de tongzhi* |

| Month/Year | Issuing body | Document title |
|---|---|---|
| May 2005 | Ministry of Education | "Suggestions of the Ministry of Education on Further Promoting the Balanced Development of Compulsory Education" *Jiaoyubu guanyu jinyibu tuijin yiwu jiaoyu junheng fazhan de ruogan yijian* |
| January 2006 | State Council | "Opinions of the State Council on Solving the Problems of Migrant Workers" *Guowuyuan guanyu jiejue nongmingong wenti de ruogan yijian* |
| May 2006 | Ministry of Education | "Suggestions of the Ministry of Education on Implementing 'Opinions of the State Council on Solving the Problems of Migrant Workers'" *Jiaoyubu guanyu jiaoyu xitong guanche luoshi "Guowuyuan guanyu jiejue nongmingong wenti de ruogan yijian" de shishi yijian* |
| Adopted in June 2006, effective as of September 2006 | Adopted at the Twenty-Second Session of the Standing Committee of the Tenth National People's Congress | Compulsory Education Law of the People's Republic of China (2006 Amendment) *Zhonghua renmin gongheguo yiwu jiaoyufa (2006 xiuding)* |
| August 2008 | State Council | "Notification of the State Council on Waiving Tuition and Miscellaneous Fees for Compulsory School-Aged Children in Cities" *Guowuyuan guanyu zuohao mianchu chengshi yiwu jiaoyu jieduan xuesheng xuezafei gongzuo de tongzhi* |

Beijing municipal policies

| *Month/year* | *Issuing body* | *Document title* |
|---|---|---|
| August 2001 | Beijing Municipal People's Government | "Suggestions of the Beijing Municipal People's Government on Implementing 'Decision of the State Council on the Reform and Development of Basic Education'" *Beijingshi renmin zhengfu guanche "Guowuyuan guanyu jichu jiaoyu gaige yu fazhan jueding" de yijian* |
| March 2002 | Beijing Municipal Education Commission | "Provisional Measures for the Implementation of Compulsory Education for Children and Youth of the Floating Population in Beijing" *Beijingshi dui liudong renkou zhong shiling ertong shaonian shishi yiwu jiaoyu de zanxing banfa* |
| August 2004 | Beijing Municipal Education Commission, Beijing Municipal Development and Reform Commission, Beijing Municipal Commission Office for Public Sector Reform, Beijing Municipal Public Security Bureau, Beijing Municipal Finance Bureau, Beijing Municipal Bureau of Civil Affairs, Beijing Municipal Health Bureau, Beijing Municipal Bureau of Labor and Social Security, Beijing Municipal Bureau of Land and Resources, Beijing Municipal Education Supervision Office | "Suggestions on Implementing the General Office of the State Council's Working Documents on Providing Better Compulsory Education to the Children of Migrant Workers in Cities" *Guanyu guanche guowuyuan bangongting jinyibu zuohao jincheng wugong jiuye nongmin zinü yiwu jiaoyu gongzuo wenjian de yijian* |
| September 2005 | Beijing Municipal Education Commission | "Notice of the Beijing Municipal Education Commission on the Work of Strengthening the Management of Self-Run Migrant Schools" *Beijingshi jiaoyu weiyuanhui guanyu jiaqiang liudong renkou ziban xuexiao guanli gongzuo de tongzhi* |
| July 2006 | General Office of the Beijing Municipal People's Government | "Notice of the General Office of the Beijing Municipal People's Government on the Work of Strengthening the Safety of Non-Approved Self-Run Migrant Schools" *Beijingshi renmin zhengfu bangongting guanyu jinyibu jiaqiang weijing pizhun liudong renyuan ziban xuexiao anquan gongzuo de tongzhi* |

| Month/year | Issuing body | Document title |
|---|---|---|
| November 2008 | General Office of the Beijing Municipal People's Government | "Suggestions of the General Office of the Beijing Municipal People's Government on Implementing the Spirit of the State Council's Working Documents on Waiving Tuition and Miscellaneous Fees for Compulsory School-Aged Children in Cities" *Beijingshi renmin zhengfu bangongting guanyu guanche guowuyuan zuohao mianchu chengshi yiwu jiaoyu jieduan xuesheng xuezafei gongzuo wenjian jingshen de yijian* |
| Adopted in November 2008, effective as of March 2009 | Adopted at the Seventh Session of the Standing Committee of the Thirteenth Beijing People's Congress | "Beijing Measures for Implementing the Compulsory Education Law (2008 Amendment)" *Beijingshi shishi Zhonghua renmin gongheguo yiwu jiaoyufa banfa (2008 xiuding)* |
| December 2008 | Beijing Municipal Education Commission, Beijing Municipal Finance Bureau | "Suggestions of the Beijing Municipal Education Commission and Beijing Municipal Finance Bureau to Provide Better Compulsory Education to the Children of Migrant Workers in Beijing" *Beijingshi jiaoyu weiyuanhui Beijingshi caizhengju guanyu jinyibu zuohao lai Jing wugong renyuan suiqian zinü zai Jing jieshou yiwu jiaoyu gongzuo de yijian* |
| December 2008 | Beijing Municipal Education Commission | "Notice of the Beijing Municipal Education Commission on Implementing Matters Concerning the Suggestions to Provide Better Compulsory Education to the Children of Migrant Workers in Beijing" *Beijingshi jiaoyu weiyuanhui guanyu luoshi jinyibu zuohao lai Jing wugong renyuan suiqian zinü zai Jing jieshou yiwu jiaoyu gongzuo yijian youguan shixiang de tongzhi* |

# Index

Page numbers in bold refer to tables, page numbers in italics refer to figures, and page numbers followed by "n" refer to notes.

38n18; vagrants and beggars 20, 23; *see also* rural–urban migration

Labor Contract Law (2007) 23
Lai *et al.* (2012) 5, 27, 122, 130; *see also* migrant schools, literature comparing migrant and public schools
Law on Promoting Private Education (2002) **61**, 76, 98, 129, **194**; *see also* private (*minban*) schools
lawyers 153
left-behind children (*liushou ertong*) 25, 63, 180n1; academic performance 25; and crime 172; psychological and behavioral problems 25
Lü Shaoqing 48, **113**, 146; *see also* migrant children's education, literature and research on

media *35*, 48, 142, *143*, 146, 148; impact on migrant children's education 158, 163, 164–5; pressure on government actors 75, 104, 106, 124, 126, 148, 156, 160; relationship with civil society actors 152, 153, 155; *see also* civil society in migrant children's education
Mentougou district 49, *51*; area **52**; migrant schools, figures **93**; outside population **52**, **93**; permanent resident population **52**; total population **52**
migrant children: decision to work 24–5, 49, 173; definition 1; figures 2, 38n12; use of terminology 10–11; *see also* Beijing, population, children of the floating population and migrant children population; migrant children's education
migrant children's education: Beijing municipal policies 59, 69–78, **71–4**, 95, 105, 130, 174, **196–7**; central policies 59, 59–65, **61–4**, **193–5**; costs of inaction 171–3; data on 6, 10–11, 26–7, 130–1; dropout rate 48; enrollment rate 26, 48; funding **61, 62, 63, 73,** 178–9; literature and research on 4, 5, 27, 28, 48, 146–7, 179–80; middle school education 114, 118–19, 133, 134, 138n18, 156; overage students 27, 54n4; policy of "two priorities" (*liangweizhu*) 3, 4, 5, *59*, 60, 65, 70, 135, 174; and

population growth and social stability 6, *77*–8, 101, 143, 145, 170, 172, 174; post-middle school/high school education 67, 133, 134, 137–8n17, 138n18, 139n29, 156; proportion attending migrant versus public schools 26, 66–9, 130–1; psychological and behavioral problems 127, 172; return to hometowns 70, 99, 104, 118, 125, 126, 133, 134, 137–8n17, 138n18, 172; *see also* civil society in migrant children's education; migrant schools; public schools
migrant enclaves 5, 22, 48, 49, 124, 138n22, 150, 173; *see also* migrant schools, demolition; urbanization, and demolition
migrant parent activists 35, *143*, 146, 156–7, 164; petitioning 156–7, 161; *see also* civil society in migrant children's education
migrant school principals' association 35, *143*, 146, 153–4, 159, 164; *see also* civil society in migrant children's education
migrant school teachers' association 35, *143*, 146, 155, 159, 164; *see also* civil society in migrant children's education
migrant schools 35, *143*; areas of concentration in Beijing 51; class size 119; closures 72, 75, 76, 85–6, 95, 98–9, **99**, 105–6, 123–4, 125, 126, 129, 133, 148, 153, 172–3; compared to public schools 27, 112, 120–3; curriculum 134, 138n18, 139n29, 172; data on 26–7; demand for 3, 5, 131–5; demolition 85–6, 119, 123, 124, 125–6, 129, 133, 148, 153, 172–3; discounts 118, 134; discovery of 47–8, 102, 142; emergence and development 2, 26, 48–9; enrollment procedures 134, 135; facilities/equipment **87**, 112–13, **113**; fees **88**, 116–18, **116**; figures (Beijing) 5, 47, **72**, **93**, 124, 125; figures (by district) **93**; food safety **88**, 89, 98, 105; funding **87**, **88**; government management of **62**, **63**, 65, 70, **71**, **72**, **73**, 76, 86–7, **87**, **88**, 95, 100, 104, 175; government support for **61**, **62**, **63**, 65, 76, 95, 100, 104, 175–6; health and sanitation **87**, 87, **88**,